Inspired to Climb Higher

Inspired to Climb Higher

The Challenges, Questions, Struggles, and Joy of Earning Your Doctoral Degree

Beverly Middlebrook-Thomas,
Jyenny Babcock,
Noha Abdou,
Helga McCullough,
Wanda Ebright,
Deborah Broom-Cooley,
Jennifer Malone, and Sallie Middlebrook

ROWMAN & LITTLEFIELD
Lanham • Boulder • New York • London

Published by Rowman & Littlefield
An imprint of The Rowman & Littlefield Publishing Group, Inc.
4501 Forbes Boulevard, Suite 200, Lanham, Maryland 20706
www.rowman.com

86-90 Paul Street, London EC2A 4NE

British Library Cataloguing in Publication Information Available

Library of Congress Cataloging-in-Publication Data Available
ISBN 9781475874204 (cloth)
ISBN 9781475874228 (ebook)

Contents

Foreword vii

Introduction 1

CHAPTER 1: My Uncharted Journey. 7
Beverly Middlebrook-Thomas, EdD

CHAPTER 2: Finding Myself in the Last Place I Thought to Look . . 27
Jyenny Babcock, EdD

CHAPTER 3: A Journey of a Mother's Love 47
Noha Abdou, EdD

CHAPTER 4: I'm Still Not Sure How I Got Here 67
Helga M. McCullough, EdD

CHAPTER 5: My Doctoral Journey. 85
Wanda K. W. Ebright, PhD

CHAPTER 6: Life Before the Dissertation Journey. 103
Deborah J. Broom-Cooley, EdD

CHAPTER 7: The Self-Fulfilling Prophecy: Dismantled 121
Jennifer Malone, EdD

CHAPTER 8: A Novel Way to Be Heard, to Earn Praise. 141
Sallie B. Middlebrook, PhD

CHAPTER 9: The Big Questions, Answered 167

CHAPTER 10: Seek Support (When You Need It) for Your
Doctoral Journey. 189

CONTENTS

CHAPTER 11: General Advice (and Help) for Writing the
Dissertation 207

References 223

Index 225

About the Authors 227

Foreword

The demands placed on leaders today are greater than ever before, with enormous challenges facing all sectors. It is no wonder that many find it impossible to consider pursuing a doctorate program on top of an already demanding life. However, if you are driven to improve, to reach new heights, and to expand your knowledge, then pursuing a doctorate degree can be a powerful motivator. If you are reading this book to decide whether to go for it, do not hesitate. What stops people short in taking the first step is self-doubt, procrastination, and fear of the unknown. Make the decision to go for it now, and turn your thoughts into action. When you do, you will rise to join the world's very small percentage of the elites who have achieved a doctoral degree.

Inspired to Climb Higher is not only for those who are exploring doctoral programs. If you are reading this book as a faculty member, staff member, or administrator of a doctoral program, you will gain valuable insights into what your students go through. You can use this book as a topic of discussion in program review and work toward improving your program to better support your doctoral students.

Being in a doctorate program is one of the best ways to grow professionally. From exploring new frontiers of knowledge to making a meaningful impact in your field, the possibilities are exciting and limitless. However, the journey can also seem daunting and scary. As someone who has been at that crossroad myself, I understand the dilemma you may face.

When embarking on a journey to a new destination, most people consult their GPS first. *Inspired to Climb Higher* can be your GPS for reaching your destination of earning a doctoral degree. The eight women contributors of this book detail their diverse experiences of the doctoral journey from a wide range of institutions, providing a sense of normalcy for your trepidations, a guiding light for your pathway, and concrete strategies to overcome obstacles. Their authentic and honest personal stories, based on real challenges, painful lessons, and joyful triumphs, give readers raw realities as well as dreamlike possibilities and practical pathways to successful completion.

There are shared themes woven throughout the eight different journeys—from the thoughtful decision-making process that leads to a firm commitment to start, to adapting to a new triple life of family-work-school, to the resilience to persist through any obstacles that arise, to tangible coping mechanisms for passage through the storms, and the signs and courage to ask for help when support is needed.

Inspired to Climb Higher provides some of the secret passages to complete your dissertation, which can often be the biggest impediment to completing a doctorate. There are more horror stories about the dissertation process than guidebooks to help you through it. The authors of this book chronicle every step of the process from topic selection to successfully defending your study, providing important tips and constructive strategies to help you navigate this challenging terrain.

Most importantly, *Inspired to Climb Higher* is a must-read if you are going through a doctoral program, because it is like surrounding yourself with eight sisters who have walked the journey ahead, staying by your side, pointing the way, and cheering you on to the finish line. Their willingness to show their vulnerability, doubts, tears, and the valleys of their emotions are meant to encourage you to lean into your own fears and doubts to find courage and determination to move forward.

The eight doctoral journeys also help you to be mindful of the balance of your priorities and life. You want to finish as a whole person, not one who has sacrificed the valuables of your soul. Keep this book close to you throughout your doctoral program, and when you are feeling doubtful, fearful, frustrated, demotivated, or lost, read it again.

You *will* finish the program with your doctorate degree. *Inspired to Climb Higher* serves as a testament to your success. By reading this book, you have already chosen to pursue excellence. Congratulations!

Ding-Jo H. Currie, PhD

distinguished faculty, EdD Educational Leadership

director, Leadership Institute for Tomorrow

California State University, Fullerton, California

Member: Advisory Board, Doctorate of Community College
Leadership, Ferris State University, Big Rapids, Michigan

INTRODUCTION

Let's face it, you want a doctorate. Something brought you here, to the place where you are right now, yearning for something more. Perhaps you've been imagining how good it would feel to be called "Doctor." Maybe you took a long look at all your achievements: a bachelor's degree, master's degree, professional projects, and conference papers and presentations—and, despite all these accomplishments, something is missing. Acquiring what's missing could make a profound difference in your life, career, family, and community.

Though you want this terminal degree, committing to pursuing it is a daunting task. You have questions, fears, doubts, and insecurities about the process and about yourself. Exactly how much work will be required? Do you have the time, energy, resources, and fortitude to see the process through to graduation? What kinds of challenges and obstacles will you face? Do you have the skills you will need to write a dissertation? All of these are questions you might be asking yourself, only the answers are nowhere in sight.

Now is the time to decide if you are ready. This book was written to answer many of the questions you have, and probably some you haven't thought of yet. *Inspired to Climb Higher* was written by eight women who have earned doctorates, and, within these pages, each of the eight shares with you the story that led to her becoming a doctoral degree holder. All of these women have been where you are right now. They have felt all the fear and trepidation you might be feeling, and they all took the plunge anyway: to climb higher by earning the doctoral degree. We believe that reading multiple points of view from diverse perspectives will help you decide if pursuing a doctorate is right for you.

THE SECRET TO GETTING THERE IS GETTING STARTED

There's a good reason why you're thinking about pursuing a doctorate, probably many good reasons. Those good reasons, coupled with a strong internal drive for success, will not only influence your decision to pursue a doctorate but also power you through the process. If the spark is lit in your mind, but you still don't know exactly what you want to do, take heart. Reading this book will help you find many of the answers you need. Committing to three or more years of working toward another academic degree is a big decision. Even if you are happy with what you have right now—you are still entitled to want more. And that's good. That's a starting point. From here, right now, you can begin thinking about your skills, your personality, your interests, your experience, and how you can use all you have to achieve what you want for your future.

Now is a good time to make a list of everything you have to offer in terms of your life's résumé, including your personal experience, employment history, professional accomplishments, areas of expertise, and sources of income. Thinking about these things should help you see all the strengths you can apply to your doctoral journey, and doing that should bolster your confidence.

If you're thinking that earning a doctorate is going to be tough, you're right. It will require a lot of difficult work. One reason people find completing a doctoral program so challenging is the personal transformation that happens along the way. In many ways, you will be leaving your old life and starting a new one. So, to accomplish this monumental goal, you will have to carefully manage your life throughout your pursuit of the doctorate.

To begin, you might have to let go of a lot of things from the past that have kept you from pursuing your future, and you might need to reorganize how you approach your daily responsibilities and your workaday world. But if you know you're not living the life you want to live, or not making the living you want for yourself with what you're doing now, then earning a doctorate could be exactly what you need to do, no matter how tough earning it might be.

ARE YOU PUTTING OFF CHANGING YOUR LIFE?

One of the reasons we decided to author this book was because we wanted to help people who are like we once were before we earned our doctorates. Each of us was someone who believed she wanted to earn the highest academic degree possible but kept putting it off because other things in our lives always seemed more urgent, or more needed in the here-and-now moments of living. After all, it's easy to put off doing things that we know will take a lot of thought, effort, and a considerable amount of time to achieve. No matter how wonderful the rewards might be, at the end of the day, the biggest question becomes "When is the right time to go back to school?"

Whether you have decided to obtain a doctorate to challenge yourself academically, push yourself to achieve something that you've always dreamed of achieving, or make a difference in the world while contributing to your field of interest in a meaningful way, you must ultimately decide on the doctoral program that seems like the best fit for you. Being a doctoral student will be a lot of work. You will spend a lot of nights reading, studying, and writing, and then reading, studying, and writing some more. Coursework and research activities will need to be juggled with family, friendship, work, and other community responsibilities. The dissertation process will, more likely than not, be demanding. The demands of doctoral life are why you need to carefully consider which program is a good cultural fit for you, in addition to how the program will help you in fulfilling your academic and career goals.

Life as a doctoral student will be both challenging and rewarding. You will be challenged academically, but you will also be rewarded by growing and developing as a person. All of us who have taken the journey and achieved this goal know one thing for certain: There's a good chance you'll come to appreciate the journey, the experience, and everything (or, at least most) of what you'll go through. You will complete coursework, conduct research, write your dissertation, and defend it. With patience and perseverance, you will get it done; in the end, you will be proud of what you achieved. There are not many moments in life that can compare to the sense of accomplishment you will feel when you finally get your doctoral diploma.

The road will be long. No doubt it will have many a winding turn. There might be times when you will feel like you are being pulled in a million different directions, but you must believe through it all that with commitment, dedication, and perseverance, you will make it. Then, once you have your doctorate, the next phase of your life and your career can begin. You'll be ready to apply what you've learned as you pursue your postgraduation goals, and you'll begin to reap the abundant rewards that come with earning your doctorate.

The next section of this book includes the stories of eight women of varying backgrounds who pursued different goals and attended eight different universities in pursuit of eight different degree paths. Although many pursued or continued in academic careers, ultimately, they all embarked upon different career paths after graduation. What we all have in common, however, is that we were all inspired to climb higher. We were all challenged to face our fears, accept the struggles, endure the pain, solve the problems, answer the questions, and navigate the challenges of earning the ultimate degree.

Each one of us knows that earning a doctoral degree is a big decision. It's a major commitment of time, energy, and resources. And it's not for everyone. You have to be sure you want to do it, and—saying so—we are not trying to talk you out of it. What we are trying to do is to get you to make sure you are making this decision for the right reasons. We hope that giving you a peek into our journeys might answer many of the questions you may have while also inspiring you to take the plunge when you're ready to climb higher. Each of our chapters includes discussions of the following topics:

- The author's personal background (who they were before beginning the doctoral journey)
- The reason the author chose to go on the doctoral journey
- How the author balanced her personal/professional life throughout the journey
- Struggles the author encountered along the way
- Coping with and overcoming many different kinds of struggles

- The author's reason for choosing her dissertation topic
- Reflections on the day the author delivered her dissertation defense
- Questions the author had before and during the journey
- Advice to those who are now considering taking this journey

The doctoral journey is filled with joys, questions, problems, and discomfort. But take it from us: it's worth it. Personal and professional growth is guaranteed when you embrace transformation. The experience offers you the opportunity to make friends and colleagues you will know and possibly interact with for life. You may even learn things you never knew you wanted to know. Not only will you change your life, but you'll make a mark upon the world, leaving a legacy of knowledge. As you walk with each of us through our journeys, we are not going to sugarcoat anything, because pursuing a doctorate is hard work. However, it's also among the most rewarding things we, the women who authored this book, have ever done. If you are sure you want to do it, then go for it! All eight of us are cheering you on and are eager to welcome you to the club.

My Uncharted Journey

Beverly Middlebrook-Thomas, EdD

Once upon a time, a young girl was dubbed by the school principal as "the quietest girl at school." It was because she didn't really speak very much beyond a whisper throughout elementary school. She was different. She only spoke out when at home in more familiar surroundings with her parents and siblings. Although she was shy and never wanted to bring attention to herself, she did well in school, always had a tight circle of good friends, and was even chosen as a senior high school homecoming queen. Near the end of her senior year in high school, one of the girl's greatest mentors and loved ones, her father, died suddenly of a heart attack. It was the first time she had experienced the death of someone so close to her. It hit hard. Her father was now gone from her life, but she felt good that she'd made him proud by being the first of his children to graduate from high school. He had already talked to her about going to college after high school and had done what he could to help her get prepared, helping her with filling out her college application. She couldn't disappoint him.

At this point, if you haven't figured it out, the girl was me, the writer of this story. The girl, now a young lady of eighteen, was accepted into Alcorn State University and that fall, traveled to Lorman, Mississippi, to begin college life. Lorman was about a three-hour drive from Monticello, my hometown, so it was a big decision for me to move that far away from home. I chose a major in business education and decided that I wanted to be a teacher like two people I admired, my aunt (my mother's sister) and my high school business teacher. I would become the first of my parents' children to attend college, and my parents and my siblings were all proud of me.

Becoming immersed in college life caused my shyness to gradually fade a bit, but not entirely. Though I managed to get by with decent grades, I took full advantage of the freedom that came with being away from home, and, often, I did not take my studies seriously. But, because I was no quitter, four years later, after completing a student teaching assignment in Vicksburg, Mississippi, I graduated with a bachelor's degree and was completely prepared to teach in the field of business education. However, I didn't go directly into the teaching field. Shortly after graduation, I accepted a job as a word processing operator for a local telephone company in Jackson, Mississippi. My inner voice of negativity surfaced, the job did not work out, and I began to doubt myself and feel the need to prove that I was good enough. Soon after leaving the job, a friend and former coworker introduced me to a nice man who was quite a bit older (fourteen years). I fell in love with his "old-school" qualities, and we soon got married. After marriage, two children, and a few more careers in Jackson, Mississippi, our family of four relocated from Jackson, Mississippi, to Houston, Texas.

In Texas, with the birth of a third child, I became more interested in the importance of my children's education and began thinking about pursuing teaching as a career. That was when I decided to get a higher degree (a master's in liberal arts), and, in 1997, teacher certification and my first teaching job soon followed. Although it brought many duties and long hours of lesson planning, teaching quickly began to feel like a good career fit. After all, it was what I had always said I wanted to do with my life. And although teaching jobs in Texas offered low starting salaries, having a master's degree meant I moved to a higher level on the teaching pay scale. With the master's degree, I also landed a job online as an adjunct professor.

After I had been teaching in my field for eleven years in a Houston-area school district, my husband and I made the decision to make a big change in our lives. With three grown children and with my husband now retired, we decided to leave Houston, Texas, to move to be closer to our daughter who lived in Atlanta. I left my teaching job, we sold our home, and we relocated to Atlanta, Georgia. Our only daughter had relocated to Atlanta years earlier to attend college, and, after finishing a dual degree at Spelman College and Georgia Tech, she got married and decided to make Atlanta her home. After much thought, Atlanta soon became our home too.

THE REASON FOR THE DECISION

When I first got to Atlanta, I was working only part-time as an online adjunct for one of the first and largest online universities in the country. The job involved interacting with students only asynchronously, so there was no face-to-face real-time interaction. When students had concerns or issues, they would schedule a call to speak with me. Teaching at a university suddenly created a thirst inside me for further education. Also, I had always admired that my younger sister had obtained a PhD years earlier, and I looked up to my sister who had always been smart and creative. Since the university I worked for offered a nice student discount for employees, the temptation was great, and I made the decision to apply for the doctoral program. Without any discussion, advice, encouragement, or opinion from anyone else, in the year 2011, I applied to and was accepted into the doctorate program and began my studies, online, as a part-time student at University of Phoenix.

Life in Atlanta, Georgia, was very different from life in Houston, Texas. With a higher cost of living in Atlanta, living off my part-time earnings, my husband's retirement, and his Social Security pension wasn't enough. So, realizing we needed to "downsize" our life, we quickly settled in a much smaller living space (a midtown studio apartment) that my daughter and her husband owned. I soon began looking for full-time work as a teacher, and, in the meantime, was spending quality time with my first grandson. He had been born as a preemie but thrived and did well as he grew stronger. We were a close-knit little family, and, although I missed living in the much bigger city of Houston, Atlanta now felt like home.

The years passed quickly, and, by this time, I worked on a few short-lived teaching jobs in Atlanta metro public schools. However, for many and varied reasons, I stopped and started the doctoral program several different times over the years. When my grandson was about ten years old, when he saw that I was often at my word processor, writing, he would ask why I was always working on the computer. I would explain to him that I was writing a dissertation which would be a five-chapter book when I finished. Later, as he got older, when he would see me researching and writing, he would ask, "Grandma Bevy, are you still writing that book?" Today, he is a sweet, long-legged fourteen-year-old, a budding baseball player with good grades. I'm proud to say that he's seriously into the game, and he's seriously a good player.

THE REASON FOR MY DISSERTATION TOPIC

My chair and committee changed a few times over the years but stabilized over the last two to three years. The first leg of the doctoral journey had included mostly foundation courses. I did well and earned A's. When the time came to choose a methodology for the dissertation, I listened to one of my classmates in the program and chose a quantitative methodology. "It's easier," they said. Of course, now I know that the method you choose to use should be based on the nature of your topic and how you plan to gather data. As far as choosing my topic for my doctoral study was concerned, since I worked as a teacher, I was advised to pick a topic pertaining to teachers or to what I taught, so I chose to write about teachers' beliefs regarding the importance of technology integration into K–12 teaching and learning.

I chose a topic related to the importance of technology integration into K–12 teaching and learning because, over the years, in my position as a business and technology teacher, I had seen that some older teachers (and a few younger ones) seemed to shy away from keeping up with the latest technology and from using it often to enhance classroom teaching and learning. They mostly used the computer for lesson preparation and administrative things like inputting grades or doing other mandatory administrative tasks that required computer use. For example, once when every teacher in my school received new classroom smart boards, one older teacher never turned it on. I found the smart board to be an excellent resource for me as a teacher, and it was a great engagement tool for my students. I found that my students enjoyed participating in class when allowed to write on the smart board while learning. I also found it to be a great way to display content and have students participate in educational games that require them to view the large screen. In fact, I found technology to be a great enhancement for teaching and learning, and I discovered there were tons of online tools and programs to use to enhance student engagement. In my interactions and conversations with other teachers, I realized they seemed uninterested in getting too involved with technology beyond what was required.

So I began to think that teachers seemed to be really set on continuing to use what they had always used, which was mostly traditional methods which included paper and pencil and worksheets. I began to wonder how much teachers really valued technology integration. Therefore, I decided to interview teachers about their beliefs regarding the importance placed on technology integration in the classroom. I believed there were many different ways the integration of technology could help enhance teaching and engage students in the classroom. As a business and technology instructor, I knew it could afford students the opportunity to learn at their own pace and provide an extra edge when it came to learning. With technology integration, creativity could be ignited, potential unlocked, and students could become more inspired to collaborate while participating in class. Also, I knew that when students were actively engaged in learning, discipline problems in the classroom were usually less likely to occur.

As a technology instructor, I also knew that technology integration in the classroom could occur seamlessly when students became engaged in lessons utilizing virtual reality. For example, a social studies teacher in Atlanta, Georgia, who was teaching her class about life in Lisbon, Portugal, might traditionally have the students view pictures in the textbook and answer questions about the lives of the people in this region. But with students who are accustomed to using technology, this method of instruction might be described as "dull" or "boring." However, with the integration of technology, the class could virtually engage with students in a similar class in Lisbon, Portugal! Engaging students on this level would require the teacher to interact with technology on a higher level. Sadly, however, rather than bothering with using technology to this extent, some teachers still prefer to engage in more traditional ways of teaching. Technology still frightens some people because of the numerous steps sometimes involved in learning how to use it, and because of the rapidly changing nature of technology.

Although using technology in the classroom has the potential to increase teacher and student engagement, concerns about technology continue to exist, and these concerns may hinder technology integration adoption. Furthermore, even though teachers support technology for teaching and learning in the classroom, the support of administrators and leaders in the school is also very important to the success of technology integration efforts. When administrators and education leaders in the school do not use technology or actively promote the importance of technology integration, classroom teachers may not be encouraged and inspired to integrate technology. Chapters 4 and 5 of my dissertation covered some of the challenges teachers encounter when it comes to technology integration in the classroom.

My topic was approved, but at some point during the last two years of my doctoral journey, my chair approached me about changing my methodology from quantitative to qualitative. What a blow that was after spending so much time focusing on the quantitative method. After thinking about how much of what I had done would have to be changed, I was against it and tried to convince my chair that using the quantitative method would be fine. But she did not agree, and she finally reassured me that a qualitative or mixed method would be a better fit since I would be questioning study participants about their beliefs. She continued to remind me that since my topic involved the "beliefs" of teachers, it would be difficult to measure beliefs using quantitative methods. "How are you going to measure the beliefs of teachers?" she asked. Soon, I saw the light and was happy that she advised me to change it to the qualitative method. It made sense, and I realized I hadn't thought through all of the challenges of using quantitative methodology for my study. After rethinking everything, of course, I realized qualitative methodology was the best fit.

Still, I often wondered why my chair waited so long to advise me to make this change. The good thing was that there would be no more focus on statistics courses. I felt like that was a win for me since I am not a math person. If I had remained with the quantitative method, I would have been required to take two more statistics courses, and I felt I had already struggled enough with statistics. Even though I thought the quantitative method would work for my study, now I am glad I took my committee chair's advice and chose to use the qualitative methodology. I'm glad I realized it was a perfect fit for my objectives.

BALANCING LIFE AND OVERCOMING STRUGGLES

It seems like a blur now, but as I recall, balancing my life during the first leg of the doctoral journey was not so bad. I was excited about the whole thing. I soon attended my Year One residency in Atlanta. "Residency" requires doctoral students to attend face-to-face meetings with professors as part of course requirements. These residences provide opportunities for interacting with professors, asking questions, and making progress on working on the dissertation study. My Year Two residency was held in Nashville, Tennessee, in 2013. I began to feel like I was making progress as a doctoral student.

My husband and I were empty nesters now with three grown children and a grandchild, and we were settled in Marietta, Georgia, a suburb of Atlanta. My husband was always very supportive and proud of me for my endeavors, but my "better half" was particularly proud of me for deciding to undertake this monumental journey. He never complained or had anything negative to say when I spent long periods of the day and night writing and conducting secondary research, or when I was required to attend my first- and second-year residencies. I knew he wanted more of my attention, but he never pressured me and seemed content to do most of the cooking and household chores when necessary.

My husband was a professional cook—a very good professional cook—and he had worked offshore as a professional chef before he retired. All our friends and family had learned to love the food he prepared and to expect him to cook when they came to see us. However, around the third year of my doctoral journey, my husband, a lifelong smoker, was diagnosed with stage 4 lung cancer, chronic obstructive pulmonary disease, and emphysema. Many years of cigarette smoking had been taking a silent toll on him, even though he remained healthy as a heavy smoker for a very long time. Soon after the devastating diagnosis, he began undergoing chemotherapy and radiation treatments. It was a difficult time for me, so I decided to take a break from my studies to be more available to take him to doctor's visits and be supportive as he began to deal with the realities of his condition and the side effects of the treatments.

Within a year of his being diagnosed, on the evening of February 16, 2014, my daughter and grandson stopped by our home for a visit. After being with them a little while downstairs, I went upstairs to check on my husband. I heard myself screaming louder than I can ever remember screaming when I found him slumped over in the bathroom. Everything else is a blur. Someone called the paramedics, and when they got there, they tried, unsuccessfully, to revive him. They tried for almost an hour, but he succumbed to the terrible invasion of his body and the damage he went through as a result of undergoing radiation and chemotherapy.

The reality of what had happened hit me like a brick. My husband was gone, and I felt completely lost. Since he passed away, I have always wondered if, at the age of seventy-five, he might have survived longer had he not undergone the chemotherapy and radiation treatments. But since I'm not a medical professional, what do I know? All I know for sure is that after thirty-eight years of marriage, my friend, my soulmate, and the father of my children was gone from this world, and I felt like a part of me had left with him.

A few months later, as I relaxed on a Norwegian cruise to the Bahamas with my daughter and my grandson, we reflected on the good times we had with him—my husband, my daughter's dad, and my grandson's granddad. It was a good idea to take that cruise; a good idea to remember my husband and to take the time we needed to mourn his loss and to remember him. It helped a lot. That year, and in the years that followed, many times, my inner voice resurfaced, and I found myself wanting to quit. Many times, I had to dismiss the constant questioning of my inner voice and engage in positive self-talk to stay determined to move on. My family, my academic advisors, and my doctoral committee chair showed a lot of care and concern for me during those trying times. In time, I was able to manage my grief and sadness while moving on. In 2015, after searching for a while, I landed a full-time position as a teacher for DeKalb County School District, the position I hold today.

As the months passed, I once again resumed my online research and writing as a part-time doctoral student at the University of Phoenix Online. Though still plagued with bouts of grief, I persevered and dealt with the ups and downs of teaching and managing classrooms in a middle school setting. As you can imagine, middle school students can present many different kinds of challenges, so classroom management was a real challenge every day. I found that I needed to take a few more short leaves of absence from the doctoral program throughout the journey just to rest and focus on my work responsibilities. However, after resuming my studies in 2021, I made the decision that I would do my best to continue nonstop with my doctoral program, all the way to the end.

After rededicating myself to the challenge, the revisions I had to make to my research were time- and labor-intensive, and many days brought me to the brink of what felt close to burnout, but I persevered. And it seemed that whenever I thought I had made significant progress, I would get back the draft from my chair with new edits in places where I thought I'd gotten the "all clear." Though I was never told, it soon dawned on me that my chair and each of the two committee members were responsible for reviewing certain chapters of the dissertation, and when there was a change in committee members there were changes to parts of the paper where I had previously been given the "okay." Although this was problematic and made me feel like I would never finish my dissertation, somehow I persevered. I found a way to believe in myself, and I kept going.

My Big Day

The institutional review board process involved answering a lot of questions to satisfy a board of reviewers of my dissertation that the welfare of the subjects of the research had been taken into consideration. It is my understanding that some institutions don't require the institutional review board process, but the day I received notice from my chair that I had gained institutional review board approval, I was elated. Absolutely elated. For the first time during my whole journey, I really felt like I had made significant progress, and I became more excited about continuing on to the finish line. From that point on, every little achievement I made helped me gain more strength, more determination, and more confidence.

A few more months passed, and, after I made more progress, soon it was just a few days before my defense. I had even prepared a slide presentation for my dissertation defense and scheduled a date to practice with my chair. Now, I would describe my chair as very strict, kind of eccentric, and a veritable stickler about many things with regard to writing and how it should be done. She always said whatever she meant and didn't hold back. She was straight to the point about any advice or suggestions and didn't sugarcoat anything. Looking back, even though, at times, it was the source of much worry for me, in hindsight, I must say that she contributed a lot to my success.

A week before my defense date, when the time came to practice the defense slides with my chair, I was a big bundle of nerves because I knew I hadn't practiced the presentation very much. Still, I had to move forward, so, as I presented it to her, I mostly read from my slides, and my chair did not hesitate to critique me for reading. Also, at one point during the reading, I attempted to explain the meaning of an acronym, but I could not recall what the letters of the acronym stood for. It popped out of my head and would not return. After a long pause, I admitted that I couldn't remember what the acronym stood for, and my chair said to me, "Beverly, that's a fail."

In the next moment, I felt my soul take flight. When my soul returned to my body, I felt the "ouch" as it became part of me once again. How could I be so nervous? How could I forget what an acronym stood for during a practice run? My chair encouraged me to practice and practice and practice some more before setting my defense date. After what I went through that day, that is just what I did. I took some time to practice in front of the mirror, on a Teams video recording, and finally, I practiced with my sister (who had earned her doctorate at least two decades earlier). My sister, who lives in another state, listened by phone and critiqued my presentation.

Soon, the scheduled day of my defense arrived (June 8, 2022, at 7 p.m.) and it seems to me that it came quickly. Days hadn't passed by; they had zoomed by. But I was ready. I was finally ready, and I had my supporters on board. About 6:45 p.m., by phone, my good friend who is a minister led a prayer as my sister joined in. I won't lie, after the prayer, I had a glass of wine and felt relaxed and ready. With my chair and the two other committee members in place on Teams, it was time.

I must explain that committee member number two had not been my favorite over the years because she always seemed to give me a hard time and was often either unforthcoming or slow to respond to my questions. We never seemed to have a good connection, and I had once tried unsuccessfully to get a replacement for this team member. However, I began to realize that the more I communicated with her, the better I got to know her, and, in time, my interactions with her improved.

When prompted to begin my defense, I was confident, I felt good in the moment, and the presentation went rather smoothly. I wore a headset, and I felt relaxed as I spoke. I felt thankful to be presenting in virtual mode, and I was glad I did not have to be in a live presentation. There was something comforting and reassuring about having a degree of control over my immediate environment. I think I would have been more nervous had I been delivering the presentation in person. The presentation lasted only ten or fifteen minutes, and when I was done, all three members of my committee asked questions, and two of them seemed reasonably satisfied with my answers. Committee member number one complimented and thanked me for not reading from my slides as she commented about how some of her previous candidates had actually read from their slides.

When I responded to a question asked by committee member number two, there was a brief and noticeable silence after my response. When I asked if I had satisfactorily answered her question, she dryly replied, "I suppose that will do." I quickly decided that her dry response was good enough for me. It was a yes, and a yes, no matter how dry it sounded, was a yes. Once the questioning was done, I was asked to leave the virtual room, and I felt an overwhelming sense of relief that was encased in anxiousness and piled on top of slight nervousness.

After eight of the longest minutes of my life, I was called back into the virtual room. As I heard the words, "Congratulations, Dr. Thomas," from my chair, they sounded like music to my ears. My mind flashed back in nanoseconds to all the years, all the toil, all the late nights and all the early mornings, all the doubt, all the work, all the rework, and all the minutes, days, weeks, and sometimes months of wanting to give it all up. It was a surreal moment for sure, but I was finally done. I messaged my daughter. I texted my grandson: "I finished my book!" I called my sister to share my delight. She had been my biggest cheerleader, and she was overjoyed. The people in my close circle of family and friends expressed sincere, resounding happiness for me.

Days later, back at work as a teacher, I adorned my door with a welcome sign that read, "Dr. Thomas." As my work colleagues saw it, they congratulated me. I had finally completed my doctorate in education in the year 2022; it was worth all the trials and tribulations I went through, and it was a good feeling to have taken the plunge, accepted every challenge, and to have prevailed. It took a while though for me and others to get used to my new handle. And, although I am not always addressed as "Dr. Thomas" at work, it's okay because I know it will take time for me and others to get used to my new designation.

At this writing, it has now been months since my doctorate was conferred. In addition to allowing me to climb higher in terms of educational attainment, I must say it was an experience of self-discovery that showed me that I can achieve anything I set my mind to that I consider worthwhile. My doctoral journey changed me and showed me that I have the emotional resilience that allows me to persevere when faced with obstacles. I overcame shortcomings and fears, and I silenced that inner voice that has always tried to keep me feeling defeated. I am hopeful, stronger, and better off for having taken on the challenge of earning my doctorate. The "icing on the cake" came through one evening in October of 2022 as I opened a package containing a hardbound copy of my dissertation. It felt so good to see my work in this final printed form, and I will always treasure it as the first book I ever wrote. I am now considering whether to participate in the commencement ceremony which, for me, will be a virtual event. I may also opt to do a photoshoot wearing my university regalia.

Though my parents didn't graduate from college, as my siblings and I were growing up, in our home they placed a lot of emphasis on the value of education. They worked hard to support six little children, and our biggest responsibility was to go to school and to learn. Even though they didn't live to see it in person (I believe their spirits know and are happy for me), getting my doctorate is one of my greatest tributes to my parents, especially my dad, who was a staunch supporter of education and always pushed us to do our best in school.

Call me crazy, but I think I would take this journey all over again, taking my own advice and the advice of others, making a few changes along the way. After writing my dissertation, the urge to write continued to plague me, so I came up with the idea to write about my journey. So, I searched for others who had completed the doctoral journey and I asked if they would be interested in writing an inspirational book about the journey they took to obtain their doctoral degree. Those who were sincerely interested joined me, and we all wrote our stories and included them as chapters in a book that we hope will serve as a guidebook of inspiration, motivation, and encouragement for others. Our book is for anyone who might be considering taking this journey, including those who have already applied to a doctoral program and might now be experiencing "jitters." We believe sharing our stories and showing how we overcame our fears and every challenge we faced will help others see that if we can do it, they can do it too.

LIFE AFTER THE JOURNEY
A few weeks ago, I responded to an email from my principal asking for volunteers who were interested in taking advantage of a free coach/mentor cohort. This opportunity would involve 150 hours of coursework and would result in two endorsements being added to the teaching certificate (endorsements including instructional coach and teaching mentor). I thought it would be a great thing to have more endorsements on my

teaching certificate, so I said, "What the heck," and I expressed my interest in the opportunity.

To my surprise, I learned that I was one of five respondents who have been selected for this opportunity. Now I am enrolled in a fast-paced course that will culminate in the summer. The courses are both synchronous and asynchronous, and I am honored and excited to have been chosen to take yet another journey of discovery. We have even been assigned a mentee, and I feel that being one of the few doctoral degree holders on my campus may have contributed to my having been chosen. It looks to me like earning my doctorate has already been instrumental in opening a new door, and I attribute being afforded this great opportunity to the fact that I never gave up and that I persevered until I completed my EdD.

Sometimes, there is something inside of me that still tries to make me doubtful that I can be successful at this, but I now know that "inner voice" does not always tell the truth. I also realize I'm not the only one who has to fight against an inner voice of negativity. I think we all have to manage negative thoughts that come at us to try to make us doubt ourselves. That voice that seems pitted against us and is 100 percent against any growth and development. No longer the quietest girl in school, I am stronger now with a lot more confidence in myself, more than ever before. I am someone who has the confidence I need to never let that voice raise an ounce of doubt in my mind ever again. Oh, it can and will try, but it will always fail, because I believe in myself, and I know I can do anything I set out to do.

Remember that little girl who didn't really speak very much beyond a whisper throughout elementary school? The little girl who thought she was different? Who only spoke out when she was at home in more familiar surroundings, with her parents and her siblings? The one who was so shy that she didn't want to bring attention to herself? I think she might have suffered from a load of doubt that might have stemmed from low self-esteem.

Low self-esteem, you see, can be the result of a person's individual personality, which can cause you to think negatively about yourself and your potential. As an adult, I have read about it and learned that, sometimes, a child who feels different from other kids at school sometimes suffers from low self-esteem. According to Firestone, Firestone, and Catlett (2002), authors of *Conquer Your Critical Inner Voice*, there is an inner voice in all of us which represents the negative side of our personality, which triggers negative moods and is against us and our ongoing development. Interestingly, Firestone et al. (2002) believe the critical inner voice exists in varying degrees in every person, and they believe this inner voice is what diminishes our self-esteem. If we "listen" to its destructive point of view and believe what it is telling us, we will often fail to challenge it. Sometimes, we will even act on it or give in to it and let it dictate our course in life. Firestone, Firestone, and Catlett believe that this process can affect our emotions and can have seriously negative consequences on our accomplishments and on our lives.

All of my life experiences have served to help me overcome much of my self-doubt, but I must admit there are times when the low self-esteem monster tries to raise its head and cause me to feel unwarranted fear. But, thankfully, I have grown into a much more confident woman, a stronger woman who conquers fear and overcomes challenges as part of my daily life. I am no longer the quietest girl in school, and I am a lot more confident now than ever before. In fact, I am someone who knows I have all the confidence I need to achieve anything I set out to achieve, and even though I know it will attempt to speak to me from time to time, I know I will never listen to that inner voice of doubt ever again.

Questions You May Ask Yourself When Making the Big Decision

There are many questions I considered the answers to before deciding to make the commitment to the life-changing leap of pursuing a doctorate degree. Many of the answers to the questions you may have will be unique to your own life situations. It is important to consider the pros and cons when answering the questions that you have about whether to pursue a doctorate degree, but finding the answers will help you make the best decision and be better prepared for success. The following are some of the questions I entertained before making the decision to pursue the degree.

Is a Doctorate Degree Right for Me?

A good way to decide if the doctorate degree is right for you is to ask yourself some key questions regarding why you want to pursue the degree. The answers to such questions may range from a desire for personal fulfillment to show your mastery or expertise in your field to career advancement reasons. When you have satisfactory answers to the questions, it's up to you to take the first step. As an educator, my decision to pursue the EdD degree was based on my desire to be among the most educated in my field.

Which Institution Should I Consider?

Institutions may vary greatly in programs of focus, financial support, and time commitment for the doctoral degree; therefore, choosing a school will involve doing your research well in advance. You will need to determine which accredited traditional or online schools best fit your needs. Learn the reputation of the school and the resources and opportunities offered. If you know anyone who has attended the school, talk to them about their experience. Do your research, because weighing the pros and cons and choosing a school that will help you be successful during your journey and in your personal and future endeavors is important.

How Do I Decide Between the PhD or EdD?

Both the PhD and the EdD are high-level terminal degrees with rigorous programs, but the program you choose will depend on your reason for pursuing the degree. The PhD degree is more suitable for those who want to conduct research or teach at the university level. On the other hand, the EdD degree prepares one to work in the field of education as a teacher or educational leader. As an EdD career candidate, you can expect to be involved in roles that are mostly practice-based, meaning you will likely manage or oversee other people. In my role as a K–12 schoolteacher and adjunct professor, the EdD degree was the best fit for me.

Is There a Good Time to Start a Doctoral Journey (Age, Career or Family Status, etc.)?

Getting a doctorate can be highly rewarding. However, choosing the right time to start is unique to each person's life situation and goals. Life will not stop. Therefore, among other things, it will ultimately depend on choosing a time when you feel that you can be confident, focused, and productive as you juggle the demands of doctoral coursework and obligations with other demands of your life. At the time I chose to enter my doctoral program, I was an adjunct professor at University of Phoenix Online. I made my decision to enroll in the doctorate program based partly on the fact that, as an employee, I would receive a considerable discount on the coursework.

PERSONAL ADVICE

Conducting a primary research study and writing a dissertation based on that study is a long and arduous journey that is very mentally and physically demanding. It is a formidable task that can be, at times, utterly exhausting as each phase of the journey has its own challenges. On the other hand, I think it is one of the most important and rewarding journeys I have taken in my life. In hindsight, I would offer four Ps that must be there for anyone who is thinking of starting a doctoral journey and staying the course. The four Ps are passion, positivity, patience, and persistence.

Passion and Positivity

Before you start this journey, you must have a burning desire to do it. That's passion! When you make the decision to take the "leap," you have to stay positive because negativity will enter your world. There will be moments, people, and things that test you. During the dissertation journey, you also have to take ownership of the obstacles you can control along the way. Don't sweat the things that you cannot control; instead, seek professional help to get over those humps. Be positive that the topic you have chosen to write about is something that you are passionate about because you will spend a lot of time researching it. It is therefore critical that you choose a subject in which you are highly interested, one you feel confident that you can enjoy researching, learning more about, and writing about for years, and finally, one that you will share the results of years of research and study with a committee of judges who are there not just to listen, but to critique the defense of your study.

If you have made the decision to start this marathon of a journey, I hope you are excited about beginning one of the most important voyages of your life. I hope you have in mind a vision of the "big picture" at the finish line because you will need to be able to bring this vision to mind sometimes to get you to the next part of your journey. In your vision, I hope you have also seen "Dr." in front of your name or the initials for your PhD or EdD that will follow your name. I hope you've seen that new nameplate on your office desk. Keeping these things in mind and being able to recall them at will, I promise, will help get you through some of the toughest days you will face as a doctoral student.

If you've chosen to go on this journey, it means you are not a person who gives up when the going gets tough. It means you have a fire burning inside and you're the kind of person who'll step over and go around any "potholes" you run into along the way. And, even if you take a misstep and fall into a few of the "potholes," you are the type of person who will get up, dust yourself off, and continue. Because you know you will not give up because you want this and because you have what it takes to get this job done. In other words, you know you have the hunger for the knowledge you need to prevail, and you have the confidence you need to stay the course. You know you can reach the finish line, and you are ready and prepared to stay positive. Even when your committee chair or perhaps a member of your committee makes you feel less than competent (oh yes, it can happen). Even when people around you sometimes make you feel like you could be in "over your head." You know you're not. You are just feeling a few "growing pains," and those are expected and should be welcomed because you are on a journey of growth. Through it all, you know you have what it takes to stay positive and to remain passionate as you continue on your journey.

Patience and Persistence

Once you begin the dissertation process, at some point, you must *become inspired and empowered to continue*, because the urge to quit may enter your mind. Keep in mind that this is a journey that can take a few years, or it can take many years. Know, however, that during your doctoral journey, you will learn a lot about yourself because, among other things, your patience and persistence will be tested.

Whoever described patience as a virtue was right. The doctoral journey will be fraught with "wait times." For example, you must wait for feedback from draft submissions, wait for the return of graded assignments, wait for answers to your emails, and so on. During such times, you must be patient. Getting stressed could cause you to lose focus, so don't let impatience affect your progress. *Lean on your support system.* I cannot overemphasize how much my support system (my family, my committee) meant to me, and how much they helped me focus and remain patient during the wait times.

Since the June 2022 defense of my dissertation is still fresh in my mind, a final piece of my advice involves the critical oral defense. The success of the oral defense will depend on how confident you are as you present your topic and how well you are prepared to respond to questions from your doctoral committee. It pays to be well-rested, practiced, focused, and ready for the defense. I think I was ready for my defense after spending many hours practicing, and I truly believe that practice is key.

Additionally, be sure to have a thorough understanding of the nature of your research topic, and key issues surrounding your research problem. Finally, it is paramount that you be thoroughly familiar with the theory and the framework associated with your research study. These things are the core of your study and will help ensure success on your "big day" as you present your topic and answer questions directed at you by your committee.

CONCLUSION

Be reminded: writing a dissertation is a daunting task. Can you believe some experts even suggest that you have a second project to work on while writing your dissertation? They believe that having other projects (such as a job) to think about can provide both perspective and distance while enabling you to remain productive as you persist with your dissertation. During my journey, I was a teacher with lesson planning to do while also having to do research for classroom activities. I found perspective and was able to achieve the needed distance from my doctoral studies by focusing on my work as a teacher when I wasn't doing work related to my doctoral studies. This helped me to persist and not give up on my doctoral studies and research. Peace and love. I wish you the best on your journey.

CHAPTER 2

Finding Myself in the Last Place I Thought to Look

Jyenny Babcock, EdD

IF YOU ASK ME, WHERE I STARTED MY DOCTORAL JOURNEY ISN'T NEARLY as interesting as where I've gotten to afterward. But I'll leave that judgment up to you, dear reader. Like a dissertation, I'll start at the beginning, lay the foundation, and then walk you through my journey to support the conclusions I've drawn about what it means to earn a doctorate. This is a story of finding myself in the last place I thought to look.

My educational path was disjointed from the start. Being a military brat meant that I went to a lot of schools; from preschool through high school, I attended thirteen institutions (some more than once) and six colleges and universities to earn four degrees, an associate of arts in business administration, a bachelor of arts in psychology, a master of arts in sociology, and an EdD in leadership. Because I moved between the US coasts and between countries, my primary education ended up with a lot of gaps. I didn't even learn to read on my own until third grade (thanks, Grandma, for making sure I didn't get left any further behind).

After graduating from high school, I wasn't sure about going to college. I don't recall my parents ever really encouraging me to go. Maybe they remember that differently. Teenagers hear what they want to. In any case, my parents didn't attend college, so I didn't think it was that important. Certainly not important enough to take on debt.

My conceptualization of COLLEGE (capitalized to signify the traditional four-year university experience portrayed in the media and by my guidance counselor) at that point came from television and looked like an Ivy League school that I did not under any circumstances belong at because my parents weren't rich, I didn't know what I wanted to do as an adult, and I couldn't possibly get into a sorority (which was a necessity to avoid being a loser). There was so much I didn't know about COLLEGE. I don't recall how, but I eventually learned about the less prestigious option of attending community college. That was at least affordable and local. Not having anything better to do at eighteen years old, I started attending community college with a vague notion that it would help me get a career instead of a job. Since I didn't know what kind of career I wanted, I studied business administration because that degree sounded like it would apply to any kind of career I might be suited for.

Though I didn't see how any of what I was learning in my community college coursework was relevant to the working world, I nevertheless applied myself to learning all I could. But I started to view community college as subpar to university. It took me seven years to finish an associate degree while working a full-time job. Although it was time to transfer to COLLEGE after earning the associate degree, I was feeling pretty burned out on school and I was even more convinced that I didn't belong.

You see, from my early teens, I had been overhearing my father vent his frustration to my mother about the discrimination he faced at work for lacking a college education. People with degrees were being hired with higher salaries or promoted over him despite his decades of experience and high-caliber performance. Because he did not have a bachelor's degree, he was overlooked to be promoted to management. His view was that performance and experience should be the basis for promotion; it was unfair for the education privileged to have such an advantage. This reinforced my notion that I didn't belong in COLLEGE because COLLEGE was for the privileged. Our family was not privileged. And we didn't want to be. So, I stopped after earning an associate degree in business administration.

REASON FOR BEGINNING DOCTORAL JOURNEY

At the age of thirty-five, I looked around and realized that the world had changed. Lacking a bachelor's degree was holding me back from climbing the corporate ladder. At least I thought it was. At the time, my title was director of marketing, so I had gotten a fair way up the management ladder. But I was starting to experience the same education discrimination my father had. So back to college I went, to earn a bachelor's degree.

Of course, I had the same problem: I didn't know what kind of career I wanted. All I knew was that I didn't want to take on debt. I'd heard the dire warnings about adults who were shackled to student loan payments and couldn't afford to live their dreams after earning a degree. I was determined to not let that be my fate, so I did one of the hardest things I had ever done up to that point: I quit my job, sold my condominium, and lived off the proceeds while I returned to school to finish a bachelor's degree.

Astute reader, you may have noticed that at this point I actually had achieved what many people hope to by that age in life: a management position and homeownership. But all I could see was that I wasn't measuring up to everyone else because I didn't have a bachelor's degree. The bachelor's degree had become my Holy Grail. I just knew it was what was missing from my life. If I could have that experience, then I'd be on the same track as everyone else. And I could have what they had—a fulfilling life!

Close to finishing my bachelor's degree, I began to search for a career I could get with a bachelor's degree in psychology. Unfortunately, I didn't think that a psychology degree qualified me for any positions outside of my former industry. So, in essence, I was going to be where I left off attending college the first time, unable to climb any higher on the corporate ladder, and stuck in the same industry I had been working in.

Looking into possible education and career paths beyond the bachelor's degree, I stumbled across the Ronald E. McNair Post-Baccalaureate Achievement Program at my campus, which provides students from underserved populations with preparation for applying to doctoral programs. That planted the seed in my mind that it was possible to earn a doctorate that would change the trajectory of my career for the better. As a first-generation student, I applied and was accepted.

The program was one of the most uncomfortable college experiences I endured. I simply didn't belong. Yes, as a first-generation college student, I was technically part of the underserved population, but all of the programming was geared toward students who were also in ethnic minority populations. I struggled to relate to the other students in the McNair cohort, and I felt extremely isolated, like an imposter. That experience made me question my decision to pursue a doctorate. There was this push and pull where I wanted to have the opportunities a doctorate would offer but I didn't feel deserving. Yet I persisted in the McNair program and applied to at least ten psychology PhD programs to support the hazy vision of becoming a psychology professor who mentors research students.

Being determined to get into a doctoral program and still debt adverse, I applied for the California State University Chancellor's Doctoral Incentive Program (CDIP). The CDIP prepares doctoral students for faculty positions by providing financial support, faculty mentorship, professional development, and grant resources. To my surprise and delight, I was awarded the CDIP in 2006/2007. But to my chagrin, I failed to get into a doctorate program that academic year.

Having failed to secure a position in a doctoral program, I set my sights on earning a master's degree. To avoid taking on debt, I took a low-level research position at my university which allowed me to use a tuition waiver to pay for courses. I enrolled in a master of education program and reapplied to doctoral programs for the following year. Lo and behold, I was accepted into a PhD program! I was thrilled and terrified in equal measure. As it turned out, the CDIP award I received in the prior year could not be rolled forward to the PhD program I was accepted into. This created a lot of cognitive dissonance for me because the PhD did not have guaranteed funding beyond the first year, which meant I might need to take out student loans at some point.

The more I thought about becoming a university professor, the more it seemed like a bad idea. For the five years I would be earning the doctorate, I would be accumulating debt and not building any savings for retirement. Then after graduating, I would face a very competitive job market for a faculty position with a low starting salary. And even if I managed to acquire a tenure-track position, I would then be under pressure to publish to make tenure. Suddenly the dreams of becoming a psychology professor didn't seem so realistic. Heck, I was approaching forty years old—too old to be upsetting my life like that. Besides, I liked my new job in institutional research and planned for the job to become a career. So, I decided to give up on the dream of becoming Dr. Babcock.

With a doctorate off the table, I committed to earning a master's degree to move up in the ranks as a research analyst in higher education. I switched to a program that emphasized research skills and eventually earned a master of arts in sociology. Fast-forward a decade into my higher education career, and I was again feeling like I had hit a professional ceiling and was being discriminated against for not having a doctorate. There is some snobbery over advanced degrees within a university.

Here is where my upbringing and my environment collided. On one hand, influenced by my father's view, I valued experience over education. Secretly, I feared everyone who had a doctorate was somehow better than I was despite my decade of work experience. I worried that they were taught something critical that I hadn't been exposed to. Those around me in the university setting valued higher education over experience. My boss at the time had confided in me that even though I had eight years of direct work experience when I applied, she nearly hired the newly minted PhD graduate with no direct experience instead. However, this same boss encouraged me to pursue a doctorate and even dangled the chance of promotion if I enrolled.

Encouraged by my boss and bored with my career, I decided once again to pursue a doctorate. Earning an EdD seemed like the best degree to support my career in higher education administration. The university I worked for didn't offer staff tuition waivers for doctoral courses, so I went looking to enroll elsewhere. My criteria for selecting an institution included regional accreditation, low cost, online modality, short program length, and high acceptance rates. Beyond that, I didn't care that much about the details. I just wanted a low bar for entry into at least a mediocre program (because I was still intimidated and felt like an imposter) that would be quick to complete. My initial motivation for obtaining the degree was to advance in my career. I didn't have any big plans to change the world; I just wanted my colleagues to see me as an equal.

I felt like my career as a higher education researcher was good preparation for the doctorate and gave me an advantage in completing dissertation research. The more I thought about earning a doctorate, the more I built up in my mind the challenges I would face until the quest became the equivalent of climbing Mount Everest. I believed that I would have to make extreme sacrifices to complete my degree like being sleep deprived from pulling all-nighters writing papers and reading journal articles. I thought I would struggle to understand the difficult materials, and I anticipated my assignments being returned covered in red ink with harsh criticism from professors. With this vision of my doctoral journey in my head, I mentally prepared myself to deal with those challenges I imagined, then took the plunge by enrolling in the most affordable, regionally accredited online program I could find. It was affordable enough that I paid for the entire cost of the program up front and then wrote off the cost on my taxes for a hefty tax refund that year.

Expectations and Experience

Insecurities about belonging in a doctoral program took root from the first assignment submitted. Feedback indicated that my paper was not written in an academic format because it included bullet points. If I had missed something so simple as writing complete sentences instead of using bullet points, what else was I going to get wrong? The struggle I expected had begun.

From that very first assignment, I was vigilant about what would go wrong. With each assignment I submitted, I expected feedback pointing out my writing mistakes and the flaws in conceptualizing the materials. But the harsh feedback never came. Of the hundreds of assignments turned in, few had comments and I rarely scored below 95 percent. I received an A in every single course.

Instead of increasing my confidence in my academic abilities, the lack of feedback made me paranoid that I wouldn't be able to maintain my performance. I didn't have a clue as to what I was doing right and could not accept that I wasn't making mistakes. Faculty were supposed to be very critical to shape me into an academic, or so I thought. I blamed myself for choosing a mediocre program (for the record, it wasn't) and started to question if I was even learning anything (I was).

The absence of feedback was causing me to struggle. Understanding the materials was not as challenging as I imagined it would be. Conceptually, I understood all the teachings. What troubled me was interpreting the assignment instructions. They were typically vague and often contained contradictory elements. Emailing faculty for clarification resulted in being told they didn't know and would need to get clarification from the curriculum designer. That further eroded the esteem in which I held my institution.

Worried about getting every assignment right, I became fanatical about addressing every element of each assignment. Looking back, I put more effort into the assignments than I needed to. At the time, I believed I needed to do a perfect job to deserve my doctorate. But it was becoming increasingly apparent to me that no matter how hard I worked I wouldn't get the feedback I needed to determine how much value I should place on my knowledge acquisition.

Sleepless nights did come to pass, but not because I got to bed late after completing long assignments. I was able to keep to a regular sleep schedule. Anxiety kept me awake most nights. A to-do list ran through my mind on a loop, and I worried about how I would get my schoolwork done for the week, be productive at work, and be available and present with my partner. In the middle of the night, I would have a thought about an assignment that seemed pressing and would need to write it down before the thought disappeared. Eventually, I kept a notebook by my bed to scribble in so I could try to go back to sleep. Sometimes that helped.

The constant anxiety and self-doubt were debilitating. There was no support I could find for the way I was feeling. Not many people in my personal life knew about the demands of a doctoral program. Now I know that the people around me wanted to support me, but they didn't know what I needed and quite frankly neither did I. I cringed when anyone asked me how things were going. I couldn't bear to share with them how much I struggled over insignificant things like understanding assignment directions; it was embarrassing. Whining about not receiving feedback was ignored. There wasn't much sympathy for my struggle since I was passing all my courses. My right to complain about a doctorate program I chose to do felt nonexistent. Withdrawing from everyone was the way I tried to cope with the feeling of being overwhelmed.

Midway through the program, the university changed the graduation requirements. The night I received the notice brought a new low in terms of depression, frustration, and anger. The institution's initial message was vague, making it appear the new program requirements would delay my graduation by a year and increase my tuition. As I read the email while seated at my desk, I was so upset that I slammed my hand down on the desk so hard that the bruise lasted more than a week. Right then, worrying about my mental health became a new concern for myself and my partner. How was I going to keep up the charade for a couple more years until I graduated?

Aside from my partner, my inner circle was unaware of my turmoil as I had pulled away so far to protect them from my chaotic and anxious energy. From the outside, it appeared that everything was fine. I was still showing up at work and maintaining my household. However, my relationships were unraveling, and I didn't have the resources to make things right. I was so wrapped up in my need to get the doctorate finished at all costs, I allowed the pursuit to eat my life.

Balancing Personal with Professional Life

At the start of the doctoral program, I tried to strike a balance between personal, professional, and academic life. I wanted to keep clear boundaries between all three while maintaining the same level of commitment and engagement as always. In my imagination, I would simply swap my downtime for studying and keep up with everything else in my life as usual. As it turned out, my amount of downtime wasn't enough to cover the needs of my academic life. Worse, due to the cognitive demands of academic life, I ended up needing more downtime than I did before I started the program.

To carve out academic time, on the weekends I quit hiking with friends. During the week, I cut back time from managing my household. My garden went untended and overgrown, cleaning intervals stretched further apart, and elaborate meals were replaced with Crockpot cooking. To my shame and detriment, I also cut back on the time I gave to my partner, family, and coworkers. My relationships suffered from neglect. Instead of going out to lunch with colleagues, I either did homework or napped in my car so I would have enough energy to deal with the second half of my day. Dinner was the one time a day I saw my partner. Afterward, I would disappear into my office to study. Holiday travel to visit family took too much time so I skipped it.

Now and then I would make some half-hearted attempt at taking downtime. But it was never enjoyable or restorative because I wasn't present in the moment. Instead, I was worried about how much classwork I still had to get done.

I gave myself over to doing the doctorate entirely. Every sacrifice was made in the name of earning the doctorate. The doctorate was my "legitimate" excuse for checking out of anything and everything. I sometimes spent twelve hours a day on the weekends doing the doctorate, to emerge from my office bitter and resentful of what the pursuit was costing me. What I didn't see at the time was my role in creating my doctoral experience. Because I believed the doctoral process should be difficult and require sacrifice, that is what I made of it. I became the architect of all that was overwhelming me. Daily emotional pain was just the journey.

Struggles Along the Way

Looking back, it is clear I suffered the classic symptoms of imposter syndrome throughout my doctoral program. I was never satisfied with my work, always taking a long time to complete assignments and wanting to get everything perfect. Rarely taking breaks, I pushed myself as hard as I could, right to the brink of exhaustion. As I studied the course materials, I was worried about someone discovering a gap in my knowledge; I felt like a fraud. And more than anything else, I didn't want to risk being seen as incompetent by asking for help. The doctoral journey emphasized all of my insecurities, even ones that I thought I had long ago resolved.

Added to the general angst I was suffering from, I encountered several trials that made the journey even more difficult to navigate. From start to finish, there was always something extra to deal with, it seemed. I experienced loss, post-traumatic stress disorder, injury, and research failure.

Early in the program, my father, who had been battling multiple myeloma cancer for a few years, rapidly declined over a week and died. When I got the call about Pop's condition and hospitalization, I made the eight-hour drive to be with my family as we hoped for the best but had to make decisions about hospice care. I had no idea how long I would be away from home, so I did the responsible thing and brought my laptop and coursework with me so I wouldn't fall behind.

I recall being torn to pieces emotionally (in fact, I'm crying now as I write this, six years after the event) from needing to say goodbye to my beloved father, feeling guilty for missing family Thanksgiving dinner the week before his hospitalization, needing to hold space for my family and my grieving, and having to complete the doctoral coursework. I recall conflicting thoughts that the coursework could wait until I felt able and that since I couldn't change the outcome of the situation, I shouldn't let it stand in the way of academic progress. While my sisters were taking their turns sitting with Pop as he slowly transitioned to the other side, I worked on my paper. Looking back, I wish I had made a different choice. But back then self-compassion wasn't in my vocabulary, so I pushed myself instead of dealing with my emotional turmoil. And the guilt I felt from not being fully present with my family as my father passed was a black cloud over the rest of my program. Part of me thought that I didn't deserve my doctorate for being so heartless and another part believed that there wasn't a point in finishing the degree if my father wasn't there to see.

By mid-program, the prolonged stress of trying to perfectly manage my life took its toll, and post-traumatic stress disorder symptoms from a decades-old car accident resurfaced. In the passenger seat, on our way to breakfast one weekend, panic struck me. I was suddenly terrified of being in the vehicle and I struggled to keep my composure for the four minutes left of the drive. That episode kicked off months of dealing with post-traumatic stress disorder symptoms, which further taxed my emotional state. My sleep became more fractured, and I retreated even further into myself. Despite feeling like I was on the brink of insanity (collapse), I managed to continue.

About a year away from finishing my doctorate, I slipped on wet stairs entering the building to my office. A coworker kindly drove me to the approved urgent care facility. Diagnosed with two sprained feet and one sprained ankle, I was sent home on crutches. The pain was considerable, but dealing with the worker's compensation bureaucracy was worse! Every week I had to return to the urgent care facility for a checkup. For months, at every appointment, I begged for more tests to be run because the swelling and pain had not decreased.

Starting from a low-resource state before the injury and being consumed with my dissertation left me without the ability to advocate for myself. Months went by before I learned I could transfer my case to a different facility. Once I transferred my case, I was able to get a new diagnosis of a broken foot and torn ligament which would require bone fusion surgery. Recovery required two months of being non-weight-bearing while wearing a cast, several weeks in a walking boot, and months of physical therapy. Unfortunately, while the surgery was successful in terms of putting my foot back together so I could eventually walk unassisted, it left me with chronic nerve pain. More time and energy were expended dealing with that.

For the record, I was truly fortunate to have a partner willing to care for me. At this point, I was busy collecting dissertation data while recovering at home. With my foot elevated, I lay in a recliner in the living room and worked from my laptop. And just when I thought that perhaps I could finish the dissertation while I was recuperating at home, another challenge popped up. My data collection efforts failed to acquire the minimum number of participants to meet my research criteria. It felt like the rug had been suddenly pulled out from underneath me again and I was between the proverbial rock and a hard place; I didn't have the stamina to start over with new research, I couldn't go on as I was being emotionally and physically drained, and I refused to become another "all but dissertation" dropout.

This is where I had to choose how to manage my life going forward because what I had been doing wasn't working. I was broken. After a lot of introspection, I decided that I would not quit; I would repair myself and find a less emotionally painful way to move forward.

How I Overcame My Struggles

Overcoming my emotional struggles came near the end of my doctoral journey, beginning with the decision to find another way to live. To figure out what needed to change, I looked outward first, recalling advice received over the years. Two specific pieces of advice came to mind: a therapist telling me I needed to treat myself more often and a bodyworker telling me that my language wasn't very nurturing despite me being a caring person. Investigating these two claims led me to explore self-compassion. After reading a book by a leading researcher on self-compassion I realized that my self-compassion was underdeveloped (okay, nonexistent).

Doing *a lot* of self-compassion exercises opened my mind to new thoughts and possibilities. Most notably that it was okay to have messy emotions and to lower expectations for myself. I quit beating up on myself for feeling bad about how I was managing my emotional states during my doctoral studies. I quit putting pressure on myself to be the perfect student, leader, employee, supervisor, daughter, sister, aunt, and partner. No longer needing to be perfect allowed me the mental space to pivot my research and resume data collection very quickly, without being overwhelmed.

As my capacity for self-compassion grew, so did my interest in coaching. My dissertation research was focused on health and wellness coaching students because when I started the doctoral program, I was focusing on my health. Health and wellness coaches help people improve their overall quality of life by addressing their health and well-being. Although I still believed in health and wellness coaching near degree completion, I was no longer looking to improve my health; I was more interested in improving life satisfaction. Life coaches, on the other hand, help people achieve their goals and reach their fullest potential. Life coaching became my new focus. After listening to a life coach's podcast for a few months,

I decided to apply their self-coaching techniques to my life and see what happened.

What happened was that I learned how to manage my mind. I know that sounds a bit mysterious and perhaps even dull. But it changed my life so dramatically that I'm a new person. Actually, I'm just more me than I ever have been. What I mean by that is I acknowledge and accept all parts of myself—the excellent, the ordinary, and the flawed. As I began to see how I am inextricably linked to all humanity, the judgment of myself and others started occurring far less often.

Through my self-coaching practice, I learned how to surrender to my limitations and push past my fears to get my dissertation done without mental drama. I recall at the start of the doctoral journey, when things felt difficult, I would tell myself "If others can do it, so can I." That language was more general than compassionate. Through self-coaching, I made my internal dialogue much more nurturing and started to tell myself that my skill and dedication were all I needed to see me through to graduation. I challenged myself to stop complaining and do my personal best, without comparison to others. My success came from integrating all of me instead of compartmentalizing, keeping school separate from work and home.

What made a difference for me was daily morning walks before I started work. On those twenty-minute walks, I would do a thought download where I acknowledged all the fears and insecurities I felt and then found thoughts to neutralize, refute, or replace those negative thoughts. Specifically, I looked for solutions to my challenges. Being deliberate with my thoughts allowed me to feel in control and direct my attention to the things I could influence and then let go of the rest. When I couldn't influence the problem, I quit worrying about it. Where I had influence, I got busy doing what needed to be done, even if it was uncomfortable. That is what life coaching taught me.

THE BIG DISSERTATION DEFENSE DAY

Some doctorate holders can recall their dissertation defense with vivid clarity. I am not one of those people. The virtual defense was a blur. The program supplied the slide template, which dictated the content and format. I scripted the entire presentation and recorded my rehearsals. With each rehearsal, I revised the script until I thought it was sufficient. The script was completed in three to four rehearsals.

I can tell you that I wasn't nervous about presenting because I had been delivering training and conference presentations professionally for some years. That meant I knew how to organize information and work the technology, and was used to anticipating and fielding audience questions. Also, I believed that my dissertation committee wanted me to succeed and wasn't likely to ask me unjust questions.

While I wasn't nervous about defending my dissertation, I felt like I should be. There was a part of me worried that I had somehow miscalculated what would be expected of me. I did feel like somewhat of a fraud because I used speaker notes instead of memorizing the presentation. Since we were not required to invite an audience for the virtual defense, I didn't, which meant it was just me, the dissertation chair, and a committee member. The chair and committee member had just a few questions and the whole thing took less than an hour. Easy-peasy!

BIG QUESTIONS BEFORE AND AFTER STARTING

Deciding to attend a doctoral program is a big decision. It's right up there with buying a house, choosing a career, or getting married because it requires a lot of resources, dedication, and time. There are so many questions, large and small, to answer before, during, and after the journey.

The first big question was where to attend. Choosing a program was easy once I established a hierarchy of wants and needs. In weighted order, I looked for a program that was accredited, offered online, cost less than twenty-five thousand dollars, could be completed in three years, did not require travel or extensive group work, and had an easy application process. Every requirement on my list was a deal-breaker. Had I not been able to find a program that fit those criteria, I would not have enrolled in a program. I know other students who prioritized institutional prestige, mentorship opportunities, and research funding when choosing where to attend. If I were younger and looking to build a career, my criteria would have been similar to those of the other students I know.

After starting the doctoral program, the next big question to answer was, what do I want to use this degree for? Ideally, this question is answered as part of the decision to pursue a doctorate so it can direct the choice of institution. If you don't answer this question at that stage, the next best time to answer it is at the start of your program because the answer should drive how you select your dissertation topic, to leverage or support your postgraduate plans. In my case, since my primary reason for getting the degree was to assuage my fear of missing out, I decided to not put any pressure on myself to use the degree for anything beyond professional credentials in the circles where it matters.

A final big question emerged about halfway through my program. A colossal question in fact. How would I graduate with my sanity intact? Phrased another way, was the investment worth it? Being in the program was costing me money, degrading the quality of my personal and professional relationships, and eroding my mental health. I worried every day that the return on my investment was absurdly small. What did the title of "doctor" mean if I was unhappy with life, unable to pull myself out of the hole it seemed I was digging in double time?

Finding the answer took a lot of soul-searching, which I've already covered. My answer was to continue, but in a healthier way than I had been doing. That was the best decision I made on my doctoral journey. But I want to take this opportunity to point out there is no shame in changing your mind about what you want out of life. If the doctorate program is not what you imagined it would be and you believe the value does not outweigh the cost, then please make a graceful exit and get on with the rest of your life. Changing your mind is not quitting. Quitting is giving up. Changing your mind is acknowledging your needs.

CHOOSING MY TOPIC

From the very beginning, I felt tremendous pressure to choose the correct dissertation topic. The pressure stemmed mainly from hearing so many times how imperative it is to choose a topic that I could be passionate about for the long haul, and that would also solve a problem of practice, and fill a gap in the literature. That seemed like a tall order.

I didn't find that magic topic on the first try. Taking a practical approach, I asked myself what I was interested in that was a pressing concern for society and that I had access to study. Working for a university seemed advantageous because it would provide me access to faculty, staff, and students.

Being in a health and wellness focus of study, I started looking into obesity. From there, I became interested in food deserts and thought about doing a study on the food available at the campus where I worked. Then a study of college student food insecurity caught my attention and that resonated with me enough that I decided replicating that study at the campus where I worked would be an ideal research project for the dissertation.

I was relieved to have found a topic early in the process and proceeded to draft a dissertation proposal and begin planning my research. During my research planning, I discovered that the systemwide office of the university also thought the study had value because they had already begun a similar study at a few campuses and would eventually be expanding to include my campus. There wasn't a way for me to lead that study for my campus, so I was back to square one, needing to find a dissertation topic.

Since conducting research at my place of employment didn't pan out, I decided to examine what ideas my interests could spark. At the time, I was very interested in health and wellness coaching. So I set out to discover a problem of practice by interviewing several health and wellness coaches. When I asked about the biggest obstacle they were facing, most coaches indicated their training prepared them well for coaching but not adequately enough to establish a thriving coaching practice. Their complaints included their curriculum lacking entrepreneurial education or that the entrepreneurial education was misleading and out of touch with the marketplace.

Bingo! I was passionate about entrepreneurship. My first recollection of entrepreneurship was selling custom-made macrame plant hangers door-to-door in my neighborhood when I was around eight years old. Over the years, I had started numerous small business ventures ranging from matchmaking to business consulting to making sterling silver jewelry. But none of those ventures became sustainable over the long term. Now I had the opportunity to help solve the problem of practice for health and wellness coaching students who needed entrepreneurial education to support their postgraduate plans. After reviewing the very shallow body of literature about health and wellness coaching students, I realized the first step was to demonstrate that health and wellness coaching students *wanted* entrepreneurial education.

I had indeed discovered a topic that related to a problem of practice and had literature gaps and would also sustain my motivation throughout the degree-earning process. I'm still not convinced it's necessary to have passion for the chosen topic because the passion that sustains motivation can stem from your passion to complete a doctorate program in general and not necessarily the research topic. However, I can say that it doesn't hurt you to have a deep connection with what you are researching because there will be challenges along the way. For me, I think my drive to finish was stronger than my passion for the topic. But if you can have both that is a good thing.

As an aside, although I initially thought that collecting data in my workplace would be an advantage and was a bit disappointed that my first topic was a no-go, I learned that it can also be risky to lean on your employer as a data source. I watched more than one colleague be promised access to data only to be left high and dry when the person granting the permission separated from the institution. I was glad I didn't have to deal with that.

Personal Advice I Would Offer Readers

Hold on, dear reader, because I'm about to go all woo on you. Every doctoral journey is unique, shaped by the student's personal experiences and expectations. The expectations you place on yourself and your program are the primary drivers of your experience. If your thoughts are filled with worries or questions about your capabilities or deservingness, your doctoral journey will be stressful in a way that leads to burnout. But when your thoughts about your ability and worthiness are at least half filled with self-compassion, curiosity, and courage, your path will be more straightforward. There will be no need for stress, anxiety, or overwhelm.

My advice to those entering a doctoral program soon is to spend some time clarifying exactly what kind of experience you want to have. Picture how you want to move through your program. What kind of student do you want to be? How do you want to manage your time? What levels of energy will you maintain? What types of connections will you form? What will be the outcome of earning the degree? What would make the outcome worth the investment of time and money? Are there other ways to obtain what you desire besides getting a doctorate? Are those ways more attractive?

For students already on the doctoral path, I offer you this advice. More than anything else, be kind to yourself. You do not need to be hard on yourself to accomplish this dream. You can be, but it isn't necessary. Even if that's the way you have gotten to where you are now. I promise you that self-compassion produces much better results because you enjoy the journey more. Managing your mind and energy throughout the journey is critical to success. Self-judgment creates negative conditions in the mind that consume energy better spent on being productive. Cultivate the ability to slip into a positive mindset on demand. Yes, this is possible. You have more control over your emotional states than you may understand.

Don't worry about meeting anyone's expectations besides your own. Partners, employers, faculty members, mentors, family, and friends will all have expectations about how you do the doctorate. Their opinions do not matter as much as your own. As an adult, you are 100 percent entitled to live your life in any way you choose to, and you are 100 percent worthy, no matter what you do. You are also 100 percent responsible for your choices. Step into the power of that. Own your choices 100 percent of the time. Forget about complaining about circumstances. Every day, choose your path to graduation.

Start leading your process right away by making decisions and moving to the next step. You don't need to overthink your choices about the dissertation. Explore your interests, evaluate the options, choose a viable option, commit to one option, and continue until you are finished or need to pivot. The sooner you choose a path, the sooner you will arrive at your destination.

No path is a straight line to graduation, only decisions that delay or speed up your time to graduation. The path to graduation will be circuitous and obscured with lots of twists and turns. The key to not getting lost along the way is trusting that the territory you explore is necessary to get you to where you want to be. When you stay curious and committed, you will learn from each obstacle, detour, and setback. Don't be in such a hurry to graduate that you put too much pressure on yourself to perform. Have patience with the process and trust in yourself.

On a practical note, be organized. Organized with your thoughts, your ideas, your documentation, and your files. If you haven't yet, create tracking files to organize your dissertation articles and create folders to organize your files. Create schedules to organize your writing activities. Schedule reminders to do the tasks on your schedule. Set yourself up for success. I cannot emphasize enough how necessary organization is to a successful dissertation and defense. Being disorganized wastes time, leads to frustration, and undermines progress. Use all the tools available to make organization easier like citation management software, whiteboards, and learning how to properly format Word documents using style guides.

My last bit of advice should be obvious, but many students, including myself, overlook this. Get help when you need it. If you need academic help, look to classmates, mentors, reputable internet sources, and various university resources like the writing center or librarian (you'd be surprised at how helpful librarians can be). When emotional support is needed, check in with your typical sources such as a partner, friends, family, and trusted colleagues. Be open to seeking additional support from professionals such as therapists, coaches, and doctors. And there's one more source of support that you should not overlook—yourself!

Starting a daily self-coaching habit can turn you into your best source of support. There are so many tools and techniques for self-coaching that promote well-being and mental fitness. A self-coaching routine can strengthen your resilience, reduce your stress level, and improve your quality of life. If you aren't sure how to begin a self-coaching routine, I recommend you reach out to a life coach to get you started. Look for a life coach who offers causal coaching, which addresses the reasons students struggle so those struggles can be resolved instead of just treating the symptoms.

You can engage in life coaching at any point in your program. A life coach will help you clarify your goals, identify obstacles holding you back, and find the right strategies for overcoming each obstacle. Engaging in coaching at the beginning of the doctoral program provides a strong foundation from which to build school-life balance, ensuring a positive educational experience. Engaging in coaching when you need assistance to resolve some difficulty can be the support that keeps you from burning out, dropping out, or taking longer than planned to graduate.

The bottom line is that earning a doctoral degree requires managing sustained personal growth over years, which is decidedly uncomfortable. Leverage all of your resources to make the best of your educational experience.

Conclusion

Starting from a hazy vision of becoming a psychology professor who mentors research students, I ended my formal education with a mission to increase the doctoral graduation rate by helping students harness their productive drive instead of succumbing to their fears. Within a year of graduating, I entered a life coaching certification program and launched a part-time coaching practice serving doctoral students called Best Self Found. Two years after graduation, I retired from my university position to devote more time to my doctoral coaching practice. I found myself in the last place I thought to look: coaching doctoral students and creating tools for them to thrive throughout the degree-earning process and cross the finish line emotionally intact, ready to achieve their postgraduation goals.

CHAPTER 3

A Journey of a Mother's Love

Noha Abdou, EdD

GROWING UP IN THE SUBURBS OF LONDON, ENGLAND, I NEVER IMAG-
ined in a million years that I would someday move to the United States
of America at the age of twenty, or even further from my imagination,
that I would eventually earn my doctorate some thirty-three years later.

My father was an oil and gas exploration geologist who worked for
the Arabian American Oil Company in Saudi Arabia in the early 1970s.
He was exceptionally gifted in the field of oil and gas exploration, with
many accolades for multibillion-dollar oil and gas discoveries during his
distinguished career. Many of his discoveries from fifty years ago still
produce oil and gas today. Many of my father's American bosses would
receive royalties from his discoveries and retired as millionaires in their
early forties; however, he would have no such rewards because my father
came from the Middle East. Instead, the only way the Arabian American Oil Company would reward and retain such a brilliant mind—who
was not a US citizen—was to transfer him to their London offices and
promote him to the head of oil and gas exploration of their European
projects.

I came from a hardworking, middle-class family. We lived comfort-
ably, but we were by no means wealthy. We lived in East Croydon in
Surrey, about thirty minutes away from London by car or train. I was the
oldest of three daughters, and my sisters and I attended an all-girls private school where I excelled in academics and athletics. I was the captain

of Croham Hurst School's lacrosse team in the fall and winter seasons and the lawn tennis team in the spring and summer seasons.

Tennis was life for me back then. I adored Chris Evert and Martina Navratilova's epic battles in the Wimbledon finals. I loved tennis so much that I won several lawn tennis tournaments as a teenager. As a result, I was nominated to be a ball girl at Wimbledon one year by my coach from the Lawn Tennis Association. Unfortunately, much to my utter disappointment and heartache, my dream of being a ball girl at Wimbledon never came to fruition.

The year I was nominated, my father had booked our family's tickets for summer travel to Egypt very early in the year, and, of course, all tickets back then were nonrefundable and nonexchangeable. So, I had no choice but to travel to Egypt and disgruntledly watched Wimbledon unfold on television from there that summer. I don't think I ever forgave my father for that.

Being studious and per the British education system, I finished all my O Levels—or preuniversity qualifying exams—by age sixteen and was headed to college in London. However, my father had other plans. Coming from a very strict upbringing, my father worried that his budding and flourishing daughter might marry a British man someday. He convinced my mother to relocate the family to Egypt, and I would enter the American University in Cairo instead.

I entered the American University in Cairo at sixteen and graduated four years later at twenty with a bachelor's degree in economics and a minor in computer science. Shortly after graduating, I met and fell in love with my husband, who lived in the United States, and we married. Fast-forward twenty years, and I then began my doctoral journey.

BACKGROUND

My doctoral journey is one of a mother's love for her child and her desperate attempt to prove to her child that you can do anything you put your mind to. My doctoral journey began with my postbaccalaureate admission into graduate school.

I had recently accepted a senior systems analyst position at a major public university in southern California. I left the hectic information technology (IT) private sector for a job that provided me with more work-life balance. Being a mother of three, I was tired of working ten-hour days and commuting at least an hour each way. So I decided to take a pay cut and looked for a position closer to home that provided me with the flexibility I needed to be there for my kids and family. I immediately fell in love with higher education and the positive, young, and energetic vibe that existed on college campuses. Walking around the campus during my lunch breaks, I could feel the optimism and larger-than-life attitude that college students exuded. It reminded me of my college days and the nostalgic memories of my undergraduate career from back in the day.

Working in IT for many years, the idea of getting a doctorate never even crossed my mind. It is not a usual degree IT professionals strive for or need to succeed. Instead, I focused on learning new programming languages, systems, and applications to help me advance my career. As such, I began to prove myself among the student affairs information and technology services team and was quickly shining in my new position. I enjoyed shutting work off at 5 p.m., taking my sons to soccer practice during the week, and attending their matches and tournaments on the weekend without worrying about finishing projects for work by a specific deadline. Life was good.

My twelfth grader at the time had just received his provisional admission offer from the same public university where I now worked. The stars aligned since I could now get some of his tuition reimbursed as he was my eligible dependent. My son was excited about starting college in the impacted major of civil engineering, along with several of his buddies from high school. My son has always been mathematically inclined since he was a little boy in elementary school. In fifth grade, he competed with a group of four other students from his school in a mathematics academic decathlon against many other prestigious schools from the southern California region and won first place. He also competed in and won chess tournaments as a young child. So, being mathematically and analytically inclined, engineering seemed a logical and good fit for him. However, he was not sure which discipline within engineering he would be interested in and, therefore, randomly selected civil engineering when it was time to submit his college application.

My Doctoral Journey

Life was rosy. I was in a good place career-wise and could attend to my family's ever-growing demands. My son was able to get into a high-demand major at an outstanding polytechnic university close to home, and my other kids were flourishing in their respective schools too. Then, one fateful day, by sheer coincidence, I discovered that with my son's newly found freedom, he was not attending his classes and would subsequently fail the quarter. The university I worked at followed a ten-week quarter system, and with the fast pace of quarter schools, once you miss a few classes, you are in a rabbit hole that is very difficult to get out of. You are so far behind that it is challenging to catch up. He was, indeed, put on academic notice, which is the step before academic disqualification from the university, and we were left scrambling, trying to figure out what happened and how to get him back on track.

We immediately started individual and family counseling but to no avail. He rebelled against his major, school, and family, and his behaviors spiraled out of control. In counseling, he shared he hated his major and always wanted to attend a university far from home—unlike his current university, which was fifteen minutes away from where we lived. I began researching how he could change his major so he could at least like what he was studying, get back to good academic standing, and ultimately transfer to another institution far from home. I quickly realized that according to the educational policies at our university, freshman students were not allowed to change their major until after their first year had finished. Unfortunately, he was stuck with his civil engineering major—which he despised vehemently—for two more quarters.

As anyone can predict, my son was soon academically disqualified and asked to leave the university. He felt hopeless and like an utter failure, and his depression quickly set in. We tried to get him into further counseling without much success, and he decided to take a break from school altogether. He lost all confidence in himself and his ability to keep up with the academic rigor of university life altogether.

Coming from a Middle Eastern background, where every family member is expected to attain a bachelor's degree minimally, I could not fathom how my son was a college dropout. Everyone in my immediate and extended family has an undergraduate degree, and many have graduate degrees too. However, my motherly instincts kicked in, and all I wanted was for my son to be well and to get his confidence back in himself; all else would follow suit. After repeated failed attempts to get him to see his self-worth, I contemplated embarking on my postbaccalaureate education to prove to my son that you can do anything you put your mind to. However, it had been some twenty-plus years since my bachelor's degree, and I was unsure if I had it in me to be back in school again. Thus, I challenged myself that if I could retake college-level calculus and pass with an "A" grade, I would be graduate school material and would subsequently apply to graduate school. So, I enrolled in a calculus class at my university with thirty other freshmen students—where I stood out like a sore thumb since I was in my forties at the time—and, hence, began my challenge.

My ulterior motive in enrolling in the calculus class was to have my son help me, since mathematics was always so easy for him and, in the process, give him his confidence back in himself. Sure enough, with my son's tutoring and many sleepless nights solving mathematical equations, I passed my calculus class with an "A." I applied for graduate school at the university where I worked using the Cal State Apply application system. Having graduated from my undergraduate institution with a good GPA, I was immediately accepted into the master of public administration program and began my postbaccalaureate journey.

When I accepted my current position at the university, I had taken a reduction in pay for the peace of mind and the work-life balance I needed at the time. So, while taking advantage of the tuition reimbursement that my work allowed for myself and my dependents (which was no longer being used by my son) was a factor in my return to school, my goal was to prove to my son that anyone can do anything they set their mind to.

Working full-time in a new position, with my youngest son now playing competitive club soccer, competing all over the state, and being back in school was very demanding, to say the least. There were many weekends when my son competed in weekend-long soccer tournaments and played many hours away from home. Sometimes, we would leave our house at dawn and return after dark. These were exhausting weekends. Therefore, I wanted to set myself up for success and decided to pace myself with my graduate program. I enrolled in one course only in my first term back in school just to test the waters and get a feel for how I would be able to handle all that was on my plate. Surprisingly, I exceeded my expectations, and I was able not only to hang in there but also flourish, despite all the responsibilities I shouldered all the time. So, in my second term at school, I enrolled in two courses this time and tested this new workload.

Being determined to prove to my son he could achieve anything he put his mind to, I managed to stay organized and kept on top of my work, academics, and my family's rigorous athletic schedule. I was determined to show him the grit and stamina he needed to succeed, not only in college but also in life in general. I managed to juggle all my competing responsibilities with grace and humility. This meant I woke up at dawn to get some of my studies done early in the morning before going to work, and on the weekends when my youngest son was competing in tournaments, I would get my reading assignments done while cheering him on from the sidelines or in between his matches. I would substitute walking around campus during my lunch break for studying or finishing off some of my school projects and assignments. Other times, I would visit the campus library during my lunch breaks to research topics and gather articles for my assignments. Additionally, I consistently allocated time after dinner to wrap up any studying I needed to do for the week so I could stay on track.

I managed to enroll in two courses per term for the remainder of my master's program, and in my final quarter, I even enrolled in three classes so I could finish and graduate with the rest of my colleagues. I must confess that I was overloaded in my final term because my mother called me one morning in early January from overseas and told me that she and my father had booked their international tickets to come to attend my master's graduation later in June of that year. She knew I was close to finishing my program. So she decided to research the spring term's graduation dates online for my university and book their tickets early so they would be reasonably priced. The pressure was now on to graduate, and I could not let my parents down—hence, I took three classes my last term, in addition to writing and defending my thesis, so I could graduate on time.

Attaining my master's degree, all while being a dedicated, working, full-time mom, empowered me to think bigger. It gave me the confidence I needed that with grit, dedication, and determination, the sky's the limit. Maybe, just maybe, I could go on to get a doctorate too? Why not? What is there to stop me? So, while, initially, I embarked on this journey for my son's sake, it indirectly benefited me as it opened my eyes to possibilities that were out there that I never imagined or dreamed of for myself. After all, it was my parents' dream for one of their children to get a doctorate. Why couldn't that be me?

Since stumbling into and falling in love with higher education, I knew I would never return to the private sector. I, immediately, began researching doctoral programs in the field of higher education leadership. I knew that earning such an advanced degree would be an effective tool for career advancement in any university setting. However, I wanted to do my due diligence and choose the right program that aligned with my career goals. Should I consider EdD or PhD programs?

After extensive research and a lot of introspective soul-searching, I realized that I was more passionate about the practical application of a doctoral degree rather than conducting research and following the tenure/tenure-track teaching route. An EdD would allow me to leverage higher educational leadership skills and prepare me for a variety of advanced roles. Being a data geek, I could then influence bringing effective, data-informed decision-making to my institution once I was placed in a leadership role.

Upon determining that an EdD would be better aligned with my career goals than a PhD, I began researching EdD programs that I could afford since money was tight and I did not want to be in debt. My husband and I were supporting my oldest son at the time, who was attending the University of California, Santa Barbara, and my youngest son was applying to Ivy League schools for admission in the fall. So, while my husband was extremely supportive of me furthering my education, paying for our kids' college tuition took precedence over mine. While the higher education institution where I worked practically covered all my master program's tuition, that would not be the case if I enrolled in an EdD program. So I investigated other prominent institutions where I might be able to gain admission as a woman of color and that might be able to offer me some form of grant and scholarship.

The associate vice president of student affairs at the institution I worked at was a trusted and dear colleague of mine, and he was also an adjunct faculty member at the prestigious University of Southern California. He convinced me that if I applied to University of Southern California, since I was a hardworking, smart, and studious woman of color, I would be just the applicant they were looking for. Additionally, my student success research interests aligned with several faculty members in the College of Education, which further improved my chances of getting accepted into their ever-so-competitive EdD program. He, hypothetically, further planned it out with me, where if I resigned from my work and we were just dependent on my husband's income, both myself and my kids would be eligible for financial aid at each of our respective universities. As enticing as it seemed to not have any college tuition burdens for myself or my kids, after much consideration, we completely refuted that proposition. My husband worked in the IT sector, and in the case of a down economy, they were usually the first to get laid off in the private sector. This worried my husband and me terribly, and I, therefore, could not leave my position at the university where I worked in a unionized environment that provided for a more stable workplace. This made University of Southern California unaffordable, and I was back to the drawing board as far as which doctoral programs I could afford.

Working in the California State University (CSU) system, I knew I would still be eligible for a small portion of tuition reimbursement for my doctorate. This made CSU a more affordable option than any of the University of California schools or any private institution, for that matter. After my extensive research, I finally concluded that either CSU, Long Beach, or CSU, Fullerton, had the best EdD programs within the CSUs that are in the southern California region. Given all my responsibilities with family and work, I did not want a school with a long commute.

Therefore, I finally decided on CSU, Fullerton, and submitted my application for the EdD in educational leadership—and so began my journey.

My Topic

Working in IT, supporting the Enrollment Services Cluster—namely the Office of Admissions, the Registrar's Office, Orientation Services, and the Financial Aid Office—I quickly became the go-to person within my circle of friends and family members who had questions about or needed help navigating our university's policies. Since my son's dropping out of college, I became a "mama bear" looking out for all my friends and neighbors' kids who attended the university where I worked. I became invested in their success in college and took it upon myself to be there for them whenever they needed help. I tried my hardest to make sure they had the best college-going experience possible, lest their fate be like my son's. Being passionate about student success, I always joked around with the functional users from the various departments I supported. I would tell them I was jealous of them since they were on the ground, supporting and guiding our students to success, while I only attended to all the various back-end data and systems they needed to do their job, which was nowhere near as sexy, in my mind.

The university I worked at followed a 4/10 summer schedule, to save on electricity on Fridays when the university shuts down. Our long and grueling summer days would start at 7 a.m., Mondays through Thursdays, and finish at 6 p.m. One Monday morning during the summer freshmen orientation season, I was going up the stairs to go into my building at 7 a.m. and noticed a young student who looked lost and confused. I, immediately, reached out and asked him where he wanted to go. Sure enough, he did not know how to get to his orientation session, and he began explaining to me that he was the first in his family to go to college and that he had never set foot on a college campus before. Additionally, he further explained that his parents had to go to work and therefore could not attend the orientation session. Hearing all this unprovoked information, the fear in his voice was palpable.

Being the "mama bear" that I now was, I proceeded to walk with him to the building where his orientation session was going to be held, gave him my business card, showed him where my office was, and asked him to check in with me later in the day. Like clockwork, he came to my office during their lunch break and sought my advice regarding the classes and unit load he enrolled in during his orientation session. The orientation advisor told him to only enroll in twelve units during his first few terms and, perhaps, later, he could increase his unit load as he grew more confident in school. He continued to tell me, in his timid yet hopeful voice, that he had big dreams to one day become a medical doctor.

Having access to all kinds of admissions data, I quickly looked him up in the system and noticed he was a straight-A student in high school and had an amazing SAT score too. He was, obviously, a very smart student. I shared with him my own master's story and how I doubted myself, enrolling in one class only in my first term, and later realized that when I set the bar high for myself, I was able to not only achieve it but to also thrive. This was all the encouragement he needed to add one more class to his schedule, and from that day on, I became his university mom and trusted advisor.

During the academic year, we would have many lunches together in my office. Because he was a first-generation college student, my office was the safe space he needed to come to check in with me on all things college related. His mother even made both of us pozole (a Mexican soup) one time, for one of our lunch meetings. He was an outstanding student with an amazing GPA to prove it. I quickly realized that my dissertation topic must revolve around student success in some way, shape, or form since that was what I was passionate about.

Keeping student success as a dissertation topic in the back of my mind, I oversaw the tracking of some recently implemented strategies at the university to help improve our retention and graduation rates, as part of Graduation Initiative 2025. Graduation Initiative 2025 was the CSU system's ambitious initiative to increase four-year graduation rates and close the achievement gaps among underrepresented minority students and their privileged counterparts. It was apparent to me there was limited research on the predictors of four-year graduation rates within the CSU and the direct and indirect relationships among variables that are predictive of degree attainment within four years for first-time students. Furthermore, in my role within the university, I had access to all the data I needed to conduct such research. Hence, my dissertation topic was now solidified.

BALANCING MY PERSONAL/PROFESSIONAL LIFE

Before embarking on my doctoral journey, I wanted my husband and me to be on the same page about the commitment we were making as a team toward my doctoral endeavor. We discussed the long hours I would need to put in studying and how I would not be able to attend most of the parties and gatherings on the weekends. I also had the same frank conversation with other family members so no one would take it personally if I could not make it to an event or family gathering. Coming from a Middle Eastern background, our weekends were always jam-packed with dinner invitations and gatherings. So I wanted to set the expectation that I am, essentially, dropping off the face of the earth for the next three years or so. My husband played a lot of golf during the weekends, and it sometimes felt unfair that I was studying while he played golf, but I reminded myself it was my choice to get my doctorate. Besides, he needed to fill the void of my not being there with something—for him, that filler was golf.

When I began my doctoral journey, my youngest son was a freshman in college on the East Coast and my husband and I were empty nesters. My middle son was also on the East Coast in college and my oldest had graduated and was working in northern California. I missed my kids so much that I poured my heart and soul into my studies, probably as an escape measure. However, it was no easy feat concurrently working full-time and being a full-time student. I was blessed to have an understanding and compassionate husband who helped me succeed in both roles—without him, none of this would have been possible.

My classes at CSU, Fullerton, were once a week on Wednesdays from 4 p.m. to 10 p.m. The school workload became quickly overwhelming, and I had to adjust fast. I noticed that I could focus more on schoolwork when I studied anywhere other than at home. At home, I was always occupied with cleaning, cooking, doing the laundry, or anything to get out of studying. So, once 5 p.m. came around during the remaining days of the week (except Fridays), I would lock my office door at work and start on my school assignments and readings. I would, typically, stay until 10 p.m. studying. However, most Fridays after work, I gave myself some much-needed time off from schoolwork. This was our movie night for my husband and me, which I looked forward to immensely to decompress from work and school. On Saturdays, I resumed my rigorous study schedule. I would pack my breakfast, lunch, and sometimes dinner, and head to my office to work on my endless papers and research assignments, since most of our assignments were due on Sundays at 4 p.m. Sunday mornings, I, again, would continue to finish my studying and at 4:01 p.m. on Sunday afternoons, it was our much-needed time for my husband and me to catch up on life. Friday and Sunday afternoons were the only times I took a break from studying, and I treasured those times.

Struggles I Encountered Along the Way

Two years into my doctoral program, my whole world was rocked to its core. Life as I knew it would no longer be the same. My father passed away. At the time, I was done with my coursework and was starting on my dissertation chapters. I had also just accepted a leadership position at another university and was barely there for a couple of months when my mother called me one fateful morning with the news that my father's health had taken a dive for the worst and that I should fly overseas immediately to go see him. I dropped work and school in a heartbeat and flew out that same afternoon to go see my father, my everything. I am grateful for the final two weeks I spent by his bedside, day and night, trying to comfort him and holding his hands. Unfortunately, even though I had a very understanding boss, I felt like I could not ask for an extension to my emergency vacation, since I had barely been in my new position for a couple of months. I returned as scheduled two weeks later. Two days after I returned to the United States, my father passed away, on October 23, 2018.

I could not be there with my mother and sisters to lay my father to rest, and that took an immense toll on me, emotionally and physically. My whole world shattered. I managed to keep it together at work, but when I came home every evening, I would just sit there lethargically watching the Weather Channel until I fell asleep. I did not want to interact with anyone, not even my husband, nor do anything outside of work. The days turned into weeks, which turned into months, and I gently pushed back on my dissertation chair when he asked why I was not sending him my dissertation chapters for review. I lost all motivation and the will to continue with my dissertation altogether.

How I Coped with and Overcame My Struggles

My husband, bless his heart, was devastated to see me throw away all my hard work from the last couple of years in my program in the ninth inning like that. He saw how passionate I was about my dissertation topic and now I could not write a word about it. After a lot of brain wrangling on what he could do to get me out of my "funk," he came up with an ingenious idea.

One Saturday morning right before Christmas 2018, he insisted I got dressed and told me he was going to take me on a surprise trip. Much to my astonishment, he took me to a car racetrack in a nearby city. I was shocked to find out he bought us fifteen laps to drive in a super fancy Lamborghini, so I could drive as fast as I wanted and could scream at the top of my lungs and get all my frustration out on the racetrack and would be able to move forward again with my dissertation. Of course, this endeavor cost us an arm and a leg.

While this was my first time driving such a fancy car, at what seemed like lightning speed, I was so touched by my husband's intention that I broke down and cried my eyes out. It finally dawned on me that the one thing my father wanted the most in his final days on this earth was to see me walk across the commencement stage and be hooded as Dr. Noha Abdou. If I did not finish my dissertation, I would be letting him down, big-time. I, then, made an oath to myself that I would do my utmost best, everything that was humanly possible to finish my dissertation so I could graduate with my cohort in the spring of 2019.

I used some mental strategies to keep my eye on the target: graduating. I changed the background of my laptop to one of the commencement ceremonies to encourage myself every time I used it, reminding myself that there was a light at the end of the tunnel. I plastered pictures of graduates in their regalia around work and home to constantly remind myself that this would be me someday soon. Finally, I got my mojo back, and it was a race to the finish line.

At school, a small group of my colleagues and I made a pact after we finished our coursework that we would always be there for each other during the dissertation writing process, as it can sometimes get very lonely. We promised each other that we would drag each other across the commencement stage if we had to. They, too, had tried very hard to get me to join them in their Saturday meetups to write their dissertation, but to no avail. Until now.

Now, I used every minute outside of my work schedule to write, write, and write my dissertation. I would stay in my office till 11 p.m. every night, running statistical analyses and pumping out chapters for my dissertation chair to review. This included weekends too. There was a time when my dissertation chair told me he had to take a day off from work so he could review all the chapters I had given him because I was overwhelming him all at once. I knew spring commencement was around the corner and I could not let my father down.

I joined my colleagues several times in the Saturday meetups at Starbucks but noticed I focused better in my office with my dual monitors. I would use one monitor to pull up all the articles I was using to cite from and the other monitor to write in my dissertation's Word document. Additionally, I always had my laptop with me wherever I went so that I would not waste one minute. Throughout this writing process, the small group of my colleagues and I would check in regularly with each other to see where we were at and to provide feedback when needed. The camaraderie we exuded during our program, and now with the dissertation writing, joined us at the hip, even after graduation. We were now lifelong friends.

My Big Day

When I was at a reasonable place with my dissertation edits, I wanted my chair and I to lock down a defense date and reserve a conference room where my defense was going to take place. I wanted to choose my place in the College of Education before all the craziness started that typically occurred toward the end of the semester and the conference rooms were booked. Luckily, I managed to secure a defense date two months out, and now, both my dissertation chair and I had a real target date to work toward. Soon after, the defense announcement email was blasted out.

My dissertation chair was a meticulous professor who was a stickler with every little detail that might become an issue with my dissertation, or so he seemed to my naive self. While I considered myself a diligent and detailed person, he raised many concerns with my dissertation. Initially, I debated him on several of his concerns, but later I ran out of steam and just wanted to finish. So I made many edits just to appease my chair and get to my defense. Little did I know that all these edits would save me from additional revisions I would need to make post-defense.

Per my chair's instructions, I made my PowerPoint slides for my defense concise and to the point, with no bells or whistles, as I only had twenty minutes to go through all the chapters of my dissertation. I needed to leave time at the end of my presentation for questions and answers, and time for the committee to discuss my research and any shortcomings or points I may have missed. Much to my surprise, I answered all the committee's questions eloquently and I passed my defense with flying colors. I had no revisions that needed to be made. Only then did I understand that every edit I made in the lead-up to my defense date, and the practice runs I had with my chair, were well worth all the pain and heartache.

My husband, without whom none of this would have been possible, attended my defense along with a couple of my colleagues with whom I had made the pact. My mother was afraid her presence in my defense would make me anxious. So she stayed in the car in the parking lot with my sister the whole time, holding a big picture of my dad so he could be with us too. After all the apple cider champagne celebrations and the pictures we took with my committee and colleagues, I ran down to the parking lot to hug my mom and my sister. I, finally, had made my dad proud and was officially Dr. Noha Abdou.

My Biggest Questions
It is not every day one decides to pursue a terminal degree, such as a PhD or an EdD. Since this is a life-changing experience, one must go into

it with their eyes wide open. So many questions that I needed answers to flooded my brain when I first pondered the possibility of pursuing a doctorate. The first one was, is it worth the time, effort, and money to get this degree in my field? Since stumbling on and falling in love with higher education, I knew I would never return to the IT world in the private sector. I also knew that a terminal degree was desirable in higher education if I wanted to pursue a leadership position, regardless of my field. Attaining such a degree would open doors for me. So, yes, it would be worth it, and my return on investment should be worthwhile.

Speaking of cost, I also pondered whether I did not want to burden my family excessively financially since we had college-going kids at the time. So, while there may have been more distinguished schools that I could have applied to and possibly attended, with costly tuition, CSU, Fullerton's rankings in their EdD leadership program convinced me that it was a rigorous, affordable program, especially since I was getting some tuition reimbursement as I worked in the CSU system. So, this was a win-win for me.

Another reason I chose CSU, Fullerton, was because their EdD was a cohort program. Being part of a cohort was very important to me. The bonds formed when you spend three years of your life taking courses alongside your peers and progressing through the program together would be the peer support system I needed lest life throw a curveball at me. Sure enough, it did.

Another question I asked myself was whether I should pursue a PhD or an EdD. I knew I was not interested in a primarily instructional and research role in higher education. Instead, I enjoyed higher education administration more, and thus an EdD would allow me to apply the knowledge I learned to practice. An EdD would give me the skills necessary to succeed in leadership levels, and that's why I chose the EdD route.

I also doubted myself and thought I could not take on such rigorous academics after graduating with my bachelor's degree some twenty-plus years ago. That is why I challenged myself that if I could retake college-level calculus and pass with an "A" grade, I would be graduate school material. I not only surprised myself with getting "A's" but also rose to the occasion when I raised the bar for myself. Thus, I felt ready to take on the world and this doctorate.

When I started my program, we were empty nesters, so I did not have to worry about attending to my kids' needs or demands. However, you must consider this if your kids are still home. But I did worry that my commitment to the rigorous program could impact my marriage. Luckily, I had my husband's buy-in from the get-go, and we both understood that we were a team going into this journey together.

While these are just a flavor of some of the questions you may ponder when considering a doctoral degree, the important thing is to address every one of your concerns before committing to this journey. Going in with your eyes wide open, with all your questions answered, will set you up for success and, ultimately, degree completion.

Personal Advice for Anyone Embarking on This Journey

Reflecting upon my doctoral journey, I have some practical, pragmatic pearls of wisdom that I wished someone had told me before I began, and when I concluded my program.

You should start the program with the end in mind, from the get-go. It is a good idea to start thinking about your potential dissertation topic from day one or before you even start the program. If there is an area that you are passionate about, start reading about all the prior research that has been done on it so you can identify the gaps in the literature. The holes you find are what you should focus on, so you can add to the empirical research that is available.

With regard to your dissertation topic, you will usually start with a general area you are interested in. Then you should narrow down the scope of your research until you eventually discover the small niche or angle you will take to add to the body of literature on the topic. Having a very focused topic makes it easier to run specific statistical or qualitative analyses, and, hopefully, adds significance to the empirical research.

As far as adding to the empirical research, we all embark on our dissertation journeys hoping to find a cure for cancer or solving for world peace, metaphorically speaking. The fact of the matter is, that will not be the case for most of the doctoral candidates, and that is okay.

Do not feel like your research was a waste of time or less than. You are sometimes not going to find statistical significance in your findings. This is part of the journey. The most important thing is that you finished and beat the odds of all those doctoral candidates that are "all but dissertation"—meaning they are done with all their coursework but have not finished their dissertation and have dropped out.

Once you have successfully defended your dissertation, while you are still on autopilot, why not publish your research findings in a journal article? It will require tweaking and reformatting your dissertation to fit the publication. However, if you wait a little, it is much harder to get back into the groove. Additionally, if a lot of time has elapsed, you may find that your research findings are no longer the latest and greatest or relevant. This is something I regretted not doing right away.

Additionally, during your coursework, you will have a deluge of writing assignments for each course you enroll in. If possible, focus your writing so you can make it fit some chapter in your dissertation. When it's time to start writing your dissertation, you can just take paragraphs from your prior work and paste them into the relevant areas of your dissertation. I wish someone had given me this advice when I first started my program. For my writing assignments, I wrote about a wide variety of topics. Then, when it was time for my dissertation, I felt like I was, unnecessarily, starting from scratch again and it was very overwhelming.

Typically, at the end of the first year in the program, all students must take a candidacy exam. During this exam, program administrators will weed out the students they do not think are proficient enough to advance to candidacy. The exam will consist of several prompts and students are tasked to solve the issues at hand or write position papers about them during a limited amount of time. In my program, we were given the prompts on Friday night, and we had to submit our papers by Sunday at 4 p.m. During the candidacy exam weekend, it is a good idea that you be in complete isolation, away from the distractions of your friends and family. Choose an area where you can be completely focused and removed from the hustle and bustle of your everyday life. Personally, I chose to take the exam in my office. I stayed in my office that Friday evening after work and prepared the outline of how I was going to answer the prompts.

Then I returned to my office early in the morning to start the writing process and stayed there until late that night. I returned Sunday morning to finalize my responses and submitted my exam.

Do not underestimate the power of a good peer support system. Luckily, my EdD was a cohort program. In a cohort, all the students are admitted at the same time, take the same courses, and progress along the curriculum together. While our cohort was not large to begin with, a group of us naturally gravitated together and began a friendship that resulted in an amazing peer support system. We helped each other out whenever anyone needed help with any subject, analyses, position paper, or problem at hand. It was this peer support system that managed to get me through to the finish line, especially when the going got tough. I am indebted to them for getting me out of my "funk" when my father passed away. The bond we formed has transcended academics and we are now lifelong friends, checking in on each other and our families on a continual basis. Since life happens to all of us, make sure you surround yourself with a good peer support system, lest life throws a curveball your way.

Lastly, don't forget to celebrate the little wins along the journey. It does the body and mind a lot of good. I used to reward myself with milk tea with boba every time I finished writing a paper. As trivial as this seemed, I looked forward to getting my boba drinks from my local juice bar. Most importantly, sit down, buckle up, and enjoy the ride!

CHAPTER 4

I'm Still Not Sure How I Got Here

Helga M. McCullough, EdD

GETTING A DOCTORATE WAS NEVER THE PLAN. ACTUALLY, GOING TO college *at all* was never the plan. When I look back on my younger years, it's a wonder that I am where I am. There are so many points in my life where my educational path could have gone very, very differently.

My mother moved to the United States from Germany on her own when she was in her late twenties. She was very smart, but she never pursued any formal education beyond completing high school. My mom had me when she was in her late thirties. I was an only child. Unfortunately, when my mother was seven months pregnant with me, my father suffered multiple gunshot wounds to the head. Miraculously, he lived. However, he suffered severe traumatic brain injury and was in a skilled nursing facility for the remainder of his life. As if that event was not traumatic enough, my mother now had to face being a single mom. I grew up without a father figure in my life.

We lived in poverty while I was growing up. I was raised in a mobile home in rural Pennsylvania. In my younger years, I remember my mom working at a gas station, cleaning houses, and working in a grocery store. She probably never really earned much more than minimum wage. She was a very hard worker and somehow managed to make ends meet. Surprisingly, I don't recall ever really feeling like I went without. Sure, all my friends had bigger, nicer homes, and name-brand clothes, but I don't think that really bothered me at the time.

67

I was a good student in elementary school. In kindergarten, there was talk of advancing me ahead one grade, but my mom felt that I already had a nice group of friends, and she didn't want to negatively impact my social life since I was an only child.

It should be noted that when I was in fourth grade, we moved to Arizona because one of my mom's close friends was diagnosed with lung cancer. There were reportedly some very good specialists in the Tempe area, so we hopped in a Minnie Winnie and drove across the country. We were only there for approximately nine months, and I really enjoyed my time there. It was so different to just be able to jump on my bike and ride to a friend's house or to swim in the apartment complex pool in the middle of November. In school, I was placed in a language arts course that was one grade level above my other courses.

When we returned from Arizona, however, we learned that the people who had been staying in our mobile home had essentially destroyed it. Because of this, my mom and I moved one town over and into a very small (well under a thousand square feet) log cabin.

When I got to middle school, I entered quite the rebellious period of my life. From seventh through ninth grades, I racked up a decent number of detentions and served some time in in-school suspension. I started both smoking and doing some social drinking, though the latter was not a regular occurrence. When I was fourteen years old, some friends and I got arrested for stealing golf carts, of all things. They charged us with three felonies and two misdemeanors. We pled guilty to one of the misdemeanors and spent a year on probation. During this time, I also let my grades plummet and did not really care about my classes.

I do not recall there being any expectation for me to go to college, though I am sure my mom was hoping for it. Neither my mom nor I had any close contact with anyone who had gone to college. It was very unfamiliar territory and just not something to which I had given any thought. College was expensive, and we were poor.

In ninth grade, I made the decision to spend half the school day at a vocational-technical school for graphic arts for my sophomore, junior, and senior years. I can't honestly say that I was very interested in graphic arts; I just wanted to get out of regular school for half a day. In my area, back then, kids attending vocational-technical schools were not typically expected to attend college.

When I was sixteen years old, the tiny log cabin my mom and I lived in sustained significant roof damage during a bad winter storm. Because of this, I ended up staying with my boyfriend, which led me to move in with him. So now I was a sixteen-year-old with no real parental supervision, living with a twenty-three-year-old who never even completed high school. We lived in a tiny, six-hundred- to seven-hundred-square-foot cottage behind his parents' house. Looking back, I am always astonished I even finished high school. The perfect opportunity was there for me to drop out. I did finish, though. I guess I figured it was "the thing to do," and I really didn't have anything else going for me at the time.

I started getting my act together and caring more about my grades in my sophomore year of high school. It wasn't until my junior year that I even considered applying to college. Again, it just seemed like "the thing to do." I had not thought about how I would pay for it, nor had I thought about my overall life or career goals. Surprisingly, I don't recall any discouragement from my boyfriend.

I applied to several state schools in Pennsylvania. I honestly had no idea about different majors or what I wanted to do for a career. I didn't have any access to or exposure to "professionals" while growing up, so I didn't even realize what many of my options were. My best subject in high school was English, so I chose that as my major for my applications. To my surprise, all the schools to which I applied accepted me. Clearly, none of them were top tier, but I still felt pretty accomplished, considering college wasn't even on the radar until just a few months prior. I even won a small scholarship through our local Lions Club.

I decided to attend East Stroudsburg University (ESU) in Pennsylvania, which was only about thirty minutes from my home. My mom encouraged me to live on campus to get the full college experience, and I am sure she did not want me commuting every day. She was probably also hoping that I would meet a nice young man who was also working toward a better life.

MY UNDERGRAD YEARS

Even though English was my best subject in high school, I was placed in a zero-credit English composition class in my first semester of college based on a writing sample I had completed during orientation. This zero-credit course was a prerequisite for some students before they were permitted to take for-credit English courses. Knowing that I was in an English composition course that seemed remedial in nature made me question whether I was smart enough to even be in college and also whether English should really be my major. I always thought writing was somewhat of a strength for me, so this was a bit of a slap in the face. Since I was a first-generation college student, I was also connected with student support services. I was very grateful for the mentorship they offered, but this also made me further question whether I was college material.

Living in the dorms was an adjustment for me. As I mentioned previously, I am an only child. I never had to share a room with anyone or really share *anything* with anyone. My roommate, Shannon, was great, and we got along fine. That said, I remember calling my mom crying about three days after moving in. I was really homesick, and I didn't particularly appreciate sharing a bathroom with so many other people. I just wanted to move home (to my boyfriend's) and commute. My mom told me that I needed to give it at least one full semester, and then we could reconsider. While it wasn't the answer I wanted to hear, I thought it was reasonable. Thankfully, that was the one and only time I really wanted to move back home. I should mention that I did go home almost every single weekend, though.

My roommate found the party scene pretty quickly. Perhaps it was a good thing that I was quite rebellious in middle school and early high school because, by the time I got to college, I really didn't have a big interest in partying. Don't get me wrong, I went to my fair share of parties and drank my fair share of horrible beer, but I also took my academics seriously. I knew there were loans involved, and my small scholarship required that I achieve a minimum GPA of 3.0. I most certainly did not want to waste anyone's time or money by doing poorly.

At some point in my first semester, I seriously started questioning whether I wanted to keep English as my major. Again, I didn't have any exposure to "professionals" growing up, so I didn't really know much about many majors or career options. I was, however, pretty certain that I did not want a career that revolved primarily around reading or writing. While I loved to read, I loved to read what I *wanted* to read, not what I *had* to read. I also liked writing, but I was fairly certain that I did not want to make a career out of it. At some point in the earlier part of my college career, I took a criminology course and really enjoyed it. I made the decision to change my major to sociology. That ended up being very short-lived because, from my limited life experience, I felt that every profession tied to sociology was either very emotionally taxing and/or very low paying. So, for a brief time, I was an undeclared major because I really had no idea what I wanted to do with my life.

In sophomore year, I pledged a social sorority. Being an introvert, this was one of the best decisions I made while in college. I met so many wonderful people and had so many wonderful experiences. I am still very good friends with many of my sorority sisters to this day.

At this point, I still wasn't settled on a major, and one of my sorority sisters, Kelly, had mentioned that she was a speech-language pathology and audiology major. She told me a bit about the program and field and said that she really enjoyed the classes and the career options. It happened to be close to the time we needed to register for classes for the next semester, so I thought I would take a class or two in the program.

That was it. I had found my major. I met with the department chairperson and asked to be signed into the program. Thankfully my GPA was very good, as they had a minimum GPA requirement for the program. This also meant that I would have to pursue a master's degree, as that was the minimum requirement to practice as a speech-language pathologist (SLP).

Despite changing my major at least three times, I managed to graduate in four years, which did not seem to be the norm among many of my peers. My cumulative GPA was 3.7, but I knew that getting into a graduate program for speech-language pathology would not be easy. Thankfully, my GPA in the major was 4.0, which I hoped would help.

When it came time to apply to graduate programs, I could not get my act together. Ultimately, I decided to take a year off and work at the front desk of a hotel in the area. I thought that it would be a really nice and laid-back job because people on vacation are always happy. Boy, was I *wrong*!

My mom was very concerned that by taking a year off, I would never actually apply to graduate school. To be quite honest, I was also worried that by taking a year off, I would never apply, and I was concerned that even if I did apply, I might not be accepted anywhere. I knew that the competition for graduate programs in speech-language pathology was fierce. Most programs received hundreds of applications per year for twenty to thirty seats. The smart thing to do would have been to apply to several programs, but ultimately, I chickened out because I didn't want to be far from home. I only applied to ESU. Thankfully, I had a very good reputation in the department and was accepted; it was a very happy and stress-relieving moment in my life. I also applied for a graduate assistantship because, again, I had no idea how I would pay for this.

MY MASTER'S PROGRAM YEARS

It was good to be back at ESU. I really loved the professors and the program. I was accepted for a graduate assistantship, so I felt that I had many extra learning opportunities, especially in the areas of testing and diagnostics. I was pretty convinced all throughout my undergrad and grad school years that I wanted to be an SLP in the schools. I liked the idea of working with children, I liked the idea of having summers off, and I really enjoyed completing my first school-based externship in the Pleasant Valley School District. The next semester, however, I completed an externship in an acute care hospital, which also happened to be right next to ESU, and I absolutely *loved* it. I loved the fast-paced environment, and I loved that I was learning something new every single day. It was both challenging and rewarding. It just so happened that I was graduating at the end of the same semester in which I was completing my medical externship, and the hospital was looking to hire a third SLP. I applied for and was offered the position. My professional career was beginning, and I was very excited.

MY CAREER AND MOTHERHOOD

I felt incredibly fortunate to secure a position at the hospital and was very excited to begin my career. The position was a nice mix of primarily pediatric outpatients and acute care inpatients. Shortly after I started, my boyfriend (still the same one from high school) and I found a fixer-upper house that I purchased. My boyfriend and his dad were pretty handy and felt they could do all the renovations the home needed.

A year or two later, I got pregnant with my first child, Samarah. After I had her, I cut back to a four-day workweek at the hospital. I knew it would be very tough financially because I was the sole supporter of the family. My boyfriend was a stay-at-home dad, so it would be hard making ends meet, but I thought it would be worth it.

Shortly after cutting back to four days per week, I received a call from the SLP department chair at ESU asking if I was interested in teaching a course or doing clinical supervision in their on-campus speech-lan-guage-hearing clinic. I asked her if I could think about it and get back to her. This opportunity was so exciting, but I also found it *terrifying*. So many things were going through my mind. I had only been practicing as an SLP for about three years, and I felt like an imposter (I still do, by the way).

I definitely didn't think I was ready to teach a course. I knew that there would be a ton of prep work, and I honestly just felt very insecure about knowing enough about *anything* to be able to teach it. I was also petrified of clinical supervision but was still considering it. I knew it would be a big commitment, and I was really enjoying having that one "free" day per week to spend with Samarah. That said, I also felt like this was an amazing opportunity and could possibly look wonderful on a résumé. I knew that if I didn't pursue this opportunity, I would regret it. So, I put my fear aside and made the decision to be a clinical supervisor at the university one day per week. That decision is what really got the doctoral ball rolling for me . . . but not quite yet.

ADJUNCTING

It was *never* even a consideration of mine to get into higher education. Like ever. It wasn't that I wasn't interested; it was just not a thought that had ever crossed my mind. I thought my professors were some of the smartest people I had ever met, and I certainly was nowhere near as smart as they were. When I started doing adjunct clinical supervision, I was beyond nervous, but I also knew that I had a great support system of faculty that I had already known for years. They were all incredibly helpful and supportive.

Things are a bit of a blur around this time. I really enjoyed clinical supervision. I also really enjoyed being back on a college campus. I did clinical supervision one day per week for several semesters. At some point in there, I also had my son, Xander, and took a semester off from adjuncting. After I returned, the department chair approached me about making it a full-time position, which would also include teaching two courses. Wow. That was terrifying to consider, but I *really* loved the place and the people. While I was extremely nervous, I knew that I would forever regret not taking the chance. I resigned from my job at the hospital and started full-time at ESU. Coincidentally, at the same time I was transitioning to full-time at ESU, they had also hired Michelle, who was in some of my graduate courses. Michelle was pursuing an EdD with a concentration in speech-language pathology. It didn't take long after starting full-time for me to realize that I *loved* academia. I also quickly realized that I wanted to make a career out of it. While there *are* positions in SLP programs that can be secured with a master's degree, they are typically clinical in nature and not eligible for tenure. I knew that I was interested in a tenure-track position, so I needed to consider a terminal degree.

MY DOCTORAL JOURNEY

I was a mother to two very small children and the sole supporter of our family. Moving was definitely not in the cards for me at the time. Unfortunately, there were no PhD programs within a two-hour drive, nor were there any online PhD programs in speech-language pathology or related fields. At the time, there were one or two online SLPD programs, but I knew that an SLPD would not be the best option for a career in academia, as the governing body for SLP program accreditation does not recognize the SLPD as a terminal degree. I started talking to my colleague Michelle about her EdD program, and it seemed like a good fit. She really encouraged me to apply.

In late 2008, I applied to and was accepted to an EdD program with a concentration in speech-language pathology at Nova Southeastern University, with a January 2009 start. The plan was to take two courses per trimester while working on my dissertation after the first summer. The program could be completed in approximately three years as long as students worked on their dissertations throughout. Well, things didn't go so smoothly for me.

The courses were not really the problem. I successfully navigated those, even managing to maintain a 4.0 GPA. It was extremely challenging to do so while working full-time and parenting a toddler and a preschooler. The problem, for me, turned out to be the dissertation aspect of the program. I knew that I was supposed to be working on it; I just could *not* find the time or motivation to get started.

It was also becoming clear that, after more than fifteen years together, I needed to end things with my boyfriend. At that point, I was facing the prospect of being a single mom and the sole provider of two small kids, working full-time, and completing my final courses and a dissertation. As if this wasn't daunting enough, I was also really beginning to worry about the permanency of my position at ESU. While I was full-time, I was on year-to-year contracts, and there were many cuts being made to higher education around that time. It kept me awake at night, and I worried constantly. Being a newly single mom, I knew that I could not afford to be out of work. Looking back now, I do not think my position was ever really in jeopardy, but I let fear get the best of me. I began looking for other options. In late spring 2011, close to when I was finishing up my coursework for my doctorate, I left academia and took a position as an assistant director of rehabilitation/speech-language pathologist at a skilled nursing facility. I cried. I most certainly did not want to leave a place and a position that I truly loved, but I also needed to do whatever I could to ensure that I could support my kids.

Quitting

Here I was, no longer in academia, making significantly more money, and not sure I would ever go back to academia. I finished up my last courses and had nothing left to complete for my degree except the dissertation. That said, I hadn't even started on it aside from choosing a topic and gathering a ton of literature. Once I finished my last courses, I was taking out over three thousand dollars in loans each trimester for dissertation services that I wasn't even using. Each trimester, I told myself that I would work on my dissertation, but I just could *not* find the motivation to do so. I felt immense guilt almost every single day.

In January 2013, I asked if I could take a semester off from dissertation services since I wasn't actually using the services. Thankfully, that was permitted, but that really was the beginning of the end. One semester off turned into several. Needless to say, after making no progress toward my dissertation, I received notification that in December 2015, my time to complete my doctorate would expire, and I would no longer be permitted to continue in my program. I was both devastated and relieved. It wasn't looking like I would be going back to academia, so why did I need a doctorate? But at the same time, I felt like a complete and utter failure that I had come so far and had absolutely nothing to show for it.

Around this same time, my mom started having some health issues. Up until that time, she had always been very active and healthy. She began exhibiting difficulty walking, was demonstrating increased weakness, and had fallen a couple of times. A neurologist that she was seeing diagnosed her with polyneuropathy. I had gone to an appointment with her and questioned the neurologist's diagnosis, asking if it could possibly be something else. He became very defensive with me when I asked for a second opinion. I ended up taking my mom to another neurologist who ran some additional tests and referred her to a neuromuscular specialist.

On December 17, 2015, my mom was diagnosed with amyotrophic lateral sclerosis (ALS), which was a death sentence. It was always just me and my mom growing up, so this was incredibly devastating news. I also was pretty familiar with ALS and recalled my grad school neuro professor referring to it as "the most awful disease." He was correct. For those not familiar with ALS, it disrupts the signal from your motor neurons to your muscles. Eventually, your muscles become nonfunctional, and you no longer have any voluntary physical control of your body. You lose the ability to walk, talk, eat, everything. All of this occurs while your mind is still sharp, and you are fully aware of what is happening to you. After her diagnosis, I found it hard to do anything, let alone the task that already seemed impossible.

I let my time expire, and I can't even explain the immense guilt I felt almost every single day. I had made it so far, took out close to a hundred thousand dollars in loans, and felt like it was all for nothing. I felt like such a failure. I also knew this made my chances of going back to academia and securing a tenure-track position nearly impossible. What had I done?

RETURNING

It was around this same time that I was scrolling through Facebook one day and saw a post from my old friend and colleague, Michelle, that she *finally* completed her EdD and was at commencement at Nova Southeastern University. I was so happy for her but also so mad at myself for quitting. I messaged Michelle to congratulate her, and she told me that her time had expired as well, but she had appealed and finished. She encouraged me to do the same. I took this as a sign but also was not very hopeful that they would grant me an extension or that I would actually follow through with it.

In October 2016, I was approved for a one-time, one-year extension beginning in January 2017 and ending in December 2017. During that time, I was required to demonstrate "noticeable progress," including an approved dissertation proposal (chapters 1 to 3). If I did not produce an approved dissertation proposal by December 13, 2017, I would be permanently dismissed from the program. It was my last shot, but I wasn't confident that I had it in me.

After I was granted the extension, I made a phone appointment with my dissertation chair. She was supportive of my return but also gave me some very strict deadlines so that I would complete chapters 1 to 3 before being permanently dismissed from the program.

It was now or never. Do or die. I knew that to be successful, I had to choose a new topic. I wasn't inspired by my previous topic, and I couldn't rely on the literature I had already gathered still being current.

THE DISSERTATION

Before I had even chosen a new topic, I had a meltdown. By this time, I had been with a new partner, Phil, for a couple of years. He was so incredibly supportive of me completing my doctorate. When trying to figure out a new topic, I cried to him that I wasn't cut out for this, it was too hard, and I would never be able to do it. I hadn't even really started working on it yet, and I was already giving up again.

I knew that I couldn't completely re-create the wheel if I only had one year to complete chapters 1 to 3 while working full-time and parenting two active kids. I began searching the literature for a study that had been completed in a related field in the hopes that I could then replicate the study in the field of speech-language pathology. I searched through physical therapy, occupational therapy, and nursing literature. I finally found a topic in which I was interested, and I thought was manageable in my limited time. I ran it past my dissertation chair, and she approved it and thought it was a great topic. I got started on gathering literature and writing. I had previously been so intimidated by the writing process, but I knew that I *had* to start somewhere. I needed to just get words down on paper and not worry about being perfect from the start. Sometimes I get so overwhelmed by tasks that I can't even start them. Then once I do start them, I realize that it was foolish to avoid them for so long.

Once I completed my concept paper, which is essentially an abbreviated version of what would become chapters 1 and 2, I felt great. I was very proud of myself, and I received good feedback. That said, I was also told that I would need to significantly expand my literature review. I recall that feedback being very deflating because I thought that I did a thorough job with my literature review and was dreading the idea of having to do more.

I was already feeling disheartened because significantly expanding my literature review seemed impossible, and then my mom passed away on Mother's Day in 2017. Even though she had a progressive, terminal illness, her death was rather unexpected by everyone, including her physician. Yes, she had been progressing somewhat rapidly in the weeks prior, but she was definitely not at the very end of the ALS progression. I did not request an autopsy, but if I had to, I would guess she suffered a heart attack. I say this because back in February 2016, she was hospitalized for a severe urinary tract infection and pneumonia. Just after she was transferred from acute care to an acute inpatient rehabilitation facility, she suffered a heart attack. She was sent to the intensive care unit, and the cardiologist recommended that she get stents, or she would likely have another heart attack. My mom declined the stents and told the cardiologist that she would rather die from a heart attack than suffer from ALS. That was very hard to hear, but I likely would make the very same decision for myself.

My mom passed away on a Sunday. When I saw her the day before, she told me, "Helga, I am so tired." I told her to go ahead and take a nap, and her response was, "No, of this," meaning the ALS. Less than thirty-six hours later, she was gone. It was devastating, but I know it was what she wanted. My mom was so independent her entire life. ALS completely robbed her of that independence well before her time.

My mom's death threw a wrench into my plans, but it also somewhat motivated me to complete my dissertation and earn my degree. My mom was so proud that I was working on a doctorate, and I wanted to complete it for her, even though I knew she would never see it. I took some time but got back to it within a few weeks.

When I say that I met my deadline by the skin of my teeth, I am not kidding. Recall that my deadline, as stated in my extension letter, was December 13, 2017. Close to that time, I received an email stating that if I did not have an approved proposal by December 10, 2017, I would be dismissed from the program. That was three days earlier than I had planned, and I truly needed those additional three days. I submitted chapters 1 to 3 to my dissertation chair and committee member very close to the deadline. It was so close that I felt the need to send a pleading email to my dissertation chair and committee member asking if there was any possibility they could approve it by December 13, 2017. I was one of *those* students. I was incredibly fearful that I was going to be kicked out for good. Oh, I forgot to mention, I also now had a job that was contingent upon my completion. We'll get to that shortly. I assure you that I breathed a *huge* sigh of relief when I received notification that my proposal was approved and that I was granted an additional one-year extension to finalize my dissertation.

In January 2018, I started a position as a tenure-track assistant professor in a speech-language pathology master's degree program with the stipulation that I needed to earn my EdD within my three-year renewable period. I was so excited to be back in academia and putting all this hard work to good use. This obviously increased the pressure to get it done but also increased my motivation.

My dissertation topic was on generational differences in work ethic among Pennsylvania SLPs. My plan was to purchase a list of email addresses for the approximately eighty-five hundred SLPs licensed in Pennsylvania from the state licensing board and then send the link to my study out to all of them via email. Much to my chagrin, lists provided by the state licensing board do not contain email addresses. Again, I was feeling deflated.

I knew I could not financially afford to send my survey out via regular mail, so what the heck was I going to do now? The best solution I could come up with, though it would be very time-consuming and cumbersome, was to cross-reference all eighty-five hundred names on my purchased list with the online membership directory of the American Speech-Language-Hearing Association and then send the consent and survey link through the messaging option within the online directory. I started this process in February 2018, and it was very time-consuming. Thankfully, I had some assistance from a student worker, which was a godsend. My survey remained open until mid-March, and I collected over eight hundred responses. I felt like I was in the home stretch at this point. I recruited some assistance with data analysis and interpretation and got to writing the remainder of the chapters. It felt incredible to submit a draft version of the whole shebang in mid-July 2018, but once again, I received some feedback that I needed to elaborate significantly on my discussion chapter. I took my dissertation chair's comments and ran with them. I was hell-bent on getting this squared away before the end of the summer and having to go back to work. I had a completely revised chapter submitted to my dissertation chair within two weeks, and her feedback was very positive. I had minimal revisions to make, and I was done with the entire process by mid-September and on track to earn my EdD in December 2018. It really felt too good to be true, and I kept waiting for the other shoe to drop. Thankfully, that never happened, and I *finally*, after *nine years* and so many ups and downs, earned my doctorate. It was surreal.

What I'm Doing Today

I am still in the same position I started in 2018 and am up for tenure this year. That is very exciting, and I am looking forward to achieving this goal. During the COVID-19 lockdown, I worked on converting my dissertation into a peer-reviewed journal article. That was a daunting but wonderful learning experience. I have presented at both the state and national levels, and I am really looking forward to some upcoming professional projects.

Advice I Would Offer to Anyone Considering Pursuit of a Doctorate

What is your motivation for earning a doctorate? That is going to be different for everyone, right? Regardless of your motivation, make a note of it and refer to it *frequently*. I would also suggest finding an accountability partner. I had absolutely *no one* holding me accountable for my dissertation. My dissertation chair was supportive of me, but she definitely was not going to hold my hand, nor did I expect her to do so. That said, I should have asked someone close to me, a colleague, or a fellow doctoral student to be an accountability buddy. I also can't stress this enough . . . *just write.* I was so intimidated by starting that I just didn't start. If I had even just committed myself to one paragraph per day or one page per week, I would have been so much better off. I think I was so stressed out by looking at the big picture of a more than one-hundred-page dissertation that I let fear paralyze me. Treat it like any ol' research paper that you will expand on later. *Just start writing.*

Also, don't be afraid to ask for help. I am sure that if I had asked my dissertation chair to hold me more accountable or put some extra pressure on me to get things done, she would have done so. I just never asked. I am not the type to ask for help, nor do I talk about my struggles, and sometimes both of those things bite me in the butt.

QUESTIONS I HAD BEFORE BEGINNING MY DOCTORAL JOURNEY
How Would I Pay for This?

I was not making much money when I started my doctorate, and I was also the sole supporter of a family of four. There was no funding available for the program I had chosen. I did not have any money in savings. I knew I would have to take out many loans to complete the degree. What I didn't realize at the time was that most positions in higher education qualify for the Public Service Loan Forgiveness program as long as the institution is not-for-profit. Thankfully, my employer is a not-for-profit, and I am on track to having the remainder of my loans fully forgiven.

Would the Benefits Outweigh the Drawbacks?

I knew that pursuing a doctorate would entail a great deal of work, leading to missing out on social and family time. I also knew that it would be very stressful, potentially negatively impacting relationships and overall well-being. That said, I really enjoyed learning, and I really wanted to achieve this goal. I also felt somewhat stale in my career, and I knew this could be a way to remedy that. For me, it really helped to keep the benefits in mind. I knew my primary goal for earning a doctorate was securing a tenure-track role in higher education. I also knew that such a position could potentially afford tuition remission for my kids, a better work-life balance, and more flexibility with my schedule.

Am I Capable?

A doctorate just seemed so prestigious. I knew that I was smart, but was I *that* smart? I always tend to feel this way when embarking on new journeys. I have always shied away from doing things unless I am confident I can succeed. Clearly, I was capable, and I am grateful that I did not let those doubts stop me.

Does This Particular Degree Have the Potential to Get Me Where I Want To Go?

I knew I wanted to pursue a tenure-track faculty position in a speech-language pathology program. I also knew that not just *any* doctoral degree was the best bet for this goal. Students wishing to become certified SLPs need to attend a graduate program that is accredited by the Council on Academic Accreditation in Audiology and Speech-Language Pathology (CAA). The CAA mandates that terminal degree holders must teach the majority of graduate-level courses in an accredited program. The CAA also specifies that they only recognize the PhD and EdD as appropriate academic terminal degrees in our field. Therefore, I knew that pursuing a clinical doctorate in speech-language pathology (SLPD or CScD) would not afford me the best opportunities for the goals I wished to achieve.

Would I Have the Support That I Needed?

I had two small children. I was working full-time. I could not afford *not* to work full-time. I knew I would primarily have to use weekends to complete the bulk of my schoolwork. Thankfully, at the time, my kids' dad was very involved in their lives and did the vast majority of child-related work. If he had not been so willing to be their primary caretaker, I likely would not have been able to keep up with my coursework, so I am very grateful that he was so involved in their lives when they were so young.

CHAPTER 5

My Doctoral Journey

Wanda K. W. Ebright, PhD

MY DOCTORAL JOURNEY BEGAN FIFTY-FIVE YEARS AGO WHEN I WAS born at Hunter Army Airfield to an Air Force family in Savannah, Georgia. My father held a degree in chemistry and was a meteorologist who would go on to work with the National Weather Service and the National Hurricane Center. My mother was a registered nurse who would continue her education with a bachelor's degree, certification, and a master's degree in public health administration. Each was the first to attend college on their respective sides of the family, and each of their mothers was educated in one-room schoolhouses in rural Georgia.

As an African American family in the 1960s, the armed forces were one of our best chances for equitable work and pay with health benefits and retirement. I was the last born, with one brother four years my senior and twins born two years later, on his birthday. As expected, we moved frequently and learned to make new friends fairly easily. Our parents required us to be engaged in one sport and one art form at all times, to keep us out of trouble. I was a gymnast and played softball for my sports. For our artistic outlets, we had to take one year of piano lessons so we could read music. Then we could change to something else. I began to study dance at the age of four, but also studied piano and sang in choirs and choruses.

I loved school, and my parents incentivized reading and scholarly work. I earned a penny per page I read, so I sought out large volumes of classic literature. I received a dollar for every "A" on my report cards and relished the role of "smart kid." Though I struggled some with mathematics, I graduated high school in the top 10 percent of my class and attended the US Air Force Academy as an international affairs major. I wanted to follow in my father's footsteps and to outrank him someday. However, it was not a place where I thrived. I left the Air Force Academy, took a break, then continued studies at Augusta College in Georgia, and then finished at Memphis State University, in Memphis, Tennessee, with a bachelor of arts in French with a history minor while living with my then remarried father.

In 1992, I married a man who encouraged me to put all my energy into dancing instead of teaching French. I was accepted into a highly competitive MFA program in dance performance and choreography at Florida State University (Tallahassee) in 1993, reaching the highest levels of both ballet and modern dance about halfway through the program, which allowed me to customize my curriculum. Here I began to research the history of Black classical ballet dancers as I sought my place in the higher education dance landscape. Upon graduation, I taught ballet, pointe, modern, jazz, composition, and dance history to grades eight to twelve in an arts magnet high school in Atlanta for four years, followed by two years as an assistant professor of dance at Kansas State University. I would then come home to the Southeast to work for eight years at Coker College, in Hartsville, South Carolina.

Why I Pursued a Doctorate

At some point in the 2007/2008 academic year, I became a tenured associate professor of dance at Coker College. I was dance program coordinator and had revamped curricula, recruiting, and marketing for my program. At this time, I started to get bored and began to seek new challenges, so I established a dance company called the Wanda Project. Beginning to seek new challenges again, I saw that Texas Woman's University (TWU) was seeking its second cohort for the low-residency PhD in dance.

I applied for early acceptance but heard nothing in the fall. In early spring I was contacted for a phone interview. I was told my research focus of excavating the history of Black classical ballet dancers had been done before and was not of interest. When asked why I wanted a doctorate, I replied "to serve as department chair or higher and to write and revise inclusive texts on dance in higher education." In response, I was told that I didn't need a doctorate to do any of those things. I hung up, cried, and gave up.

Around early April, I received a call saying that I'd been accepted into the summer 2008 doctoral cohort at TWU and asking if I would be accepting my spot. I asked for a day or two to consider it, since it meant arriving in Texas in under two months' time, canceling summer travel plans paid for by a relative, leaving my husband and kids, and paying for tuition and textbooks with short notice. I was furious, elated, confused, and terrified, all at once.

I knew several scholars with doctorates who were pompous and arrogant, and I never wanted to be one of them. I didn't want to publish to impress other academics. I wanted to publish things most of the American public could read, using language most could understand. I was reassured by a few treasured colleagues that I would be me, no matter what rank or title I might hold. I discussed it with my husband at the time, who reassured me that it would be an investment in us and in our family. It would require sacrifices from all of us, with our daughters rising into the sixth and eighth grades in the fall after the initial summer residency in Texas. I took a deep breath and accepted my slot in the cohort.

The low-residency PhD in dance at TWU required a five-week summer residency, fall and spring terms each with one week in residence for presentations and feedback, a three-week summer residency in the second summer, fall and spring terms with one-week residencies, and a final two-week residency in the third summer. All coursework would be completed during that time. After this, each member of the cohort would be on a personal time line, based on their work and readiness to move forward. The qualifying exams, prospectus proposal and defense, dissertation stage, eventual dissertation defense, and commencement would all be completely individualized.

Struggles along the Way

When June came around for the initial summer residency, my mother stayed with the kids and my husband and I drove from Fort Mill, South Carolina, to Denton, Texas. I was moving into graduate student housing with two members of my cohort, and we needed to buy groceries, a microwave, and other cheap supplies for the five weeks. We drove around so I could get acclimated to Denton, and I had a complete meltdown as all my insecurities and the "mom and wife" guilt consumed me.

I loved my roommates and my cohort colleagues, but we all had very different study methods. They preferred talking things out as a group and quizzing each other. I preferred solitude in a private study room of the main campus library, where I could focus. I'd always prided myself on having an exceptional vocabulary, but I constantly encountered words I'd never seen or heard of before in scholarly texts. I was continually having to read and reread while looking up what seemed like at least one word per sentence, hoping to comprehend any given paragraph once read through.

The philosophy books we were reading seemed like a foreign language, and I was trying to grasp the barrage of challenges to what I thought I knew. Nothing was absolute truth, history was only a story from one person's perspective told for a particular audience, for a particular benefit to some party, and it was always crafted at the expense or omission of others. Objects and images were no longer real, but relational, as meaning completely shifted based on the lens and personal baggage of the viewer or participant, the desired end result of observation or critique, and the intended end user of the research.

In effect, everything seemed a lie, including whatever research each of us planned to explore, author, and publish for global consumption. We were also required in one class to plan the delivery of online courses in our field. Already in my forties, I was not at all a digital native, and the idea of teaching dance studio or theory courses entirely online seemed ludicrous in a world unaware that someday the COVID-19 pandemic would require literally every academic discipline to rethink what was possible online.

Balancing the Personal and Professional

Coping with the stress of beginning the doctoral coursework was a mix of both healthy and unhealthy mechanisms. I stress-ate and -drank a great deal, gaining at least five pounds per residency. I sought and found a church home in Denton. This was not a priority for other members of my cohort, so I went to church alone on Sundays to a Lutheran worship service. They had an outreach that provided stuffed animals to comfort those under duress, so I'd pick one up, hold it throughout the service, and I'd cry every single week.

I missed my husband, I missed my kids, and I missed my dog. I missed my mother and my friends. So very few people knew what I was going through and how genuinely difficult it was. We were reading ten books at a time and being asked to synthesize it all into a two- or three-page paper, remembering both to crystallize the authors' varied perspectives and use them in combination with our newly informed perspectives to generate original, supported theories. While in this first residency, I was offered a new job, a promotion to department chair, and a significantly higher salary to move from where we lived in Columbia, South Carolina, to Charlotte, North Carolina. We would have to sell our house during the market crash, find a new home, find a school system where both girls could start in the same middle school for a tiny bit of mutual comfort, and my husband would have to transfer with his job, if possible.

I spoke with my doctoral advisor, Dr. Penelope (Penny) Hanstein, about whether to take the job. She laughed softly and said that you don't just turn down an opportunity like this. She saw me as an emerging arts administrator like herself, and she further counseled me accordingly. I had to accept that with these major upheavals during my coursework, I could not expect to graduate when my peers did. I needed to get okay with that because the others were either not teaching, were adjuncts instead of full-ime, were not yet tenured, and for the most part were neither parents nor married. I was a tenured associate professor with a spouse, two kids in middle school, a new job and what became multiple relocations, and a charge to create new arts degree programs from scratch while pursuing my doctorate.

Several things helped me through these two years of coursework. My cohort became so close-knit and supportive as a whole that we scaffolded each other through personal, professional, and academic challenges. We accepted various study styles, with most of my cohort engaging in study groups to discuss readings while I studied alone in a quiet room of the library. We accepted everything about each other, including race, gender, social class, nationality, and genre of dance, since it was a doctoral program in dance. We took turns breaking down under the stress of coursework and putting each other together again. We helped each other revise our writing and talked out what we didn't understand about the readings.

As I finished my coursework and prepared slowly for my qualifying exams, my doctoral advisor announced that she was retiring. That meant I would have a new advisor for my dissertation committee. It was around this time that my marriage rapidly started to decline, though I had missed or misinterpreted signs along the way. We moved my mother into our home to help with our then teenaged daughters. My husband asked me to step down as department chair, put my dance company on hiatus, and pretty much just come home after work, to prioritize our marriage, and I did. He asked me to stop working out before work in the mornings, so I was around longer, and I did. I completed my qualifying exams and flew to TWU to defend them.

At my prospectus defense, I learned that in my efforts to be as scholarly as possible in my writing, the committee felt I had distanced myself so far as the researcher from my writing that now they could no longer see my personal analytical voice. In retrospect, I think the same could be true at that time for how I was present as a professor, a wife, and a friend. My new doctoral advisor told me she was unhappy in the job and would be leaving after only one year, so I would get a third dissertation chair and advisor. My husband and I entered marital counseling, but I also undertook my own individual counseling, to take ownership of healing my childhood and early adulthood traumas that heavily influenced my marriage. Then he announced he was leaving, and I filed for divorce so I would have clarity about division of property, custody of two children, and responsibility for the kids going to college or other career training. This, he said, was a declaration of war, and he moved to California.

I was assigned a third advisor, one who had also taught several of my courses. She was frustrated because all the members of my cohort originally assigned to my initial advisor and then the second advisor were now landing on her, in addition to her original roster of doctoral advisees. I struggled with a third person's ideas and suggestions about how to change everything about my approach to my topic, my writing style, my sources, and the points I wanted to make as a researcher. One daughter was beginning college at Duke University, so I needed her to be able to focus on school, not on whether I had the money to keep her there. The other daughter was struggling with high school and bullying while missing her sister terribly. I was thousands of dollars in debt from my divorce lawyer and private investigators, and my third advisor was diagnosed with breast cancer that was advancing rapidly. With so many things to worry about, I often stopped writing for months at a time.

Overcoming the Obstacles

With all these challenges to my writing focus, I found it easier to periodically disappear for a long weekend or fall or spring break and to work intensely for a short period of time, rather than to block daily writing time. When TWU began offering dissertation boot camps, I signed up for accountability and support while blocking a few days or a week at a time to make a lot of progress at once. I remained in counseling and worked with my primary care physician to start minimal doses of antidepressants and antianxiety medications so I could remain stable for my kids while making progress with my dissertation. My colleagues and cohort members served as readers for feedback, a close friend managed all my formatting problems, and I sold both the marital home to pay for Duke and TWU and almost everything inside it to keep food on the table and gas in our cars for myself and my youngest daughter.

Approximately a year after filing for divorce, I had a breakthrough and realized I was the only person really stopping me from finishing my doctorate. I realized all I had handled while in the dissertation phase. I had simultaneously created an interdisciplinary bachelor of arts program in visual and performing arts with concentrations in dance, theatre, film, graphic art, studio art, and sound art; a bachelor of arts in dance;

and minors in dance, theatre, photography, and animation at Johnson C. Smith University. I had gathered data on five historically Black college campuses, passed and defended qualifying exams and a prospectus for the dissertation, and adapted to three different advisors. I would not be denied this accomplishment. After these realizations came to me, it was easier to write, edit, and finish.

I completed my dissertation defense in the summer of 2017, graduating in August, but attended my hooding ceremony on campus in December of that year. That fall, a dear friend urged me to apply for an associate dean position at Winthrop University in Rock Hill, South Carolina, about half an hour south of Charlotte. The week prior to my doctoral hooding ceremony in December 2017, I was asked to interview on campus. I asked to attend my ceremony first, and I interviewed a day or two after my commencement ceremony. Less than a week after that, I was offered the job. My salary increased by approximately forty thousand dollars per year. I got a financial advisor, became a solo homeowner, and also became an empty nester.

The COVID-19 pandemic came and started to taper off, and in my fourth year as associate dean at Winthrop University, I decided to test the waters and see what work I still needed to do to eventually become the dean of a college of visual and performing arts. I applied across the country to a handful of positions but realized I did not want to leave the Southeast. I refined and narrowed my search and applied to Columbus State University in Georgia, expecting to be eliminated at some point, and to discern where I needed to hone my interview skills or materials. The search firm saw all that I had accomplished before in my materials but noted that I had not bragged enough about myself for a search committee to notice. I was urged to create a bulleted list of my accomplishments, so the firm could include it for the search committee. I did and became a finalist.

The search firm talked me through my answers to typical general search questions, so I could do my thinking and clarifying prior to arriving on campus. I was offered and I accepted the job as dean, and my salary jumped by another seventy-one thousand dollars per year. I bought a house, am continuing to invest for retirement, and started building generational wealth for the future of my family. I started to notice doctoral or dissertation support communities on social media and joined whenever I could in order to provide encouragement to people struggling with distractions from writing, discouragement due to critical feedback, parenting while researching and writing, or fear that their relationships would suffer because significant others and family or friends did not understand the doctoral process or the need to pursue it.

Why It Was Worth Doing

As a woman of color and as a mother, it is so important to me that students of color see themselves reflected in higher education leadership roles. It is important for both male and female students to witness a woman leading without apology or allowing her authority to be undermined. It is important for campuses and communities to see that a woman can be both a good mother and an effective and ethical leader of people and steward of resources. It is important for visual and performing artists as well as their peers to see that a ballet dancer can be a respected dean and an equal among academic role models in executive positions, especially that an artist can make six-figure salaries with benefits. The country is quick in times of financial crisis to challenge the need for college. While I agree that not everyone needs a college degree, I also insist that some of us absolutely need one to reach this level of self-sufficiency.

Once I had completed my bachelor's degree in French, and my then-fiancé convinced me to pursue dance as a career, I thought through what job would allow me to dance, teach, choreograph, research, write, and present at conferences. The answer was "dance professor." I completed my MFA in dance and, seeing the dearth of resources on dance in higher education that include people of color, or historically Black institutions and historical figures beyond Alvin Ailey and Arthur Mitchell, I chose to focus on these things. I noted that the people who wrote and edited higher education textbooks held doctorate degrees and that in search committees for jobs, those with doctorates sifted to the top of the rankings right off the bat. Because of these things, I knew I would need a doctorate in addition to my master's degree in order to be taken seriously as a leader or administrator and as an author or editor.

Regarding search committees for colleges and universities, I observed that in the arts there is a persistent rift between professors of the practice with an MFA and researchers/writers with a doctorate. Those with an MFA tend to feel those with doctorates get them because they aren't highly skilled, technical artists, hence the belief that those who can't do, teach. Those with doctoral degrees tend to feel MFA practitioners pursued them because they cannot write or speak well. This keeps both groups feeling superior while continuing to promote a false dichotomy, a sense that there are only two options available to everyone. Part of my strategy has been to attain both my MFA as a practitioner and also my PhD as a researcher, author, and presenter. This discourages in searches any implication that I am less than other candidates with only one or the other of these types of degrees.

QUESTIONS

There are several important questions to ask yourself if you are considering pursuing a doctoral degree.

Do You Enjoy Conducting Research?

It's important to know that the purpose of a doctoral degree is to contribute new knowledge or a new interpretation to your field of study. That requires you to select one or more research questions, develop a research project, choose a methodology, conduct the research, sort and analyze data, and then write and publish the findings and analysis. If you find all of this distasteful, a doctorate will be torture for you.

Do You Enjoy Writing, or Do You Dread It?

If you enjoy the writing, that is helpful in doctoral study. If you struggle with clarity of thought, grammar, punctuation, or spelling, you will likely need to budget for an editor. An editor will not write your papers for you, but they will let you know where your thoughts are unclear and where you need to review and revise grammar issues. I had a lot of trouble with formatting and sought a colleague's help with that, so I could focus on the writing itself.

Do You Want to Be an Educator, or Is It the Only Career You Could Think of in Your Field?

As a professional dancer, I have known many peers in dance who considered teaching as the only option they could think of once their performing years came to an end. This is not an ideal reason to teach and could lead to resentment and bitterness on the job when the educator is asked to do unpleasant or unsatisfying work. If you have a passion for education and for being the positive change your field needs, then doctoral study may be right for you.

If You Want to Be an Educator, What Ages and Levels of Education Do You Most Enjoy Teaching?

You want to be sure to pursue a degree program, institution, and research topic focused on the demographics of most interest to you. It is your passion for your topic and the students whose lives you will change that will get you through the time and effort required to complete a doctorate.

What Are the Qualifications for and Salaries Attributed to Teaching Those Ages and Levels?

I have encountered many people who were surprised by the change, or lack of change, in their salaries upon completion of their doctoral studies. Monetary gain can be a motivating factor, but it should not be your only motivating factor. Do your research before starting a doctoral program. If you know you want to teach K–12 in your hometown, know the typical salaries there in public and private schools. Know how much the pay increases upon completion of your doctorate.

What Funding Exists to Offset the Expense of Your Doctoral Study?

Be sure to ask the schools to which you apply about departmental scholarships, graduate school scholarships, fellowships, student employment options, and the Academic Common Market. Ask financial aid if they are aware of any additional opportunities for which you should apply. If you are already teaching, your institution may offer professional development funds that can help offset the cost of tuition or textbooks.

Will You Be Able to Work Full-Time While Pursuing Your Doctorate, or Is That Frowned Upon?

Some doctoral programs require you to be in residence on campus at all times, which would make keeping your day job difficult or impossible. Some programs are low residency, as mine was. It allowed me to continue to work full-time and keep my benefits while pursuing my doctorate. I did have to manage one week in residence each fall and spring, and multiple weeks in residence each summer.

If You Are a Parent, Do You Have Help with Your Children, Your Home, and Your Finances so That You Can Focus on the Overwhelming Amount of Reading and Writing Necessary to Finish the Degree That You Start?

My husband and I established blocks of weekend time when he would take the kids out so I could read, write, and make notes for my classes. At my job, I found holes in my schedule that allowed me to book a study room in my campus libraries, so I could do more reading and writing. You will need to plan the necessary time and block it as an ongoing commitment to yourself.

Does the History of Your Marriage or Relationship Suggest That Prioritizing Your Studies Will Bring You Closer to Each Other or Drive a Wedge Between You?

Not every doctoral student who is in a committed relationship struggles as a result of their studies. However, I recommend taking the time to think through past levels of support from your significant other when you have taken on huge tasks. I also recommend that you discuss the blocks of time you will need to read and process an overwhelming amount of information, so you can write and speak about it. I am certain many partners feel neglected at times and wish the entire process would move more quickly. Know that you control the pace of your research and writing, but the pace of degree completion is up to your advisor and committee. This is a long commitment for you, but it may feel like an eternity for the most supportive significant other.

If a prospective doctoral student enters into coursework without having thought through all of these things, they may be set up to fail bitterly and discourage all others from pursuing degrees.

Topic Selection and Methodology

While my initial approach to telling my doctoral journey focused on what I felt and experienced while moving from applicant to student to candidate and then graduate, I also want to share with readers the actual steps I took to choose a topic and to devise and implement my research plan. I had just started my courses in my first summer residency when I was offered a new job as chair of the Department of Visual, Performing and Communication Arts at Johnson C. Smith University (JCSU). JCSU is a historically Black university located in Charlotte, North Carolina. Up until this point in my career as a professional dancer, teacher, choreographer, and professor, I had only trained in and attended predominantly white institutions (PWIs).

I had immediate concerns about whether my own training, education, and experience had adequately prepared me to design and implement arts curricula in a historically Black college or university (HBCU). I naively assumed that I could look up dance degree programs in other HBCUs as a starting point, and I set out to find them one night while in residence at TWU. At that time, there were 106 HBCUs. Some are large, others small, some public and some private, many with a religious affiliation, some land grant institutions. That night, I looked up the websites for all 106 schools. Online I saw representations of dance in photos and online catalogs, but for all that searching, I only found three existing HBCU dance degree programs, and I was to create the fourth. Some schools were four-year institutions, and some were two-year institutions. I found some dance minors, and other dance programs with neither a degree nor a minor, and I found registered student organizations and clubs that offered dance, but only the three leading to degree completion.

I wondered what it meant that I saw depictions of dance both inside and outside of the curriculum on practically every HBCU campus website, but that the vast majority of the campuses offered no degree program in dance. Is it that HBCUs believe dance is of the people and does not require formal training? Is it that dance is an integral part of life for people of color, but it is not considered a viable career field? Is it evidence of the church's ages-long, love/hate relationship with the body as both something sacred and something profane and in constant danger of perversion? I exhausted the 106 websites and started to search for books about dance in HBCUs, but found none. I turned to a search for articles on dance in HBCUs and again found almost nothing written. In truth, there was no real literature to speak of on the topic.

I took my concerns to my faculty and asked if I might be looking in the wrong place or manner. To the contrary, they insisted that this meant I had encountered a very rare thing indeed: a truly new research topic. It would be difficult to pursue, and I would have to track down artifacts and keep up with emergent themes arising from the data collection phase. It was important to me that all these different types of HBCUs (large, small, public, private, four-year, two-year, etc.) not be essentialized as being exactly the same in their approaches to dance. I also wanted to avoid the trap of my dissertation being seen as ranking the existing campuses or approving of some traditions and insulting others. I needed enough schools to generate abundant data to sort and code for the dissertation without drowning in data.

I selected five subject schools, including large and small, public and private, with a degree, a minor, or just a program, so that they could not be lumped together in a dismissive way. Because at the time I had a daughter looking hard at colleges and giving brutally honest feedback about what she saw in online presence and printed materials from schools, I opted to use only extant data rather than surveys or interviews. There was so little literature that I needed to open the topic in a way that paved the way for additional research to come.

For proximity, so I could get to each campus over a weekend, I selected JCSU in Charlotte, North Carolina; A&T State University in Greensboro, North Carolina; Benedict College in Columbia, South Carolina; Spelman College in Atlanta, Georgia; and Savannah State University in Georgia. In my data collection phase, I gathered institutional and dance mission and vision statements. I scoured digital and physical archives for each school, looked at websites, dance facilities for instruction and performance, dance curricula, library holdings, and You-Tube presence of dance for each school. Archival data included school and local newspaper articles, catalogs, yearbooks, photographs, posters, and programs from approximately 1935 to the time I started data collection in the early 2000s. Each data source yielded maybe two or three captioned photos or articles. I truly was gathering the slightest threads of artifacts and trying to craft meaning from them.

My original idea was to sort and code the data, reporting on each campus as if to draw a portrait of the ways that dance exists on each. However, that yielded a result that felt much like a book report. I thought about sorting by types of dance, still in order of school. This also did not make a compelling argument for why this research data was important to anyone outside of the HBCU world, and my point was that American higher education includes that occurring in HBCUs because they are American higher education institutions. Then I found the way.

Just as I had found when I accepted the job at JCSU, there were things my PWI background prepared me to see in this milieu and there were other things that were new to me. I stumbled over each new thing, asking questions and seeking understanding without questioning or challenging the validity and purpose of each instance. This gave me a sense of stumbling upon buried treasure throughout my first year or so on the JCSU campus. This was what I wanted my readers to feel if they were coming to the research from the world of PWIs.

Sorting and coding again, I split the data into things that someone with my PWI background would likely find familiar when visiting an HBCU dance program. It included practices like classes offered in multiple genres of dance at various skill levels, marching band auxiliary units, registered student organizations, school social dances, and physical education classes. This was followed by data about things people with my PWI background would likely find foreign to them because I did not recall seeing their equivalent activities or practices on PWI campuses where I had worked. This included things such as African diaspora traditions of call-and-response or ring shout dances, and the honoring of spaces of the diaspora. For example, data reflected homecoming or other event practices themed after places like Jamaica, the West Indies, ancient Egypt, or African countries like Nigeria or Uganda.

In this manner, the dissertation and subsequent book led the reader down the path of discovery, starting from a place of comfort before ushering the reader into a new land, full of wonder and beauty. Rich, long-held traditions are still practiced and honored in these places, and it does not in any way threaten the existing Western European canonical literature or practice of concert dance. As I see it, this is an outstanding model for the diversification of American higher education as a whole, so that our diverse nation can make room for the histories and practices of all the demographics coexisting in our nation to be included in our textbooks, practices, and lessons. This is the reason I sought both my MFA and my PhD, to make education as a whole more diverse and inclusive by taking my place in the leadership role that helps make decisions, and to be seen by students and colleagues as a woman and person of color who is both capable and confident.

THE DEFENSE

In the twenty-four-hour period prior to my dissertation defense, I learned that no matter how I sent my dissertation to my committee, the formatting was destroyed. In the years I'd been in the dissertation stage, I had worked on so many different versions of Microsoft Word and Google, on multiple generations of both Apple and Dell computing devices, that nothing would hold its formatting. Determined not to delay my defense, I spent the entire night before the defense retyping the entire dissertation from beginning to end, so I could send it without formatting problems. I slept a few hours and flew to Texas to defend.

I arrived in the lecture hall early on the day of my defense. I wanted to ensure the technology was working properly, but of course, it was not. My dissertation committee helped me troubleshoot the technical issues, then took their seats and we began. My defense did not involve reading the paper but giving an oral presentation about my topic selection, research questions, methodologies, data collection, and analysis. I talked about how I chose my subject schools for the study, what I hoped to learn when I started, and emergent theories arising from the collected data. I supported this information with visual references and slides. Time seemed to stand still, but I believe I spoke for approximately forty-five minutes.

Following my presentation, I sat with my dissertation committee members, listened to their feedback, and attempted to answer their questions. At this time, my advisor sent me out of the room so the committee could discuss my writing and my presentation. Again, time stood still, and I waited in the hallway for what felt like half an hour or longer. My advisor came, brought me back into the room, and told me I had passed my defense.

To say I was ecstatic after nine years of work and sacrifice is an understatement. The committee gave me a moment to ride the wave of elation and then sat me down again to list many, many things I had to revise and resubmit to actually graduate. My all-night typing session had led to enough typographical errors that the committee almost questioned my ability to write. It was because my advisor had seen so many drafts of my best writing that she convinced the others this was an anomaly that needed explanation rather than a failure to pass. I agreed to edit, revise, resubmit, and go through all steps required by the graduate school at TWU in order to be approved to graduate.

I thought my advisor meant for me to fly home and make these changes by an agreed-upon deadline, but she meant for me to make the changes immediately. I was exhausted and bewildered, but we picked up a pizza and headed straight to her house to begin revisions. I worked all night yet again, applying all the changes requested by my committee, on the same laptop on which I'd retyped the dissertation, so I could leave updated copies with the entire committee and the graduate school before getting back on the plane to South Carolina. It was over.

ADVICE

If you or someone you care for is contemplating whether to begin the doctoral journey, please take the time to help think through the answers to every question you can imagine about how to make the completion of the degree both possible and useful. Know how you best study, alone in quiet or with a group, with a set writing time each day or week or if you prefer to be sporadic about when you can go into writing overdrive.

Design your methodology so that you can easily get to any sites or resources you need for your research. Remember that your dissertation is not necessarily the last thing you will ever write or publish. Don't hold on to control of it so tightly that your committee will not let you defend or pass. You have the rest of your life to write the way you want to write on subjects of your choosing. You will get it done by simply accepting the feedback you receive and applying it. Get done, get out, then write as you like, but only start a doctorate if what you want to do and what you want to be requires one; then think about how your life will change to make completion possible.

On the social media doctoral and dissertation support groups, I so often see people asking if the degree is worth the time and expense. Unhappy people rush in like predators to say a doctorate is a waste of time, energy, and money, and that they have not advanced enough in their careers to justify their choices to obtain them. This frustrates me not only because they are discouraging people as a result of their own lack of research and planning, but because they made a decision to obtain a degree specifically for money, not because it helped to advance knowledge in their chosen field of study. Anyone who enters into education at any level without thinking through their own intrinsic motivation, prospects for employment in the field, average starting salaries, and rate of upward mobility in the field has set themselves up for disappointment and debt.

You will feel empowered and inspired to do more once you complete your doctorate. Since obtaining my PhD, in addition to working to excel in my academic career, I researched and wrote a book (Guffy and Ebright, 2019) about the history of dance on historically Black college campuses.

You are capable, and my PhD has been worth everything I went through to acquire it.

CHAPTER 6

Life Before the Dissertation Journey

Deborah J. Broom-Cooley, EdD

THE IMPORTANCE OF EDUCATION AND GIVING BACK WERE ESSENTIAL elements imparted by family that encompassed my mind, body, and soul for as long as I can remember. I was born prematurely in the early 1950s in New Orleans, Louisiana, to Simon Broom Sr., a laborer and jazz musician who played trumpet, stand-up bass, and trombone with several marching bands, and Carrie Howard Broom, a full-time secretary at the Algiers Navy base. Later in her career, my mother transitioned to the New Orleans Public Schools as a secretary in the administrative office of the principal at Walter L. Cohen Sr. High School in Central City New Orleans. That decision enabled her to receive her three children returning from school daily. On Sundays, she served as a consummate organist and singer for two churches in the community: the Beulah Baptist Church in Central City New Orleans and alternating Sundays at the Rising Star Missionary Baptist Church in the Carrollton area, which was our family's home church.

Both parents provided a solid foundation that celebrated a love for music, education, community, and cultural traditions for my oldest brother Simon Jr. and youngest sister Valeria Arnette and me. Musicians and singers were always present and prominent on both sides of the family; their gifts were always on display in a city known for its music, art, culinary flair, and cultural holidays. The transference of our parents' musical gifts allowed my siblings and me to continue utilizing our talents in numerous churches and community choirs throughout the New Orleans area from youth to adulthood. My siblings were academically gifted and talented and needed little attention or tutoring from our mom in their formative years. Valeria and I attended People's United Educational Center run by People's United Methodist Church while Simon Jr. attended Hume's Educational Community Center.

My premature birth, accompanied by intellectual growth complications, presented my parents with numerous challenges, but my mother provided me with extra emotional, social, and academic support to overcome those deficiencies in my early years of development. That additional assistance would positively impact my trajectory and determine my educational, social, emotional, behavioral, and physical growth and success over a lifetime. She never complained or identified any academic shortcomings between her children, believing steadfastly that we were all academically smart and capable of anything; negative statements never came out of her mouth regarding my academic abilities. I clearly remember her working with me after school and on weekends regarding my reading and math skills, such as retrieving books from the community mobile library known as the bookmobile and school library; intense math facts review, especially multiplication or times table drills; writing; and speaking. All of that assistance enabled me to perform at and sometimes above grade level. The hard work certainly paid off once I entered high school and several postsecondary institutions.

In retrospect, my parents were not perfect or without struggle but knew how to provide love and foundational support for us in our formative years; they were in their thirties rearing a growing family. Thus, we were able to endure the death of our mother from leukemia at thirty-nine years of age in August 1963. Simon Jr. was fourteen, I was nine, Valeria Arnette was seven, and my newly widowed father was a young-looking forty. As siblings in this union, the devastating loss tied us together intricately and intimately throughout our lives due to this untimely and painful experience in our early years. Throughout our lives, we steadfastly stayed true to the foundation our parents gave us; we understood that our very survival and successes depended on it.

Losing a mother at any age is like losing your footing and balance on shaky ground. I instantly realized the urgent need to grow up quickly, learning all that was needed in order to become independent and self-sufficient because a part of my closest protection was gone, and my footing was off balance. While in the hospital and before her death, Mother wrote copious instructions regarding our care and schooling and gave them to my father and brother before collapsing into a coma. Simon Jr. was responsible for looking after and keeping up with us, ensuring that he and we continued our education beyond high school into higher education. Once the plan was revealed to my sister and me, we were reminded of our mother's wishes throughout our lifetimes.

Now, Dad and his mother Beulah Richard Broom, a Cajun/Creole French speaker, oversaw the next phase of our lives. My paternal grandmother, affectionately known as Ma'ma by all her children and grandchildren, lived in southwest Louisiana, in a small town called Raceland, located forty-five miles outside New Orleans in an unincorporated part of Lafourche Parish. Parishes are known as counties outside of Louisiana. At the time of my mother's death, we were on summer vacation visiting my grandmother and other relatives for the first time. We arrived in June and Mother transitioned in August.

When we first met our paternal grandmother, we were asked to call her Ma'ma, and always responded to her questions by saying, "Yes Ma'ma" and "No Ma'ma." She was sixty-three years old, and five feet, four inches tall with high cheekbones, long white hair, large almond-shaped brown eyes; she smoked a pipe and carried a long stick. Beulah was short, but she was in charge, and everyone knew it. She was rearing three other grandchildren whose mom died several years prior to the death of our mom. Cousin Jackie, who was one of those three siblings, assisted me and my sister in translating and understanding our grandmother, who spoke Cajun/Creole French mixed with English.

We remained with her for one year; our dad left us in her care and went back to New Orleans to prepare for our return. Prior to our return, my grandmother constantly fed, housed, loved, guided, nurtured, and disciplined all six of her motherless grandchildren. Funds during that time were limited, and she was living off her pension which during the

1960s was called relief, but her reputation and credit were good in the community. Many of her children, friends, family, and church provided and assisted her with our rearing. No funds that I know of were provided by my dad to support us, despite numerous contacts made to him by my grandmother. She endured the hardship for a year, protecting all her grandchildren entrusted in her care. Regardless of the language barrier experienced by some of us, we knew love, care, and concern when we saw and experienced it.

Ma'ma's encouragement, training, and support were boundless; I observed her carefully and learned how to cook, clean, feed chickens, and get eggs from the henhouse every morning. Being raised in the city most of my life was different from daily living in rural southwest Louisiana known as Cajun country. The rancid smell of sugarcane was foreign to us, along with chickens running around in the backyard with an outhouse (toilet) in the back of the house. A large cemetery sat behind the outhouse; all in all, it was initially a culture shock. The adjustment from city kid to country kid was slow but it played a major role in me being able to mentally endure and adjust to new things under unusual circumstances. However, my siblings and I were able to make the mind-blowing life transitions with the love and support of our huge families, schools, and churches.

Overall, the community, wherever we resided, served as a vital support system, enabling us to fully heal, move forward, and become productive and educated people. This moment in time allowed us to never forget what others did for us by always reaching back for those who may need us. We were most fortunate that while living with Ma'ma, in Raceland, we had relatives who taught in the local elementary and high schools, and one of them taught and nurtured me in the fourth grade. Victoria Hadley understood that I was still in shock and grieving over the loss of my mom; she counseled and consoled me during those moments of tears and utter sadness displayed in the classroom during that time. Fourth and fifth grades are a blur to me, and I can't recall my school days during that most grievous time of my young life.

Mother had been deceased only one month before school started in September. A new school and friends meant my siblings and I were forced to make the necessary adjustments. After the school year ended, we endured yet another transition: moving back to New Orleans and attending the New Orleans Public Schools. I don't recall my fifth-grade teacher or school experience, but my aunt by marriage was a teacher in the new school. In sixth grade, teacher Victoria Hadley's sister Louvenia Hadley Broom became my teacher, and the counseling, support, and academic rigor began in preparation for school integration and junior high school. My mother and Louvenia were best friends and attended Straight College together (currently Dillard University). They were both married to two brothers, my dad Simon and his brother Willie. Again "the village" was there to support me in my new environment of change and to reinforce my mom's vision and desire for her children.

In retrospect, my grandmother understood that our spiritual and emotional healing was vital in us moving forward and accomplishing all the things my mom had hoped for us. Mother provided the guidance and all we had to do was follow it; her siblings and friends understood the directives and all sides of our families came together to inspire us to achieve in every area of our lives. Those early life experiences taught me invaluable lessons as an educator and leader in how to nurture and support students in the K–12 and postsecondary experiences during their crises, turmoil, and dramatic life changes.

The mentality of unwavering support and understanding for young people evolved from my childhood experiences of being motherless, enduring multiple transitions from birth to adulthood, and a determination to succeed enabled me to encourage and guide students throughout my professional career. This emboldened me to share personal stories of overcoming life challenges, engulfed with a myriad of successes and failures that ultimately determined my destiny. The level of observation and sensitivity toward students identified as students with disabilities in special education and alternative education was heightened as a result of early loss, navigating life's transitions, and a need to be seen, heard, loved, and supported.

After a year of living in Raceland, Louisiana, Dad moved my sister and me back to New Orleans with mom Ivory (his new wife), and her four children, with one on the way. My brother remained in Raceland with Ma'ma completing high school. He went on to become valedictorian of his graduating class at C. M. Washington High School and received a full music scholarship to Johnson C. Smith University, a historically Black college in Charlotte, North Carolina. My sister and I attended New Orleans Public Schools, excelling and successfully graduating from Marion Abramson Sr. High School; we moved on to higher education and the world of work.

Understanding the love and support our parents gave us, along with both sides of my family, community, and church, we gained strength to endure the many challenges that lay ahead in achieving our personal, academic, and career goals. I was further convinced more than ever that being a native New Orleanian with a Creole French background encompassing cultural and community mores served as a linchpin for promoting continuous academic study, professional development, career advancement, and healthy social and emotional growth. The ultimate culmination of these elements supported my rationale for giving back to a unique community via educational initiatives while preserving the rich and distinct culture of Louisiana. Like a wonderful and delicious gumbo, all these ingredients and experiences melded together were needed for support after the death of my mother and the furtherance of her vision impacted my decision to return to school to complete my doctoral studies program.

The culmination of a carefully planned and executed academic course of study, and varied life and work experiences, positively impacted my forty-three-year career in education, ministry, and philanthropic endeavors. The expectations of goal setting and high academic achievement were always at the forefront of family discussions, career choices, and ongoing conversations relative to cultural sustainability and legacy building. Ultimately, the institutions of higher learning, and a variety of teaching and leadership opportunities, led to my foray into dissertation study and choosing the topic relative to high-stakes testing and the graduation rates at a suburban high school.

Before my dissertation journey began at Argosy University, I was a full-time teacher/leader with twenty-eight years of combined training and experience in the K–12 and postsecondary environments. My teaching career journey began with the New Orleans Public Schools after graduating with a bachelor of arts in Spanish education in 1978 from Southern University at New Orleans, which is a part of the Southern University System in Baton Rouge, Louisiana. The Southern University System is the only historically Black college and university system which has five schools within a system of operations located in Baton Rouge, Shreveport, and New Orleans, Louisiana. While at the New Orleans campus, I received a full university scholarship after my freshman year in addition to a book scholarship and an invitation to join Sigma Gamma Rho Sorority, Inc., Gamma Upsilon Chapter. The freshman year was paid in full by my mother's two sisters, whom I lived with for a year in Destrehan, Louisiana. Family turmoil with my dad and mom Ivory forced me to make a life-changing decision to leave a blended family of twelve and move forward with the vision and directives of my deceased mom, to continue my schooling and journey into higher education and beyond, no matter the obstacles. Again, family and the university community embraced and supported me by providing formidable opportunities for academic growth, professional development, and career success.

During the following years at Southern University at New Orleans, I became a Fulbright-Hays Fellowship recipient to the University of Costa Rica, in San Jose, Costa Rica, in Central America in the summer of 1975. I pledged Sigma Gamma Rho Sorority, Inc. Gamma Upsilon Chapter, participated in the Alpha Mu Gamma (Foreign Language Honor Society) in 1973/1974, became president of the Pan-Hellenic Council in 1975, and was selected for Who's Who in American Universities and Colleges 1974/1975. My life was full of love and support from university professors, Sigma Gamma Rho Sorority, church, family, and friends, even though my living conditions were unstable and fraught with uncertainties. The love, hopes, and dreams of my mother kept me going despite the myriad life challenges encountered during my college years.

After graduation, New Orleans Public Schools hired me to teach Spanish I and III at Marion Abramson Senior High School, from which I had graduated years earlier. It was awesome but strange teaching and leading with my former teachers who nurtured me during my high school years. They were excited to see the fruit of their labor; I had gone to college, studied abroad, achieved numerous honors, and returned to teach at my old high school. During my second year, I was recruited to teach in the English as a second language program (ESOL) as an itinerant teacher in grades K–12. I was assigned to five schools with a bilingual teaching assistant for eight years. As a team, we worked with international populations in three elementary schools, one high school, and one junior high. My teaching tenure also extended into the community night school and mirrored my day school population serving multilingual students from Central America (Honduras), Cuba, Haiti, Vietnam, and Cambodia.

While teaching and serving in leadership positions in the school district, the State of Louisiana offered to pay for graduate school for all educators desirous of returning to school for a master's degree and above. Of course, I leaped at the chance to improve my teaching and leadership skills and became certified as a reading and curriculum specialist by pursuing an MEd in curriculum and instruction with a concentration as a reading specialist at the University of New Orleans, formerly Louisiana State University at New Orleans, graduating in 1981. In order to effectively reach my ESOL students and operate in various leadership positions, I returned to University of New Orleans two years later to receive my master's plus thirty graduate hours in educational leadership and ESOL in 1985 and became certified in areas of ESOL, educational leadership, reading specialist, and curriculum and instruction. Of course, the State of Louisiana was responsible for all of my higher education free of charge and for that, I will be forever grateful.

After eight years as an educator in Louisiana, windows of professional growth and opportunities opened for my spouse and me in 1987. We relocated to DeKalb County, Georgia, a suburb outside the perimeter of Atlanta known as Doraville. It was a rapidly growing, up-and-coming international community, convenient to our new places of employment. I was initially hired by the Atlanta Public Schools to teach Spanish I, III, and IV at North Fulton High School in the International Studies Baccalaureate Program. The school was located in the Peachtree Hills community, an Atlanta community called Buckhead. Years later, North Fulton and Northside High School merged to become North Atlanta

High School, which moved into the IBM Building in North Atlanta. I taught one year at North Fulton and returned to Atlanta Public Schools several years later as an ESOL itinerant contract teacher for two years serving international students in elementary, middle, and high schools throughout the system.

During my hiatus from the public school system, I became a full-time mom with two sons and a husband on a fast-track career in law enforcement. To stay engaged and maintain my teaching and leading certifications in Louisiana and Georgia, I taught and provided leadership as an ESOL, reading, and Spanish adjunct for the following schools of higher education: DeKalb Technical College (DeKalb County, Georgia), Interactive College of Technology (Chamblee, Georgia), and Atlanta Technical College and Morris Brown College's Upward Bound Summer Program (Atlanta, Georgia).

In 2004, I returned to full-time teaching for the DeKalb County School District at Columbia High Math, Science, and Technology Magnet School as a reading specialist and ESOL teacher. Again, the embrace and support I received from colleagues after a long hiatus from public education was what I needed. Numerous teaching and leadership opportunities were presented to me, and I accepted them to provide experience and support to fellow colleagues and students. While at Columbia, I served on the Consolidated School Improvement Committee, school council, SAT prep and ESOL teacher/leader department, language arts curriculum trainer, and high-stakes testing examiner for the Georgia Milestones Testing Program. Those opportunities provided me space to serve my school and community for which I lived, supporting both Columbia High and Snapfinger Elementary Math, Science, and Technology Magnet School. My sons attended both schools, and my oldest completed high school during my teaching tenure; the youngest finished four years later.

My decision to complete my EdS and EdD degrees in educational leadership was made while teaching at Columbia High. It was fertile ground for educational research with a plethora of current educational problems and concerns in need of realistic and data-driven solutions. I was in a fertile place of support and ideas because many of the administrators and teachers had attained their masters, educational specialists, and doctoral degrees and were committing research to practice. Initially, I wanted to begin the doctoral journey focusing on reading, math, and technology literacy for children, which would provide motivation, inspiration, and support for future educators and students needing educational support. Further study and research would afford me opportunities to reach a diverse audience, targeting current issues for the exploration and implementation of viable solutions for improving student academic achievement.

On the other hand, I believed that topics such as "high-stakes testing" and "high school graduation rates" were also relevant, viable, and needed innovative research and immediate strategies to affect positive change and increase academic achievement among high school students. I further believed that targeted study of such topics could lead to greatly needed long-term instructional and assessment solutions for low-performing schools. To seek this level of study was not for me only but for the greater good and enlightenment of my profession, the community, and the families within the community. My gateway was to reenter public education and complete my doctorate after a ten-year hiatus, in order to make a positive and long-lasting impact in the field of education, by strategically targeting literacy and high-stakes testing issues in the K–12 environment.

TOPIC SELECTION AND RATIONALE

In the summer of 2004, I accepted a position to work at Columbia High School as a reading specialist in the DeKalb County School District. This school was in my community, and it was there my oldest son would be starting his senior year. I was initially apprehensive; however, excitement about resuming my public education career and completing my doctoral journey after a nineteen-year hiatus from graduate school became my focus. I had not taken graduate courses since the summer of 1985 after completing my master's plus thirty hours in educational leadership and ESOL certifications.

As an itinerant reading specialist, I moved to different rooms for instruction in various parts of the building teaching Reading Across the Curriculum, ESOL, and SAT prep. The high school was large and housed over two thousand students in a middle-class, multigenerational community of homeowners in southwest DeKalb County. On one occasion, while moving to my class, I noticed what I interpreted as stress and tension emanating from administration, faculty, and students in the classrooms and hallways regarding the pending high-stakes test known as the Georgia High School Graduation Test that was administered in the fall and spring of each semester. It was administered to first-time test takers in the eleventh grade and twelfth grades who needed to retake sections of the exam for graduation and receipt of a high school diploma. This high-stakes test consisted of five components: English language arts, math, science, social studies, and writing (essay).

Because the passing rate in 2004 for Columbia High School was 45 percent, a plan for academic support for students, developed by administration, faculty, and staff, encompassed mentoring and coaching activities that were held before school, after school, and on weekends in the test content areas. The goal was to increase the passing rate from 45 percent to 80 percent or higher. I too had a deep concern regarding the low passing rate which prevented students from receiving their high school diplomas. Instead, they would receive certificates of attendance at graduation if all sections were not passed. They would have to retest until all sections were passed. This was a stressful situation for all concerned as it related to the overall assessment achievement success for ninth and tenth graders and graduation passing rates for eleventh and twelfth graders.

The plan of support was implemented, and I participated fully in mentoring juniors and seniors, teaching social studies during the academic support hours for all eleventh graders. This commitment involved morning, afternoon, and weekend tutorials; on weekends I taught the SAT prep course. The low Georgia High School Graduation Test passing rates became a problem needing a solution which led to the development and research of my dissertation topic: "An Investigation of the Impact of High-Stakes Testing on the Graduation Rates at a Suburban High School in the State of Georgia" (Broom-Cooley 2007).

Balancing Personal and Professional Life During the Journey

During my journey, I balanced my personal and professional life in a variety of ways. Personal strategies were implemented to set aside quality time for family fun activities and mini-vacations, continuing workout sessions alone twice a week at the Wellness Center, and monthly massage sessions for de-stressing and self-care were necessary and adhered to, unless there was a family emergency or travel for school. Work and ministry strategies included training and delegating leadership duties and responsibilities to ministry workers in my absence, maintaining honesty and open communications with school administrators, and ensuring that classes were covered for attendance and instruction during absences. The graduate school academic strategy included a self-care mental health plan for survival and restoration from coursework, dissertation writing to defense. Most importantly, keeping all relationships informed was vital in communicating to family, friends, coworkers, and church family in detail, regarding my return to graduate school and entering dissertation studies. Everyone knew of my impending status and mostly complied with my wishes. Therefore, I encountered no misunderstandings regarding my absence from events or lack of telephone conversations because all important parties were properly informed.

Struggles in the Journey

Turning fifty years old in 2004 and returning to a full-time teaching job at Columbia High School was a shocking turn of events for me that called for gradual adjustment after my ten-year hiatus from the K–12 public school setting. Technology used by employees in the operations of daily school life was new. I had to learn to use a variety of technological programs and systems to successfully complete the duties and responsibilities of my new position. Additionally, I was a full-time mom to two teenage sons, monitoring and supporting their academic journeys through middle and high school, and my husband was involved in his career journey as a senior criminal investigator for the Fulton County District Attorney's Office; he was also a master instructor for the Fulton County Public Safety Training Department.

During this time of adjusting to a full career, I received an acceptance letter in the fall of 2004 for the doctoral program in educational leadership from Argosy University in Sarasota, Florida. I was excited and understood that this time around the financing was all on me. My previous degrees were paid for by the State of Louisiana and Southern University at New Orleans. Classes were starting soon, and I had a short window of time to arrange funding and register for my first class which was a hybrid, beginning online and concluding with weekend classes on-site in Sarasota, Florida.

So, with great sacrifice, I arranged with the university to pay my tuition bimonthly and they agreed. My family did not go lacking, and my spouse and I divided up our financial responsibilities. I was fortunate because the DeKalb County School District's pay scale was lucrative for experienced and veteran educators. Pay raises were given every year I was in my graduate program and traveling to Florida. For the next three years, I sacrificed part of my monthly earnings to pay for classes and travel to Florida. Classes began in late fall of 2004; I completed my EdS in educational leadership in the fall of 2006 and my doctorate in educational leadership in 2007. With every degree was a $5000 to $7000 pay raise. However, two years later the school district experienced monumental financial shortages, all personnel were placed on furlough, and pay scales were lowered by thousands. Employees experienced six years of furlough status due to the school district's financial deficit.

Meanwhile, amid adjusting to graduate studies, traveling to Sarasota, Florida, occasionally for on-site classes, and balancing a full-time teaching job, with family duties and responsibilities, Hurricane Katrina hit and devastated my hometown of New Orleans, Louisiana, in August 2005. So, from 2004 to 2005, in the midst of all the transitions, turmoil, devastation, and overwhelming disbelief, I had to pause and think about the strength I used from my past lessons of endurance. Overcoming the situations I confronted in my youth assisted me in gaining my balance to continue on with my studies. My mother's work, faith, vision, and love were forever before me. The pain and love for my city, supporting those who were now relocating to Georgia, some at Columbia High School, to continue their education, became my focus.

Dealing with all the emotional struggles of displaced family members and friends after a horrific hurricane was a lesson in hope and perseverance, one I knew well. This was where I had to navigate teaching all students, inspiring them to go forward and sharing parts of my life's struggles and successes. As completely overwhelmed as I was during that season in my life, I kept on going with prayer and support from my Argosy University professors and classmates, church family, colleagues, friends, and immediate family. My support system sustained me; I remained positive and focused to continue with my doctoral program.

COPING STRATEGIES FOR OVERCOMING ADVERSITIES

To cope with and overcome the struggles and challenges I encountered in the first year of my doctoral studies, I consistently prayed, meditated, and asked God for directions. Doing this is what kept me focused. As a ministry leader, I informed church leadership regarding my return to school, and I sought support and prayer from my team. Reaching out to my church provided the strength I needed to "set my proverbial house in order." Next, my family and I met to discuss my return to graduate school, my travel schedule, in-home study hours, and solicitation of their support and help with household duties.

Second, I informed my school administration team at Columbia High School of my return to graduate school and reassured them that I would complete all my teaching responsibilities in a timely and consistent manner. I also assured them that competent substitute teachers would teach my classes with minimal disruptions during my absence. My first courses were all hybrid (online and face-to-face) which allowed me to spend minimal time in the classroom.

Third, coping with the devastation and disruption of Hurricane Katrina, with the assistance of administration, faculty, and staff at my high school, I was able to focus on teaching and supporting displaced students who were coming in from New Orleans, Louisiana. My great-niece and nephew lived with me and my family during that time and were attending Columbia High School. We all supported each other during this sad and horrific time. Talking, sharing, and listening to each other assisted in overcoming many of the obstacles and adversities experienced during my time of study. Deep reflection and gratefulness would permeate my thoughts when encountering negative situations. Being still, silent, and separated was my motto when coping appeared impossible. However, the dissertation journey continued despite the distractions.

DEFENSE DAY . . . A DAY TO REMEMBER

In August 2007, I transferred from Columbia High to the DeKalb Truancy School. On October 4, 2007, at 9:30 in the morning, while teaching class, I received a telephone call from my dissertation chair, Dr. Larry Reagan. She congratulated me and informed me that my defense was for October 12, 2007, at Argosy University, Sarasota, Florida, in the Administration Building at 10:00 a.m. Dr. Reagan asked that I check my email regarding preparation for the in-person defense and forms that needed to be completed for closure. Notifying my principal was immediate regarding my impending absence date and dissertation defense. I immediately reserved an airline flight, hotel, and car for October 11, 2007, a day before my defense. Per Dr. Reagan's instructions, the dissertation secretary needed two CDs, a flash drive of my edited final dissertation, and completion of all the forms for closeout and graduation. For my defense preparation, I initiated some safeguard actions. First, I loaded two flash drives with my dissertation defense PowerPoint and sent the information to two email accounts for presentation. Next, I prepared six portfolios with hard copies of my defense PowerPoint, just in case the projector malfunctioned, and finally, I purchased thank-you gifts and cards for my defense committee to present after the conclusion of dissertation defense.

My big day began as I arrived at the Argosy University Sarasota's Administration Building a full thirty minutes early. I submitted to the secretary the two CDs containing the final copy of my dissertation and one flash drive, and completed the forms needed to conclude the process for graduation. At 9:50 a.m. on October 12, 2007, the secretary escorted me to a small meeting room, and I was ready to greet the committee and present my defense. The projector was set and ready for my flash drive, and I calmly greeted the committee, then I passed out copies of my defense PowerPoint and explained the rationale for the portfolios.

After about ten minutes into the presentation and responding to questions, the projector stopped working. The chair of my committee paused the session and asked the cochair, Dr. Imhulse, to assess the problem with the projector. Since I had given the team the portfolios in advance, the chair asked that I proceed. Within five minutes, the projector started working, and I was able to continue the presentation and continue responding to questions from my committee. After answering deep, probing statistical questions, I concluded my presentation. The committee asked that I step out of the room while they completed their rubrics and engaged in deliberation. I went to the secretary's office and just stood there for a long ten minutes; my mind and heart were calm and at peace. I knew that my defense was accurate and honest. After a phone call from the committee, the secretary walked me back to the room to hear the conclusion my doctoral committee had reached. When I entered the room, the committee was standing, very solemn and stoic. Dr. Larry Reagan announced, "Congratulations, Reverend Dr. Deborah J. Broom-Cooley, you have successfully passed your defense and we are so proud of you!" We all hugged and cried in each other's arms for about five minutes. After composing ourselves, the committee asked that I consider mentoring other doctoral students in the dissertation process after observing the skills I utilized in proceeding through the program with seriousness and excellence. Upon immediately agreeing to the proposition, I began mentoring doctoral students. To this date, I have helped twenty students who received their doctorates from different institutions in various courses of study. Because I agreed to fulfill that one special request from my doctoral committee, many friendships have been forged and support has reached those in need of understanding and support during their dissertation journey.

Finally, I presented gifts to the committee for their support and for their confidence in me during my course of study, including my dissertation writing and defense. Because of the excellent guidance and instruction from Argosy professors, I was able to research and draft my dissertation in five months following institutional review board approval from the university and the DeKalb County School System.

FINDING SOLUTIONS TO THE QUESTIONS

Prior to embarking on my dissertation journey, I had a variety of questions and concerns. It was my hope to complete my educational journey in a unique way; I did not want to continue in a traditional learning environment, attending all my classes in person during a weeknight. Immediately, I understood that returning to graduate school in the era of online teaching and learning meant navigating multiple platforms of learning for flexibility and ease in successfully completing my doctorate. The transition was initially challenging; however, my teaching job and graduate school experiences assisted me in understanding the new ways of learning. Additionally, the multiple opportunities to mentor educators in the Atlanta Public Schools and DeKalb County Schools afforded me a unique perspective in asking probing questions and making appropriate decisions regarding my doctoral journey by asking the following: (1) What institutions of higher learning would provide diverse teaching and learning experiences in the field of educational leadership that would implement practical and applicable strategies in the twenty-first-century learning environment? (2) Would the faculty, department chairs, and auxiliary personnel have the training, experience, and sensitivity in guiding and supporting all doctoral students in multiple disciplines? (3) What would be the cost of my doctoral journey for three to five years, and how would it be financed? (4) What employment opportunities and career advancement might be available after completion of my program? (5) What personal and professional sacrifices would occur during my tenure in doctoral studies?

From multiple professional encounters, I found the best-suited institution for completing my specialist and doctoral degrees in educational leadership that would prepare me for meeting my academic and career goals ahead. The professionals at Argosy University had vast career, knowledge, and work experiences in leadership, in and outside the field of education. Dissertation defense teams were supportive, direct, caring, and professional; they were known as no-nonsense, experienced in guiding doctoral students in multiple disciplines. A great institution of higher learning, knowledgeable content professors, and an experienced defense team assisted me in completing my doctoral journey in three years. After deciding on the institution, I developed a plan to pay for courses for the next three years: travel, hotel, and other expenses. I was familiar with various career options that would be available after attaining my doctorate; all I needed was to enter and successfully complete the program of study. Once beginning the EdS program in educational leadership, I had questions regarding topics I wanted to research in leadership, but I wasn't certain, so my writings were centered around a variety of current topics and issues. It was vitally important that I develop a plan of action for time management and effectively communicate that plan to family, friends, coworkers, and organizations in which I held membership.

PERSONAL ADVICE FOR A SUCCESSFUL JOURNEY

Before starting your dissertation journey, I would advise you to question your motives for seeking a doctorate. Think about how you plan to use it in the future, for personal and professional reasons. First, evaluate the cost and time needed to complete your coursework from dissertation writing to defense, and how the financial cost will impact you over time. Reflect on this important investment to make sure it is worth your time and effort. Second, select the right institution, one that reflects your values and would provide professional support from professors, academic deans, and personnel from your program of study throughout the doctoral journey. Third, please talk with your immediate family and seek their support in developing a plan of action for family time, completing household chores, schooling, and emergencies. Fourth, carve out daily study and research time with no interruptions, so that you can complete a myriad of assignments and research tasks. If you are employed, keep in mind your duties and responsibilities to your employer. Any problems, concerns, or issues that may impact your daily routines and obligations should be discussed immediately with supervisors. Always maintain an open line of communication to avoid any misunderstandings. Finally, find a mentor and doctoral group that would provide needed support during your journey. Please allow for alone time to reflect and rest from conducting your dissertation research study and writing. Find the best way for you to remain focused, because everybody's journey is different and unique.

CHAPTER 7

The Self-Fulfilling Prophecy: Dismantled

Jennifer Malone, EdD

I AM DR. JENNIFER JOYCE MALONE. I AM THAT BLACK WOMAN WHO made it to my appointed destination: completion of my doctoral degree and finally being offered a "seat at the table" where I knew I belonged after my mother spoke "truth" over my life. I am a first-generation college graduate. I grew up in Kansas City, Missouri, in the urban core. I received a bachelor of science degree in special education in 1985 from Truman State University. In 1992, I was granted a master's degree in special education from the University of Missouri–Kansas City. I earned an educational specialist degree in 1996 in the area of education administration also from University of Missouri–Kansas City. Lastly, I was awarded my doctorate in 1999 in the area of educational leadership from Saint Louis University.

I served for eighteen years as a PreK–12 special education teacher and an additional eighteen years as a K–12 principal. I am now in my "dream" position at a university as an assistant professor in the Department of Education. It's important to note that before reaching my latest position I was an adjunct professor for sixteen years at two different universities.

WHY I PURSUED MY DOCTORATE DEGREE: EDD

I pursued my doctorate degree because my mother said so: "You will be a doctor one day: walking on a beautiful campus with a tan-colored briefcase tucked under your right arm." A mother's dream for her daughter became the daughter's assignment. But, first, there was some dismantling to be done, more than the eye could see.

"You can't have a donut; go sit down, dummy." I wanted white socks to my knees and black-and-white saddle oxford shoes, just like the white girls. Maybe then the teacher wouldn't call me "dumb" and would allow me to have a donut. These were the words that resonated in my head throughout my journey as a student in the American educational system. For most of my formative education, this was my truth. The creation of the "self-fulfilling prophecy," a system that is supposed to be inherently designed so that all children succeed. These words were spoken over my life from the impressionable age of nine. These same words would continue to shape my life as it became my personal and professional mission to dismantle the "self-fulfilling prophecy" that was spoken over me.

My mother demanded that all eight of her children speak "proper English" in our home. She would say, "Don't embarrass me in front of these white people," whenever we went out in public places where white people might be present. My father was one of the first African Americans to integrate within the Kansas City, Missouri, Fire Department. He opened the door for many men of color to join the department. Nobody ever talked about that. He saved more lives than I can count.

Every chance I got I told my children how beautiful, handsome, kind, and smart they are because I knew I could not trust the public school system to perform this essential duty. In my everyday life, I modeled what it means to embrace diversity and to love and accept everyone, regardless of their ethnicity or background. I needed to prepare my children for when they would become students in the public school system. Delpit (2006) coined the phrase "other people's children." Other people's children walk boldly and confidently through glass doors in large brick buildings daily, only to be told that they are not enough and that they need to be more to make it in today's society. My parents could not have prepared me for what lay ahead once I entered the classroom doors as a little Black girl.

In tenth grade, I recall a history class that was a requirement for graduation. I was inquisitive about the content and wanted to know how Black people contributed to America. Public education did not provide me with the tools to answer this question with fairness and equity. Not seeing myself in the curriculum stood as a reminder that I was Black and not white.

I became a "doctor of education" for the very reasons written in this chapter. My mission has always been engulfed in the aim to dismantle any negative self-fulfilling prophecies consciously or unconsciously assigned to myself or any Black child.

Telling my story in fragmented pieces was exhausting. My story is my truth, and it needed to partake in its wholeness. It was time to be done, and I was finally ready. I was no longer afraid or ashamed about what I experienced as a child, youth, or young adult.

My story was written for the unheard and unseen children who were neglected by the American education system. I write specifically to help others dismantle the self-fulfilling prophecies that may have been spoken over their lives whether done consciously or unconsciously by people in institutions that were designed to educate all children and give them the tools to have a voice and a future. I write to set myself free while at the same time creating a space to allow others to do the same. This is why I pursued my doctorate.

I wasn't supposed to go to college; no one from my neighborhood ever pursued a college education. The expectation was to land a good job and remain there for the next thirty to forty years and have a nice nest egg for retirement. No one ever talked about college. Whenever I brought up the subject, people would either remain silent or enter into a long discussion about their plans for that dream job or a career in the military.

My high school academic advisor informed me that I was not college material and that I should seek what I considered a mediocre education at a trade school instead. I didn't even know what a trade school was. Once I researched and uncovered the definition, I knew this place was designed for children like me, who were made to believe these unspeakable lies.

Historically, career and technical education was seen as a first resort for students who weren't considered college material. It was a system that tracked predominantly low-income students and students of color into career and technical classes, then known as vocational education (Butry-mowicz, Amy, and Fenn 2020).

I refused to believe this, yet another deception, and continued my quest to attend college, far away from the discolored world that had been my existence all my life. I did attend college at a small midwestern university where I majored in special education while engaging in sports, track and field to be specific. I did not enter college based on my high GPA from high school, which was 3.5. I was offered a chance at college because I was an athlete. This is the entry point for many Black students. Jackson (2022) ascertains that Black students are ten times more likely to receive an athletic scholarship than their white counterparts. While white students from my high school bragged about their academic scholarships, the majority of the Black students discussed their athletic scholarships in private. My scholarship would serve as my ticket into higher education, as is the story for so many other Black children.

My high school track coach worked me hard, but it paid off in the end because he secured a full scholarship for me at his alma mater. He believed in me more than any other authoritative figure in my life at the time, including my high school guidance counselor, who insisted that my ACT scores were too low to be considered for any entrance into higher education. Of course, they were low—no one helped Black students to prepare for the ACT. We were casually told to sign up for the test, show up, and take it. I don't remember my score; however, it must have been insufficient. Still, I simply could not accept this as my fate. I could not imagine this for my life. I told my guidance counselor that I wanted to give college a try because I was not ready to be an adult. His act of unconscious bias was duly noted. His attempt to breathe fire onto my existing self-fulfilling prophecy was met with resistance. I witnessed the same sad story far too many times within my neighborhood. Young girls would graduate from high school, get a job, snag a boyfriend, and have multiple children. The thought of this life always struck fear in me. I did not want my life to go in this direction. I knew I was made to do something more, something magnificent, something to make the skies open up. In my seventeen-year-old mind, I didn't need to be pretty or smart to make it; I just needed to know how to run. And thus began my journey into higher education.

DISMANTLING THE SELF-FULFILLING PROPHECY: ITS ORIGIN

In the fall of 1980, I enrolled as a freshman at Northeast Missouri State University, now known as Truman State University. My athletic virtuosities earned me a full scholarship or as many of the kids say today, a full ride.

Majoring in premed was extremely challenging for me. My high school teachers did not prepare me for the level of commitment and dedication required to acquire success in such a program. My high school academic experience lacked regard for the collegiate future of Black children.

"I bit off more than I can chew," I told my college academic counselor. As much as I loved chemistry, the other premed courses were overwhelming and uninteresting to me. During my sophomore year, I would change my major to special education. It was one of the best decisions I ever made. I knew I wanted to become a teacher.

We were instructed to write our first college essay in English 101. I was clueless as to what an essay paper was. I didn't even know how to write a paragraph. As one can surmise, my first essay writing piece was more like three sentences on paper. My instructor assigned me to a remedial writing course, which was designed to support students who lacked college-level writing skills. If only I had that one teacher other students from my high school spoke so highly about, maybe I wouldn't have needed a course to teach me how to write a simple paragraph. I made my way across campus to the writing lab, a place that was quiet and bright. Instructors were students from the college: all white and smart. I find it ironic that the students at my current institution who support students in need of writing support are all non-Black. In the writing lab, they taught me how to write an effective paragraph, and then an essay paper. It took approximately two weeks for me to master the task of effective and fluent writing. Being able to write gave me a newfound joy, and that joy was teaching.

College life came with juggling academics and sports. Track practice took place two times daily, in the morning and the evening. Classes were in between the two practices. I kept this tight schedule for three years until I decided I was more interested in becoming the first one in my family to graduate from college than in running track. Needless to say, I had to finance my final year of college by working full-time in the summer as well as during the school year.

I wasn't prepared for the rigorous work required of a scholar; however, being a first-generation college student meant I had to represent and bring one home for the team, meaning my family, my neighborhood, my church, and the community. Whenever I would come home on breaks, I was frequently acknowledged as the "college girl." I walked to the local corner store and was graced with free candy and chips regularly. My community supported me, and this was displayed through their actions. I completed my undergraduate degree.

Shortly after completing my undergraduate studies, I became pregnant with my first child. After returning to my childhood neighborhood, I fell in love with a young man who lived only a few blocks away from my family home. I wanted to fit in, so I did what most girls from my neighborhood would eventually do and gave birth to my firstborn, not understanding the challenges I would face in the years to come. Having my beautiful son in my arms, following the loss of my mother, gave me a new attitude toward being a single parent. I was going to make a difference by being an example for my sweet baby boy. I was a first-year teacher, a single mother, and a daughter of a loving and caring mother, for a short while.

THERE'S MORE TO BE DONE: FACING STRUGGLES AND OVERCOMING

My mother passed away during my first teaching experience; however, before she departed, the words she spoke over my life would churn in me forever and would eventually guide the trajectory of my quest to dismantle the lies I was told as a girl.

Attending graduate school was another distress. Many people told me that my current degrees were enough and "You blessed you got those." My mother thought otherwise and instilled in me the desire to do more. She said to me when I was pregnant, "One day, you will be on a college campus and people will refer to you as 'doctor.'" I certainly could not conceive these words and continued to exist per the lens of the lies I had been told all my life. However, my thinking began to shift when she left me in 1985. Something in me wanted to believe her vision for me. I wanted to see myself through the eyes of my mother: the one who loved me and believed in me the most.

I began my journey to seek my master's degree. I received a master's degree in 1992 and continued my journey to receive two additional degrees, one being a doctorate in 1999.

I took the GRE three times before I was finally admitted into a doctoral program. I traveled to the University of Kentucky in 1996 only to be told, "You need to work on your presentation." A close friend insinuated my failure to gain acceptance was due to me missing my first flight. After all, I was a single parent and needed to ensure proper care was in place for my eight-year-old son. His words did not make sense to me at all. And I did not give up. Since I had obtained two previous degrees from a local university, my attention was drawn there. I obtained a master's degree and an educational specialist degree from this particular university only to be told, "You need to increase your GRE scores." I took the GRE again only to receive an even lower score. I recall being told by someone, who obviously didn't know my grit, "Maybe you don't need to pursue this degree." This statement alone made me even more determined to gain acceptance into a doctoral program.

There is a secret test that exists for admittance into the world of academia. This test holds the power to either permit students access to this destination, or it can derail and cause distress and doubt in the minds of Black scholars who seek entry into doctoral programs in higher education. The GRE is the test in question. Today, many higher education institutions have waived the GRE as a standard for admission; however, this was not the case from 1994 through 1997. Many Black students seeking admittance into doctoral programs were faced with this assessment on more occasions than one. Some students studied, prepared, and seated themselves in the stale classrooms only to be told their score was not good enough for entrance into any graduate school. My scores were simply not good enough. I ordered the practice booklet and studied day and night for months. After my third attempt, I chose a different strategy.

I searched diligently and found a program that I thought was willing to meet my educational pursuit in Saint Louis, Missouri, at Saint Louis University. I called the department directly after submitting a letter explaining the fact that I was simply not a good "test taker." The chair of the department returned my phone call and we set a date to meet in person on campus. I was thrilled, to say the least. The department chair was kind and understanding. He wanted the program to have more diversity and agreed to allow me admittance. The terms for my admittance were that I would be on academic probation for my first semester. I had to prove that I was fit to occupy this very important space in academia.

This narrative would be the backdrop for several spaces I sought to enter. This is true for many Black women. There is a ceiling that exists for many Black women who aspire to achieve higher-level positions in their field. We put in the work for many years and satisfied all the requirements to break through the glass ceiling. That glass ceiling often becomes concrete for a large percentage of Black women. A concrete wall reflects the barriers that women of color face more accurately (Babers 2016). I liken the majority of my experiences to being sold to the highest bidder; standing stone still on the auction block waiting to be noticed by the ones who hold the key to my acceptance, while all the time hearing my mother's voice, "you belong in that space."

THE ART OF BALANCING PERSONAL AND PROFESSIONAL LIFE AS A SCHOLAR

In my doctoral program, I was the only Black in every class. Surrounded by all white scholars, I began to display responses to the "imposter syndrome." The "imposter syndrome" is defined as the "failure to believe you are as smart, skilled, and deserving of success as your peers and live in the fear that this 'lie' will be uncovered by others at any given time" (Clance 1985). I had to prove that I belonged in this cohort; therefore, I began to make attempts to "fit in." I would go out to eat at "fancy" restaurants with them and when making references to my current job, as a special education teacher, I fabricated my real duties to match their stories. This was exhausting and expensive; I was a single parent trying to impress those around me with a teacher's salary. I decided enough was enough and made the decision to focus on the people in my life who I knew loved and supported me. I had a huge team of friends and family who would do whatever it took to propel me in my journey to obtain my doctorate.

The importance of friends and family cannot be stressed enough. I come from a large family; I have four sisters and three brothers. I was the first sibling to receive a bachelor's degree and certainly the first to make it to graduate school. My family was my source of strength and provided unconditional love to me and my son. My extended family included my close friends, my church community, and some collective members from the school where I taught. This populace of individuals and groups is where I found peace and encouragement whenever I launched myself in a direction that was not subservient to my purpose.

It's important to note that some people who were in my predoctoral life, didn't remain on my doctoral trajectory. If someone proved to be toxic or negative, they were no longer a welcomed guest in my life. This is an imperative note for those currently on this path. You must be very selective about which people can occupy a seat on the bus toward your destination. Everyone you know is not always for you. This is not to say they are bad people; it simply means some people have to be put on hold until they are invited back into your life. Some are extended a long-awaited reentry, while others are not.

Needless to say, I lost a few friends on my path to my doctorate. I also gained some; one, in particular, stands out to me. This would be my husband, who just a week before I was to graduate, read my dissertation in its entirety. He provided words of affirmation and encouragement. This was new territory for me because I refused to date while pursuing my degree. I wanted to keep distractions to a minimum as much as possible. Dating seemed to interfere with my goals. I decided being single was best for me while on my journey. I missed out on a variety of activities and events; however, my priority was full completion of my doctorate and to graduate with my cohort. My concerns centered around caring for my son, working as a teacher to provide food and shelter, and remaining grounded in my studies. There was little room for anything else.

COPING AND OVERCOMING STRUGGLES

I never experienced the daunting task of looking for childcare because one of my dearest friends accepted my son as her own. She waited for him to arrive at her home and would feed him and ensure he completed his homework for the following school day. I never had to worry about my baby when I was in class.

During weekend classes, my family stepped in and cared for my son. The only task required of me was to show up on time both for arrival and departure.

My church family served as a sanctuary of refuge for me during my doctoral studies. My pastor would often brag about my accomplishments to the congregation and displayed a sincere interest in my research. Often, the pastor would allow me to share my research with him and others in the church who expressed interest. One such item that stands out to me is the book *The Mis-Education of the Negro* (Woodson 1933). The pastor would ask me to read passages from the text to him. We would often dialogue about its contents. He was so passionate about my research that I felt it developed into a sincere connection to him, his ministry, and his congregation.

While it was my duty to teach during the day and attend classes at night, my number one priority was my mental health, which allowed me to be a mother and a student simultaneously.

I made sure I didn't sign up for every single committee sent my way at school; instead, I concentrated on those extracurricular activities that were aligned with my mission.

I kept my eyes plastered on the prize and did not allow myself to become envious or jealous of the accomplishments of my friends. Many of my friends got engaged, married, and started families during my time as a doctoral student. I made it a point to celebrate with them, but only for one day, because the duties of completing my dissertation took precedence over any and all celebrations that lasted more than one day. While others were enjoying life, I toiled through the night, reading articles, organizing various pieces of research, and writing my dissertation. There was no time to be wasted.

WHY I CHOSE MY TOPIC

I decided to concentrate my research on America's current curriculum because being a teacher for many years taught me that the Eurocentric curriculum was not meeting the needs of our Black students. With that being said, I chose to focus on the hidden curriculum for my research topic. This area was important to me because my own experiences with the American education system were so brutal. There appears to exist a distinct problem in our American public schools regarding the achievement of African American students (Honeman 1990). Honeman avowed that American schools are failing African American students due to the lack of appropriate instruction. Honeman's research confirmed that advocates of African American students are seeking new and innovative ideas to help African American students succeed. I too was in search of a different way to teach Black children in our American schools; thus, my dissertation was titled "The Effectiveness of a Culturally Centered Curriculum on Achievement Scores of African American Students in Urban Elementary Schools." I would conduct my research using an urban school in the Midwest that practiced "Afrocentric" teaching and learning in grades kindergarten through fifth.

While I thought I had it all figured out regarding my research topic, it would take me one complete semester to receive approval from the institutional review board for me to conduct my study. I thought this was strange because all of my white counterparts gained IRB approval during their first semesters and would frequently have discussions regarding their research after our weekly class session. Once I gained IRB approval, it was time to demonstrate my established hypotheses through my research. The conclusions from my research demonstrated that the curriculum does impact standardized test scores for Black students. It unveiled my belief that a culturally relevant curriculum can impact the test scores of Black children in a positive manner, thus giving Black students access to higher education.

I never received a grade lower than an "A" in my doctoral work. My story is all about dismantling the lies I was told and embracing the truth about who I was and would become. I graduated in May 1999 with a doctor of education degree in educational leadership. The first in my family, then, and still today.

THE BIGGEST DAY OF MY LIFE: MY DEFENSE

The day was sunny and warm. I exited the home of my dear friend in Saint Louis, Missouri, to make my way to the campus of Saint Louis University, where I was to defend my dissertation. My friend and I prayed together before my departure as she believed in me and was one of my truest cheerleaders. I never paid for lodging while in Saint Louis because my friend provided this for me and my son, along with childcare, meals, and a loving place to call home for the two summers while fulfilling my residency requirements.

I arrived early and took a seat in the lobby. My committee chair greeted me and instructed me to follow him to the meeting room. Before entering the room, he whispered in my ear, "You know your research better than anyone in this room." He was my ally and believed in me from our very first meeting when I presented my case to him for admittance.

Once in the room, I felt a sense of peace which led to confidence. The questions came from every angle, and I tackled each one as if I were an expert on the subject. I was an expert because I was the one who had done the research and dissected the results in a meaningful way. I knew my research, and I was very passionate about the topic.

After two hours of questions and dialogue, my committee chair casually walked me to the door and said, "Congratulations." He went as far as stopping others on campus to tell them about my success. He was so happy for me. I'll never forget my chair and how he fought for me every step of the way. This made me understand the concept that "one does not have to look like me to be for me."

THE DAY OF MY COMMENCEMENT CEREMONY

The day of my commencement ceremony was met with my tribe of supporters from family and friends to church members including my pastor and First Lady. They rented a van and traveled the four-hour journey from Kansas City, Missouri, to Saint Louis to see their "girl" receive the honor of a doctor of educational leadership.

I sat in the huge arena in my doctoral regalia. I felt like a queen sitting on her throne waiting to be summoned to her stage. I was a proud candidate for the degree of doctor of educational leadership.

When they called my name, one would have thought I was the only graduate in the auditorium. The roar from my tribe shook the arena, and all I could do was cry with tears of joy of course. My chair carefully and methodically draped me with my doctoral hood and whispered into my ear, "You are going to do some amazing things." I will never forget his words nor his acts of unselfish kindness. Both were duly noted. Following the auspicious ceremony, I was greeted with hugs, kisses, and congratulatory words of affirmation from my team.

BIG QUESTIONS TO CONSIDER WHEN DECIDING IF A DOCTORATE IS RIGHT FOR YOU

Why Do I Want a Doctorate Degree?

This is a question that must be answered on an individual basis. Every person has a different why for wanting to pursue a doctorate degree. I encourage you to be very clear when answering this question because your answer will be the light that guides you when times get tough and become difficult, especially in the beginning when you are trying to find your footing. I personally desired to pursue a doctorate degree in order to set a high, yet attainable bar for Black children to aim toward. I knew they needed a voice and an example of what Black excellence looks like. I had a mission to prove the self-fulfilling prophecy was a fallacy. I needed to be the one to make a difference in the classrooms across America whose curriculum was historically built on the goal of preserving the Eurocentric curriculum.

Which University Best Meets My Needs?

One has to decide on which higher education institution best meets their needs, both professionally and personally. I chose Saint Louis University because this particular institution displayed a keen interest in diversity and inclusion. Again, I was accepted into their doctorate program, not based on my GRE scores, but rather, based on my research platform and my unwavering desire to pursue the degree. The campus location was a four-hour drive from Kansas City, Missouri—close enough to make the journey to and back during the summers of my residency. I also had a very close network of friends in Saint Louis, so I was well aware there was no need to concern myself with lodging, food, transportation, and most importantly, childcare. Not only was the university located in Saint Louis, but they also had a satellite campus which was only a couple of miles away from my home where my cohort and I would meet for class once weekly.

What Am I Passionate About?

I encourage one to think about what they are most passionate about concerning their field. This will serve as a backdrop when forming your research question. It's important to keep a journal with you at all times during the process of entertaining your research question. I wrote down everything that came to my mind for at least a year before making a solid decision on my question. Then began the deconstruction process: which question or topic brought me the most satisfaction? Finally, I chose my research question based on my deliberate analysis of my journal entries. I shared my topic with my chair who was then able to support me in the process of narrowing it down to something that could be accomplished within my two-year time frame.

Forming your hypotheses should be fashioned in a manner that allows you to formulate solid research-driven answers. Your focus should be hinged in the context of solving a current problem or adding further solutions to a recently solved dilemma. I caution you to steer away from questions that you might not find an appropriate answer or solution to per your research. It would behoove you to look carefully at your literature review while seeking answers to your research question(s). It is not an admirable practice to gather literature that does not serve your research purpose. Your literature gathering should be significantly tied to your question. You do not want unnecessary articles, books, magazines, and other publications to clutter your mind and thinking. Staying focused on your question requires you to cross-examine any and all inquiries for substantive information that can support you in proving your hypothesis.

What Do I Want to Accomplish through My Research?

It's important to know with certainty what your end goal is regarding your research. Answer these questions: "What am I seeking through my research results? What am I attempting to prove?" This is going to serve a stupendous purpose as you outline your research question. Being confident in answering your research question will serve as your hypothesis. Your literature review should be robust enough to support your research topic and answer your question.

Joining an online research organization is very helpful. Some of the major research platforms are ResearchGate, Google Scholar, JSTOR, Library of Congress, Google Books, and of course your university library. These sites will be instrumental in allowing you to narrow your research focus simply by entering your topic into the search bar. You might have one hypothesis or several. I chose to have five hypotheses because my research question required results from several grade levels. I questioned the impact of the Afrocentric curriculum across sundry grade levels. Your research results must be tightly aligned with your question(s). If the configuration is absent, your research might possibly be viewed as invalid in nature.

How Will I Pay for My Classes?

I believed in the principle of "if they make room for me it will come." I am referring to funding your doctorate. I was accepted into my program late; therefore, there was no time for me to apply for scholarships or funding. My chair suggested I take out a second mortgage on my recently purchased home. I knew there was not enough equity there because I had bought my house just three months before I began my doctorate. I did what many of us do: I applied for student loans. I paid for my master's degree as well as my educational specialist degree out of my own pocket. I wasn't financially able to do the same for my doctoral degree. I attended a very prestigious university which called for steep tuition. Student loans would be the answer for me. If you have scholarships and internships available for you to apply for, that might serve as a more lucrative route for you. I was also blessed with a full-time teaching position in a local school district while pursuing my doctorate.

Who Will Serve as My Support System?

Knowing who is for you during this process is key to your success. I am a very gregarious person. That being said, I had a large number of friends and acquaintances around me all the time. Once I began to dive deeper into the doctorate work, I began to realize which people, both individuals and groups, should remain in my close circle. If drama was your forte, you had to be put on hold and I would "see you on the other side." My circle of support included my family, church members, my pastor, and my very close friends. These people became my tribe and propelled me to greatness on more than one occasion. They listened to my writings, proofread my writings, and provided a shoulder to cry on if needed. They provided shelter, sanctuary, love, and so much more. You might also consider joining a group on Facebook. There are several assemblies, and this platform can provide support for individuals on the doctoral journey. I joined at least two of these myself.

My father, who was well into his seventies at the time of my studies, would find so much joy in listening to me read my chapters to him. He called me "doctor" even before I was entrusted with the title. He was to pass away only two years following the conferring of my degree.

Am I Too Young or Too Old to Pursue My Doctorate Degree?

People told me I was too young to pursue a doctorate degree and should put my dream on hold until my son finished high school. This didn't sit well with me, and I dismissed this theory swiftly. My son needed to witness his mother achieve "greatness."

I was thirty-three years old when I began my journey to become a doctor of education and was thirty-five upon my completion. There are no age restrictions in the world of academia. I have students in my current position who are my age, and some are even older; some are younger of course. It doesn't matter your age; instead, it's your desire for your life and fulfilling your dreams and desires. You can accomplish this feat at any age.

Are My Writing Skills Up to Par?

I had achieved two graduate degrees prior to my doctorate; therefore, I had an advantage regarding academic writing. One piece of advice I can offer is to invest in purchasing the latest edition of the *Publication Manual of the American Psychological Association*. I procured my copy of its current edition, and it served as my academic writing guide during and after my doctoral degree. Being an academic calls for academic writing. The seventh edition of the *Publication Manual of the American Psychological Association* is available online in the form of a PDF.

In the event you need support in the area of writing, there are numerous online resources available to you. I found Citation Generator, Scribbr, Research Rabbit, and Grammarly to be most helpful, and the best part is that these platforms provide free services. Citation Generator will be useful when you are at the point of citing your literature review sources. Grammarly is known for checking your document for proper structure and word usage. Scribbr has a reputation for providing editing services as well as checks for plagiarism and clarity. Most university campuses have writing labs on-site. This might serve as an additional layer of support for you when formulating your research question. There is an abundance of online groups and platforms designed to underpin your writing by providing editing and proofreading services. The majority of these services are available for free; however, there are a handful that require a fee. I caution you against using the services that ask for a fee or subscription. Paying for your classes can be financially burdensome. You don't need an extra expense on top of your tuition.

ADVICE TO THOSE CHOOSING THE PATH OF A DOCTORATE

Dismantling any lies you've been told should be your first priority, not just by the ones in pursuit of the doctorate degree, but everyone who has a keen interest in making our world a better place of acceptance and love for all, especially in academia.

Accountability means taking a look in the mirror and asking yourself, "Am I dismantling the lies or am I magnifying them?" This is a question only you can answer for yourself. Determine what you are passionate about and what brings you joy. Ask yourself the question, "What needs to either change or be brought to light?" Envision yourself answering this question through your research and sharing your results with others, for the good of course: with an overwhelming goal to make things better as a result of your research. For me, I had a mission to change and eliminate the errors of the curriculum on our Black students. My desire was to give educators a new way of teaching and learning as it pertains to Black children. With this in mind, it's important to choose the right higher education institution for you. Find out which institutions support your area of research, talk to faculty members about your research interest, meet with current doctoral students, share your research ideas with family and friends for feedback, and lastly, pray for wisdom and guidance. Once you have settled on a research topic, allow space for your research to become a part of your soul: with the intention of becoming an expert. Talk about your research every chance you get; this will only make your voice stronger upon your defense.

Don't be afraid to look to others in your field of research for advice and direction. You will be amazed at what you might uncover just by reaching out to those who have walked in the path of your research topic. Remember, it's all right to be selective about who you welcome into your life while you are on your mission. From the moment you determine your topic, it's imperative that all future conversations are aligned with your topic.

As I stated earlier in my chapter, everyone who you think is for you may not be your ally. Most importantly, do not allow a test to define your destiny. If the GRE is giving you anxiety, try a different approach to your destination. Allow your research to become your best friend, your traveling buddy. I brought my research with me to church, basketball games, soccer games, and any other event that might be long-winded. I had no time to waste, and every second counted toward my "big day," which was my defense.

Understanding and having the foresight to speak about your research is paramount to your success. Build your knowledge base regularly, including both past and present theories that surround and support your topic. Become very familiar with authors who have successful publications in your area of research. Attend conferences and workshops both virtually and in person that will propel you to a deeper understanding of your work. It is also beneficial to join organizations that are aligned with your goals. For instance, Learning for Justice is a platform that I am associated with, as this organization provided me with current information including webinars, literature, and a variety of resources that proved to be invaluable to my study. There are a host of resources available simply by searching for your topic in groups or organizations.

Writing a dissertation can and will be a very overwhelming task, especially when you have doubts. Once you begin the writing process, it's important to erase any and all negative thoughts. Surrounding yourself with positive people who you know will provide candid and meaningful feedback is paramount. Keep in mind that all feedback is not actionable feedback; in other words, you are not required to respond to every piece of advice you are given. If you act upon all advice, you will be thrown into a vicious cycle of trying to please everyone. Make a T-chart, one side highlighting the feedback you will utilize and the opposite side highlighting the points that you might not use. This process will decrease the probability of you becoming overwhelmed and engulfed with making copious and unnecessary changes to your writing.

WHAT AM I UP TO TODAY?

Today, I am a professor on a college campus focusing on teaching, scholarship, and service. People refer to me as Dr. Jennifer J. Malone. I disarmed the lies and erased their power. I am living my dream because of a believing mother and a determined spirit. Breathing life and not death is what she exemplified on my behalf. Now, I am exercising this same principle for others who may have been told some untruths.

Educators must program themselves from telling lies to our children. Children believe what they are told. Instead of repeating lies, whisper to them that they are beautiful and can be and do whatever their heart desires.

Imagine an educational system right here in America, where the principle of simply "being for me" was the staple for entering the classroom as a teacher of young and impressionable minds. These minds are filled with untarnished thoughts just waiting to welcome the wonders of the world and the magic of having someone who is for the whole of them in front of them daily. Being light and generating the "light in their eyes" (Nieto 2010) as they learn to be thinkers of critical content without boundaries concerning who and what they might wish to become. I encourage every educator to be this and more for our children, particularly our Black children, who for so many years have been left behind and introduced to avenues not aligned with higher education. My children were welcomed into the world of academia by way of the example I set for them. Currently, my daughter is a researcher and a high-achieving scholar at my very own alma mater, Saint Louis University. Oh, how the tables have turned. She studies women and gender-related issues and has aligned herself to serve in this capacity all while acting in the role of a researcher as she dares to dream and make her reality of creating a space for people who have been marginalized and told lies their entire lives.

Lastly, live your life on purpose during and after your doctorate. I live my life on purpose by employing this daily principle: "Do all the good you can, by all the means you can, in all the ways you can, in all the places you can, at all the times you can, to all the people you can, as long as ever you can," by John Wesley, 1799 (Quote Investigator 2016).

CHAPTER 8

A Novel Way to Be Heard, to Earn Praise

Sallie B. Middlebrook, PhD

I DON'T THINK MANY PEOPLE WHO EARN A DOCTORAL DEGREE START out in life with earning the doctorate as a goal. I know I didn't.

I remember being little, living in a small house on a small farm, in the Mississippi rural country with my parents, two older brothers, one younger brother, one older sister, and a younger sister who came along when I was eight years old. I remember having a lot to say before I was school-aged, but with so many of us around, I often felt unheard. I remember sometimes feeling like I needed to be alone, somewhere away from the crowded little house. If someone made me angry (which happened a lot), I would storm out and stomp my way up a big hill near our home where I would pay a visit to a big pine tree with a unique curvature in its middle. I would sit on the lap of and discuss my troubles with a tree I named "Connie Bea." Everyone knew I visited Connie Bea when I wanted to be alone (I had a vivid imagination, and she was a very understanding tree).

I remember that learning was always celebrated in our home. Our father finished high school and trade school, our mother finished high school, and they both wanted more for us. From the time I was old enough to carry a sack until I was school-age, I performed farm chores and gathered vegetables from sunup to sundown. After sundown, I remember that learning—showing what you knew—was a sure way of getting noticed and getting praise in our home. Proof of learning and evidence of developed skills was a sure way to get seen and be heard by my parents. I remember learning from my older siblings who were school age before I was. I learned to read, write, and all my numbers before I ever spent even one day in school. I remember showing off what I knew to my parents, being heard, and earning their praise. It felt good.

When I was in the fifth grade, I had a teacher who started taking our class on trips to the school library. After learning how to check out books, I borrowed library books every week and spent most of my leisure time reading. Books lit my soul on fire, and, starting around age ten, my favorite place to be was in the library. I read everything. Fiction, nonfiction, biographies, autobiographies, magazines, newspapers, anything and everything that captured my attention. I read everything, and everything I read inspired me.

My school became racially integrated when I was in middle school, even though we, as students, protested integration. Still, eighth grade was the end of our Black school. It all happened without our consent, and when I finally got to high school, two teachers made lifelong impressions on me. One of them was my eleventh-grade English teacher. A Black woman. I remember her because she loved books and literature as much as I did. She assigned books for us to read and essays for us to write, and she played records containing literary stories in class (the 1970s versions of audiobooks!). Records that told interesting tales about interesting characters using only voices and sound effects.

In the twelfth grade, I had another great teacher. A white man who taught speech always encouraged us to be creative and to use our imaginations when writing, speaking, or presenting. Ironically, we hardly ever wrote or presented speeches in speech class. Learning, for me, included showing who you were by sharing what you loved. With this in mind, I remember creating a radio play (which I recorded to share with my class using a tape recorder, and for which I produced my own sound effects), and I also wrote a stage play. In that class, writing became my way of getting noticed and gaining praise for my knowledge. My efforts. My speech class and my speech teacher thought both my radio play and my stage play were exceptionally well written, and my teacher asked if he could share my work with the school. I consented, and, one day, near the end of the day, before it was time to head out to the school buses, we all heard something that got everyone's attention. A story was being told over the school's intercom system. It was my radio play, with my voice as the storyteller, and with all the sound effects I made and recorded to make the play come alive. That evening, on the bus headed for home, my friends and neighbors gave me a big round of applause. Then, just weeks later, my stage play found its way out into the public. It was a Christmas play, and, thanks to my speech teacher, people from my speech class performed it at an assembly for the elementary school in our town. Well, it received so much acclaim, we were asked to stage the performance at our high school too. I was the director of the play, and after it was performed at our high school, our town newspaper, a weekly, printed a story about it and my picture appeared in the newspaper as both writer and director.

Well, that did it for me. I now knew how to use what I'd learned to be heard and seen by others and to earn acclaim and praise. Wow. It felt good, and it told me what I wanted to be when I grew up. So, after high school, at age eighteen, I left my hometown and went away to college. After being offered an academic scholarship, I chose to attend Jackson State University (JSU). I had been a country girl my entire life, so I thought it might be nice to learn how to be a city girl. JSU was in Jackson, Mississippi, the capital of the state. With an academic scholarship in hand, I decided that studying in the capital city would be good for me. I intended to study English because I dreamed of becoming a writer of novels, especially after I learned a famous author I admired was a professor in the English department at JSU. Thinking about all I was going to learn about writing and creating literature, I psyched myself up so much I could hardly wait to begin taking any and every class taught by Dr. Margaret Walker Alexander. The woman was, after all, the author of one of my favorite novels—a work of fiction titled *Jubilee*. I read that book my senior year in high school and reading it changed my life. It opened my eyes to history I had not been taught in history class, and it made me know without a doubt that I wanted to become a writer of novels. I wanted to use our mostly untold history, and our good and bad legacies, as my inspiration to create and write contemporary stories about my people.

Once I got to JSU, I found out the famous author was no longer serving on the English department faculty, and the news devastated me. I was so disappointed, I considered leaving school altogether. But I stayed, and before long, I made a friend who lived in the same dorm as me. She was a mass communications major and thought I might want to consider it too as a major. I had no idea what mass communication was, but she explained it to me. It was her goal to work in television broadcasting, and, knowing I wanted to be a writer, she suggested I might want to study print journalism. That way, I could work as a professional writer to earn money while also writing novels. Hum. Maybe I could become a news reporter. Maybe I would enjoy writing news stories and sharing my writing with newspaper readers. I would be learning, I would be writing, and I would probably be helping someone in some way. Best of all, I would be showing what I knew, perhaps getting noticed and even earning praise for my skills. It sounded like a good plan, so I decided to become a mass communications major.

Besides going to class and doing my best in all of them, I worked different jobs, and every now and then, I even had a crush and a boyfriend or two. But I spent a great deal of time reading books, my favorite hobby. So I didn't spend an inordinate amount of time dating, even though I hoped to meet the love of my life in college. Then, in either my junior or my senior year (I can't remember which one), I felt like I'd won something big and important when a woman from *Ebony* magazine came to work on the faculty of the mass communications department. Not only was she from *Ebony*, but when she worked for publisher John Johnson, she was over the company's book division. The book division, I thought. The department that published books written by famous authors like Lerone Bennett Junior (October 17, 1928–February 14, 2018). The magazine *Ebony* was then far removed from what it is today (and I think the original version was much better), and I believed this Black woman was truly a godsend to the mass communications department. She started a real newspaper that the department published, and, finally, I and other mass communications students were able to be real news reporters. We wrote articles and had them published in a real newspaper. We created portfolios showcasing our work, which helped us get jobs after graduating.

And, four years after I started my journey at JSU, I earned my bachelor's degree in mass communications with a concentration in journalism. I graduated at the top of my class too, with a 3.98 GPA.

After getting my bachelor of science degree, I worked as a newspaper reporter and writer, and, for a brief time, as assistant editor of a small magazine start-up. Working for the start-up magazine, *Sunbelt, Black Life in the South*, made the biggest impression on me. Started by Mississippi businessman Thomas Espy (brother of former US Secretary of Agriculture Mike Espy), it was a magazine targeting primarily southern Black readers, and the editorial content was directed at these readers. *Sunbelt* was where I fell in love with publishing.

Here is an interesting story from when I worked at *Sunbelt, Black Life in the South*. It was either 1980 or 1981. I knew our executive editor had sent several copies of the publication to the president of the United States, who, at the time, was Jimmy Carter. Then, one day, after 5 p.m., I was surprised at work when several "men in black" wearing dark shades came into our offices in the Barnet building in Jackson, Mississippi. You see, it was during the time when Jimmy Carter was running for reelection, and his campaign had made its way to Jackson. He could not come by our offices to pay us a visit, so, he sent his mother, Mrs. Lillian Carter, to visit us. Most of the staff had already left for the day, but a few of us were working late. And that was how I met, shook hands with, and had a nice conversation about our publication and my role there with the mother of the president of the United States! It was and still is one of the most profound moments of my life. Because of that and other amazing people and moments, I found myself loving working in magazine publishing. I was an interviewer, I wrote stories, and I believed I was helping someone in some way with information the magazine provided. I was showing what I knew, getting noticed, and earning praise for my skills. Who could ask for anything more?

But my joy was not meant to last. Getting enough advertisers to bring in the revenue we needed to continue publishing was always a big problem for the publication, so, unfortunately, the magazine folded after existing only several years. Still, I internalized the mission of *Sunbelt*, and even though I've worked as an editor for other magazines in more recent years, I have never found more purpose in my work than when I worked at *Sunbelt, Black Life in the South*. Showing the world the joys and challenges of living in the South as a Black person became part of me. Still in my twenties, once the magazine ended, I decided to go back to school to work on getting a master's degree in English. I thought it would allow me to focus at least some of my time on writing fiction. But a lack of commitment to these plans soon came between me and that degree. What happened? After completing more than two-thirds of a master's in English, I caught the copywriting bug and decided to get my master's degree in advertising instead of English. I think I felt that understanding more about advertising and how it worked would benefit me if I ever decided to start my own magazine. I had already learned that publishing was a sure way to learn, show your knowledge and skills, help others, and get notice and praise from lots of people for doing something you loved.

So I stopped short of earning my master's degree in English. With only three courses and a thesis paper left to complete, I chose to leave Mississippi and started pursuing a new master's degree at the University of Illinois, in Urbana. There, I was among a blessed group of graduate students called James Webb Young Scholars. James Webb Young Scholars were people from all around the nation who had been selected to be recipients of the competitive and prestigious James Webb Young Fellowship. I was a James Webb Young scholar. James Webb Young was a "Mad Man" way before advertising professionals became popular on television. The very first chairman of the Ad Council, Mr. Young was voted Advertising Man of the Year in 1946, long before I was born. I enjoyed everything about my time at the University of Illinois where I became a research assistant for faculty in the advertising department. At University of Illinois, I not only completed my master's degree in advertising, but I also took lots of courses in literature, once again fueling and feeding my dreams of becoming a writer of novels.

WHY I STARTED MY DOCTORAL JOURNEY

First, I want you to know that teaching at a university was never my dream, never one of my lifelong career goals. I wasn't one of those little girls who always dreamed of being a teacher, and I never dreamed I would become a college professor. I enjoyed helping others by sharing knowledge, and I was always interested in writing. It was my love of writing that led me to a place where I ended up pursuing a master's degree in advertising, and pursuing my master's degree in advertising led to a new goal of becoming an ad agency copywriter.

All of this happened during a time when major advertising agencies across the nation were under fire for not hiring Black Americans. However, by the time I finished my master's, the "pull" from the advertising industry had slowed to a stop. Without providing specific examples (of which there are thousands), the move to recruit Blacks had come due to the fact that there was a preponderance of negative images of Blacks in advertising, in particular, and in the media in general. There was also an absence of Black models and actors in advertising and in general market media, and this is what led Black civil rights organizations (led by the National Association for the Advancement of Colored People) to begin demanding that major mainstream advertising agencies increase the numbers of Black employees in non-menial, decision-making roles. At this time, the ten major New York firms employed about twenty thousand people, and fewer than thirty of these were Black Americans who held creative or executive positions at these agencies.

The advertising industry went from actively recruiting Blacks to being seen as a place that was "anti-Black" by the time I completed my degree and started interviewing for jobs on Michigan Avenue in Chicago. I, someone who had received the prestigious James Webb Young Fellowship that paid for my education, went from one interview to the next with no one offering me a job, even though I graduated with a high GPA from a university that, at the time, was considered to be in first place among the best in the nation for the study of advertising.

Side story: Living in a college town (a college city) in the North, I experienced being called the N-word for the first time in my life. No kidding. No one had ever called me that vile name in my twentysomething years of living in the South. And then, one day, I was walking to my apartment, which was on campus. Walking with several friends who lived in the same apartment building, most of whom were Asian, most from Vietnam. They were beautiful women who had beautiful brown skin. In fact, my skin was lighter than most of theirs. So, when a pickup truck drove down the "fraternity row" street where we were walking on the sidewalk, one of its occupants yelled the N-word at us, shouting "Hey N-words!" Well, one of my Asian friends believed he was talking to them, so she yelled back, "We're not N-words! We're g—ks!" The sickening, awkward moment was quickly dissolved by my friend's response, and we all laughed all the way home. What the ignorant young man yelled at us was not funny, but the way my friend chose to deal with it was refreshing.

After completing my master's degree in advertising at the University of Illinois, Champaign-Urbana, my goal was to work as a professional in the advertising industry. But I had no idea how hard it would be for a Black woman to get hired in that industry. After going on several interviews with no job offers, I realized it was going to be an uphill proposition. So, with no job offers, when one of the professors I stayed in touch with from my undergraduate alma mater asked me to apply for a teaching position there, I did, and that is how I ended up becoming a university professor.

Still in my twenties, I accepted the offer to join the faculty of the mass communications department at JSU in the fall of 1984 and was hired to teach courses in advertising and print journalism. During this time, I was still keeping an eye on the advertising industry, both as a scholar and as someone who still planned to work in an agency one day. The more I taught courses designed to teach others about the industry, the more I wanted to work as an ad agency copywriter. However, my constant research and reading revealed that Blacks who worked in the mainstream of the industry for the biggest white-owned agencies were becoming increasingly dissatisfied with their employers and their discriminatory racial practices. Many of these workers were unhappy, so they complained and were quickly finding themselves laid off and out of work. Many of those who continued to work in the agencies were unhappy too as they faced mountains of disappointment trying to advance upward in these companies.

After teaching at JSU for two years, I realized I was not a happy camper. In my late twenties, I wasn't ready to be a college professor, and I didn't know if I would ever be ready for an "academic" position. Teaching at the college level was a big job filled with all kinds of challenges and responsibilities, and it was a never-ending job. Even after preparing lectures or discussions for classes, after doing research to bring new knowledge or new examples from the professional world to class that I did not find in a book, even after teaching and advising students, there were always papers I needed to read and grade. The work never ended, and I felt like I was still unprepared for the job. I believed I needed to work at least a few years in advertising before I could begin to enjoy teaching about it, so I left the university and moved to Houston, Texas. That was where my older sister lived with her husband and their young family.

My goal, again, was to get a job working in advertising. With no luck in Houston, I moved to Dallas, where my younger sister knew someone who knew someone who knew someone. The last someone was a Black man who owned an advertising agency. A Black-owned agency. So, using my sister's connections, I got an interview, presented my portfolio, and was hired as a consultant for research and copywriting. I had finally made it into the advertising industry after years of trying to get there, and the agency where I worked was one of the agencies of record for the city's bus system, Dallas Area Rapid Transit. I got a chance to work with other writers, researchers, and ad designers on print, television, radio, and outdoor billboards and promotional campaigns for Dallas Area Rapid Transit and for other clients, including the NBA's Dallas Mavericks.

But I was a consultant. Not a permanent employee. So, in 1988, I applied for, interviewed for, and was hired to become a member of the faculty at the University of Nebraska–Lincoln. I had gained experience in advertising and had served as a researcher and a copywriter for print, radio, and television advertising, all to be the best professor I could be. At University of Nebraska–Lincoln, I soon became interested in serving as an academic advisor to student groups entering national advertising and marketing competitions, and that's where I found my "sweet spot," my joy in teaching. My students entered competition after competition, and we were soon winning third-, second-, and first-place prizes in national advertising and marketing competitions. I met one eligible, single Black man when I was in Nebraska, and he and I dated, got serious, and I even ended up accepting a marriage proposal from him. But marriage wasn't meant to be, and we ended the relationship after spending more than six months together. Then, as it turned out, the Nebraska winters were just too cold and snowy for me. After one where I found myself literally knee-deep in snow, I decided it was time for me to head back south. So, I interviewed for a teaching position at the University of Florida (UF) in Gainesville, and I left Nebraska after living and working there for four years.

In 1992, I began serving as a member of the advertising faculty at a huge university, and I knew if I wanted to get tenure there, I would need to earn a doctoral degree. I could have pursued my degree at UF while teaching at UF, but I didn't want to work and study in the same department. Still, I knew if I wanted to continue working in higher education, I was going to need a doctoral degree. I had already applied and been accepted to study in a doctoral program at the University of Tennessee, Knoxville. At the time, however, I felt it was best for me to continue working at UF because I was helping to support my mother financially. My father passed away when I was fourteen, and even though my mother worked for many years, she was now retired and had started experiencing health challenges. After thinking about it for a while, I decided it wasn't the best time for me to become an unemployed, full-time graduate student. Instead, I needed to keep working and saving as much money as I could, just in case my mother's health took a turn for the worse.

By 1994, in my mid-thirties, I felt like I was Dorothy, standing at a crossroads on the "yellow brick road" with a puzzled look on my face. I had to make up my mind about the right way for me to go. I was the only one of nine children our mother gave birth to who was still single and without children (my younger brother had passed away in 1985, at age twenty-seven). Therefore, I knew if my mother's health got worse, I would—most likely—be the one who would go home to Mississippi to look after her. I had applied and been accepted to study in the doctoral program at the University of Tennessee, Knoxville, but that would have meant leaving my job, which I did not want to do. But, since I was already working full-time on the faculty at a major US institution of higher learning, I needed to pursue a doctoral degree in case I decided to apply for tenure. Only I was not sure I wanted tenure. After all, I did not like living in Gainesville, and I never wanted to become a college professor. Therefore, I had to ask myself why in the world I would put myself through the torture chamber I'd heard the "publish or perish" tenure process could be.

Finally, I remembered something my mother once told me. She said it was always better to have something and not need it than to need it and not have it. So, after having several conversations with my department chairman about my goals as a member of the advertising faculty at the UF School of Journalism and Mass Communications, I decided to continue working full-time while pursuing my doctorate through distance education. Once I made that decision, I conducted some research and found out that two people I admired, Nelson Mandela and Charles Shultz, both had learned and earned degrees through distance education. After many months of deliberation, I made my decision based on my needs at the time. And heck, if distance education was good enough for Nelson Mandela and Charlie Brown's creator, then it was good enough for me too.

With encouragement from friends I respected and admired, who were already tenured university professors, in 1994, I applied and got accepted to study in the doctoral program of Walden University, where I would study to get my doctorate in business administration and management, with a specialization in marketing. From everything I saw and read, I believed Walden had one of the country's best distance learning programs. It was regionally accredited, had excellent academic advisors, and provided top-notch library, research, and technical support. They also had a residency program that required attendance at regional seminars. And, once a year, in the summer, Walden doctoral students had to attend seminars at Indiana University in Bloomington, where the school also maintained a library program. The best part for me was, by choosing to study through distance education, I was able to continue working full-time at UF.

I finally made up my mind to pursue my degree through distance education at Walden University. I made my choice, took a leap of faith, and over the next two and a half years, I earned my doctorate through nontraditional study at a nontraditional university. I have to tell you, my experience as a nontraditional graduate student was like no other. I found it to be a new, challenging, and wonderful way to learn. For me, it became a fantastic exploration that helped me expand my thinking and reasoning abilities through my studies, by meeting lots of new and interesting people, and by traveling to places I might never have visited to attend required regional seminars. I was glad I chose Walden University and the distance mode of learning, and glad I took that leap of faith that was benefitting me in many immeasurable ways.

WHY I CHOSE MY DISSERTATION TOPIC

Distance education was new to me, and it was new to most of the students I met while I was completing my coursework. I was learning so much, not just about business and management, but I had become intrigued with this "self-directed" mode of study. While I was completing my courses, I learned how to use databases to conduct secondary research. I had been using computers and teaching students how to create advertising campaigns using computers and software for many years. So it was easy for me to learn to use other computer applications and software while conducting research for papers I had to write as I was completing my coursework for my doctorate.

When it was time for me to decide what I wanted as my area of research, one thing I felt was needed was more information on how distance education providers could use the universe of adults who were studying through distance education to reach out to other working adults. People like me. Working folk who did not know about distance education and distance learning. So, for my dissertation topic, I chose something like: "Using the relationship between doctoral degree students' personal values, degree expectations, and degree program satisfaction to create distance learning marketing communication strategies."

I chose this topic because I wanted to use my background in advertising and marketing as I conducted my doctoral research study. I also wanted to learn as much as I could to advance my knowledge of marketing and advertising as I conducted my first primary research study. Finally, I wanted my study to discover information that could help distance education providers develop strategies that would help them communicate more effectively with adults who might want to continue their education without leaving their jobs.

Pandemic considerations aside, today, there is a lot more interest in nontraditional education alternatives as more and more traditional colleges and universities have added distance components to their repertoire of offerings. And, as more students earn their degrees through nontraditional institutions, the image of online and other distance alternatives is also becoming updated. Schools such as Kaplan University, the University of Phoenix, and Walden University (my doctoral alma mater), for example, have gained prominence and notoriety through the years based on the competence, quality, and proven capabilities of their product (their graduates).

How I Found Balance for My Life

I worked, full-time, as a college professor while pursuing my doctorate. Teaching two, three, and four different classes, for me, meant preparing and updating lectures; actually conducting classes (not handing them off to assistants—which I never experienced the luxury of having); scheduling and conducting meetings with students (during office hours) to help them with class projects; being an academic advisor; grading papers; attending and contributing to departmental, intradepartmental, or university committee meetings; and serving as academic advisor to student groups entering national advertising and marketing competitions. Once my workday was over, I usually left the UF campus. Some days, however, before leaving campus for the day I would have to go to the library to do research or to check out books I needed to complete my doctoral coursework. I never thought about it while I was working on my doctorate, but it was actually a blessing to have the UF's library as a resource I could use to read, check out, or order books I needed through the interlibrary loan system.

After finishing everything I needed to do on campus, I would go home and begin my school day as a doctoral student. I completed work for any courses I was enrolled in which involved a lot of research and a lot of writing. Since I was single with no children, I never had to juggle a husband, kids, or any type of family life. But, even though this was true, my life was still filled with a lot of other things I wanted or needed to do. I was renting a two-story condo that I had to keep clean and maintained, and I was also into physical fitness. I walked as my preferred method of losing or maintaining my weight and that meant after completing household chores, I had to find at least an hour a day that I could devote to walking. I usually chose to walk on my treadmill, but sometimes I would choose to take a mile-long walk outside.

Managing the phone and unnecessary conversations took a lot more tact and diplomacy. Unfortunately, it also called for me to let go of a friendship. Everyone in my life knew I was working a full-time job while going to graduate school full-time, studying for an advanced degree. Soon, a longtime acquaintance began calling constantly, keeping me on the phone for hours and hours at a time. At first, I didn't think much of it. My friend and I lived in different states and never saw each other in person, so I was willing to keep in touch by phone until the calling got to be too much.

Being on the phone started to interfere with either my writing time, my research time, or my study time. Once that began to happen, I had to ask myself if this person was a real friend, especially after I delivered my standard speech on how little time I had these days. So, this so-called friend knew I wanted and needed to devote most of my spare time to my studies. But this person kept calling and calling, wanting to talk for more and longer periods of time. I had to come to the conclusion that this was not a good friend. This was an enemy, in disguise. Good friends observed boundaries and respected each other's time. I had no other choice. I ended the "friendship." For good. To this day, I do not question my choice. I did the right thing.

HOW I COPED AND OVERCAME STRUGGLES

There is a saying that attitude is more important than facts. It goes on to say that what happens to us is not nearly as important as how we respond to what happens. Attitude, therefore, is more important than anything else to a sense of well-being. Simply put, I believe if we have the right attitude at any given time in life, we can triumph over anything. It is said the two most difficult things to handle in life are failure and success, and

I have found that attitude is the thing that makes the most difference in how I handle each of these things.

I must tell you there were many moments when I was completing either my coursework or my research when it became very tempting to give in to negative emotions. But my *attitude* is what always saved me—after I learned I had to work hard to keep it positive. I did my best to incorporate time management best practices into every day to make time for my many responsibilities and my coursework. By doing this, I was usually able to carve out quite a bit of quiet time within the chaos that often was my day. Now I'm going to share with you a few of my time management favorites. I hope you'll find the following tips helpful.

I prioritized my goals whenever it was possible. On the weekend, I would take a few moments to think about the week ahead. Using one of my collected day planners or books of blank pages, I would make a list. First, of all the things I needed to do, things I had to do. Next, I wrote down the things I wanted to do, and finally, I wrote down the things I would do if I had the time. Once my week got started, I spent the bulk of my time and energy on those things that were "musts," and I got as many other things done as possible if they were really important to me.

I chop, chop, chopped big jobs into smaller ones. Whenever it was possible, I whittled big tasks down into a series of smaller tasks, and then I worked on the smaller tasks in intervals until the big job no longer existed. Smaller tasks were not nearly as intimidating, so once I was looking at multiple smaller tasks, it was easier for me to complete every task.

I set time limits for "unpleasant" chores. I gave myself a set amount of time—for example, ten or fifteen minutes—to perform tasks I knew I hated. For example, I hate vacuuming. Therefore, I learned to set my oven timer and only allow myself to vacuum for ten minutes at a time. If more vacuuming was needed, after spending time doing something else . . . anything else, I would devote another ten minutes to vacuuming. Get it? By giving myself time limits and then sticking to them for those must-do tasks I absolutely hated, I was able to get my housework done with time to spare.

I never wasted a waiting moment. Any time I found myself somewhere waiting on something, if possible, I used that time to write or to plan what I wanted or needed to write. It could be for one of my courses, or it could be one of the chapters I was working on when I was writing my dissertation. I kept a notepad with me at all times so that I could jot down ideas that might come to mind whenever I had to wait in line for something I needed.

I practiced phone fasting. Realizing that spending too much time on the telephone could be the biggest time waster of all, I learned to see my phone as a tool to be used only for "must-have" conversations. I learned not to allow other people to determine what I was going to do with my time. If it was important or necessary for me to talk to someone by phone, then by all means, I would talk to them. But if I saw a call as one that was really more "nothing" than "something," in terms of what I needed to do, if I answered the phone, I learned to kindly and gently shut the conversation down quickly.

MY BIG DAY

I didn't believe this until I earned my doctorate, but after earning it, I came to believe that for me—and maybe for most who earn one—earning a doctorate is not just about earning a doctorate. I believe earning a doctorate is about proving something to yourself. Something that you believe you need to prove, and earning the degree just happens to be the way you have chosen to prove it. Earning any degree provides visible proof that you can do something that takes time and effort; something that you plan and set out to do. After all, a college degree is something most people respect—inside and beyond the academic arena. And that's what the doctorate was for me. It was visible proof that I could achieve what I set out to achieve.

While completing my degree, I made up my mind I was not interested in applying for tenure at the UF. I did not enjoy living in Florida, so why would I want to stay there? Then, just several months after earning my doctorate, my mother's health started getting worse. My aunt let me know she believed someone needed to go home to stay a while to look after my mother, her youngest sister. I had also decided, despite being an academic advisor to students winning first place in national advertising and marketing competitions, university teaching was not for me. I loved directing those marketing and advertising teams because I loved the practical side of media communications. That helped me know I wanted to do something else with my life, and none of those things involved doing academic research and writing academic research papers. I enjoyed teaching, yes. And I enjoyed serving as advisor to student teams entering national and regional marketing and advertising competitions. I even enjoyed serving on committees and helping to complete assignments that helped students in some way. But I was from a "practitioner" world where I was most comfortable. I fit into corporate environments and was "at ease" working as a communications practitioner. Conducting interviews and writing for a magazine that had a noble purpose for people I believed in; working for a Black-owned advertising and marketing firm doing research and writing for print, radio, and television; working with artists and graphic designers and learning how to create and prepare visual communications designed to get attention from a target audience whose attention was desired, that was the world I loved. A world where everything was not so "academic."

Of course, all of the aforementioned realizations came after my "big day." After I delivered the results of my doctoral research study. Going to school from a distance and learning from a distance meant I would be delivering my dissertation defense from a distance too. The chairman of my dissertation committee prepared me well for what to expect, so I knew I would be delivering my defense to my whole committee, which, at that time, consisted of the six people I had worked with while completing my doctoral study. I was allowed to have one member on my committee who was "outside" of the Walden doctoral program. Therefore, for more than two years I had the pleasure and the challenge of working with one of my UF faculty colleagues, a very smart man who helped me structure my research study and who guided me in analyzing the results of my quantitative study. I had prepared a questionnaire which I had mailed to the entire student body of the doctoral program at Walden University, which, at the time, was more than eight hundred students. I had gotten responses from more than half of those I mailed the questionnaire to, and, to me, that alone meant my study was a success. In the months leading up to defense day, I chatted with my advisor and with members of my committee to help me determine what to prioritize in my presentation.

In the days leading up to defense day, I studied. I read every chapter of my dissertation over and over as a way of preparing myself for any possible questions any member of my committee might send my way that day. My faculty colleague let me know I needed to be ready for any question so, to be thoroughly prepared, I made notes. I purchased plastic tape, and I taped notes from every chapter of my dissertation on the walls all around the living room of my apartment in Gainesville, Florida, just to remind me of what I thought were the most important parts of my study.

My defense was going to be done by speakerphone, and I would be sharing the results of years of work through a virtual defense seminar attended by my whole doctoral committee, which included my faculty colleague from the UF. My big nerves are what I remember most about my big day. I was so afraid, even though I didn't believe I could be more prepared to defend my study. Preparation is one thing and presenting to a group of people who already hold the degree you're trying to earn is another thing. The intimidation was palpable, but I had made it this far and there was no way I was not going to finish what I started. That was how I learned the true meaning of courage. It did not mean acting while having no fear. It meant acting while being consumed with fear. It was what I had to do. And it is what I did. Defending my study from a remote location certainly had some negatives, like not being able to look people in the eye as I spoke and as I responded to their questions. But it also had some positives, like not having to look people in the eye as I spoke and as I responded to their questions.

I delivered my defense more than twenty-six years ago, so a lot of things about that day have become a bit fuzzy in my memory. But I do remember that I loved the virtual platform. Not being "there," in person, somehow gave me a feeling of control. Being able to control my immediate environment and having notes on the walls (most of which I did not have to use) gave me a feeling of security. It helped to enhance my confidence. Having notes to look at, which my committee could not see, also helped me when it was time for me to respond to the toughest questions I received that day, all of which had to do with the quantitative results of my study.

I remember standing for the whole presentation. Even though my committee could not see me, I stood while delivering my defense, and standing allowed me to remain focused while feeling like I was doing something important. I believed it enhanced my delivery skills and enabled me to connect with my audience—even though I could not see them. In the end, my presentation was a culmination of everything I ever learned. My high school English classes. My high school speech classes. My college journalism classes. My communications work experience. My love of writing. My dreams of writing books and novels. At the end of my presentation, once I was told I had passed my dissertation defense and that I was a PhD, Dr. Sallie Middlebrook, I felt like a ton of bricks had been lifted off my soul. I knew I had added something else to the person I was. Something that would help me in my writing; something that would help me get noticed while doing things I loved, earning praise from me, the person who—for me—had to matter first and had to matter the most.

MY BIGGEST QUESTIONS

Using hindsight, I can tell you it is important to address your biggest concerns prior to selecting a school so that you will know what questions you need to ask, and what things you need to look for as you consider and compare institutions.

While there are many questions you will need to find answers to, what I am presenting here represents some of the most important considerations for those considering studying through distance education. You might want to ask if you would make a good "distance learner." Will you be able to manage your time well? Will you enjoy completing your courses and your research without face-to-face instruction? How will it feel to be an independent learner? Will you love it, or will you hate it? Will you be making the biggest mistake of your life? Will you regret your decision to go off the tried-and-true path to enlightenment by taking what is still a less-traveled route to the PhD? Will your degree be respected after you earn it? Will you respect your degree after you earn it?

I had earned both my bachelor's and master's degrees from traditional brick-and-mortar institutions, so I was a bit skeptical about straying from the conventional path for my doctorate. I had a lot of questions, and I wasn't able to find many answers, but I took the plunge anyway into the nontraditional mode of study. Oh, there were naysayers who "poo-pooed" distance education, but I ignored them. Why? Because I saw distance education and the technology it embraced as part of the future of education, and I knew those naysayers were "dinosaurs" with feet firmly planted in the past. And today, more than twenty-six years later, I'm still glad I took the distance plunge.

Some of the most important questions I had are questions you might need to ask. It is not easy to provide a list of questions and answers because the questions and the answers will vary depending on both the student and the specific higher education provider. In other words, considerations about earning your doctoral degree are personal, based on your needs and preferences. However, as a doctoral-degree graduate of a university providing distance education, exclusively, and as someone who has read survey responses from more than five hundred adult students learning through distance education, many of the major concerns I and other students had many years ago (when I conducted my research study) are still relevant today.

Is the School I'm Choosing Regionally Accredited?

If you are considering distance education providers, you will need to be concerned about accreditation because it is important to employers, licensing agencies, and financial and lending institutions. Accreditation is an ongoing process that schools must go through periodically, and accreditation can be attained or lost. Therefore, you need to know if the distance providers you are considering have continually maintained the standards of quality that are required by regional accrediting agencies.

This, I believe, is the first and most important question you should find the answer to as you look at distance providers. It is extremely important for a college or university to earn and keep regional accreditation—the highest (and most important) form of accreditation that any college or university, traditional or nontraditional, can attain. You need to know that many employers, licensing authorities, and financial lending institutions view regional accreditation as the standard, most vital indicator of quality when it comes to colleges and universities.

Most distance education providers are aware that potential students are concerned about whether schools have attained regional accreditation. Schools that are not regionally accredited are considered to be "diploma mills," and you should avoid them at all costs. Accreditation information is usually contained in marketing and advertising materials used to reach prospective students. If you are unable to find this information in printed material, you should contact the school's administrative offices or check out their website to find out if they're regionally accredited. Depending on the region of the nation where the school's main offices are located, the school should be accredited by one of the following six regional accrediting authorities in the United States: Middle State Association of Colleges and Schools (Commission on Higher Education), New England Association of Schools and Colleges (Commission on Technical and Career Institutions and Commission on Institutions of Higher Education), North Central Association of Colleges and Schools (The Higher Learning Commission), Northwest Association of Schools and Colleges and Southern Association of Colleges and Schools (Commission on Colleges), and Western Association of Schools and Colleges (Accrediting Commission for Community and Junior Colleges and Accrediting Commission for Senior Colleges and Universities).

Will I Be Able to Manage My Life and My Time so That I Can Devote Needed Time to Reading, Research, and Study?

The question of time management is important. Education and learning require a great degree of time management and self-discipline. Doctoral students who do not learn to manage their time effectively while pursuing a degree often find themselves getting nowhere fast. Learning and/ or adhering to good time-management habits was the main problem area cited by respondents to my national survey. If you decide to study via distance education, you should first determine your own needs and how you like to study, keeping in mind your lifestyle and what you plan to accomplish as a result of your education.

After looking for a school that offers a program of study suited to your needs, learning preferences, and lifestyle, you need to think about, ask, and answer questions related to things that will help or hinder you as you strive to accomplish your educational goals.

I've Decided to Pursue Distance Education, but if I Later Decide to Transfer to a Different School (Traditional or Nontraditional), Will I Be Able to Transfer the Credits I've Earned?

If you decide to study through a "nontraditional" education provider (distance education provider), you will need to ask and get answers to questions you might not need to think about if you choose a traditional university. These days, especially post-COVID-19, more and more traditional schools are offering degree options using distance learning/distance education modalities. This fact, alone, has enhanced the "image" of distance education/distance learning. Some people who choose a nontraditional provider sometimes decide to transfer to a traditional university to complete their degree. The problem is some providers of online/distance education offer courses that may not be transferable to state-supported/public or other private colleges and universities. Therefore, you need to ask if you will be able to transfer your credit before choosing between nontraditional or traditional schools, and before committing to any distance provider.

Most schools have policies governing transfer coursework and will only transfer certain coursework completed at US and foreign colleges and universities/institutions that meet/have obtained the proper academic accreditation standards. For this reason, if you know you might need to be able to transfer your earned credits to another institution, you need to find out about the transfer policies for the school you're attending, and for the one you're planning to attend in the future.

WHAT ABOUT FINANCIAL AID TO HELP PAY FOR SCHOOL-RELATED EXPENSES?

Many providers of distance or nontraditional education allow students to apply for the same types of financial aid as students attending traditional colleges and universities. Distance education institutions, when they are accredited, are eligible to offer certain types of financial aid. Since there are so many different kinds of financial aid, and since schools may have different offerings, when you request information about a particular school, you should always ask them to send you information about their arrangements for student financial aid.

Life after Earning the Doctorate

One of the most important things I learned as a result of my doctoral study was realizing I could write a book. It's true. The doctoral dissertation is a sort of book comprising five chapters, and after writing mine from start to finish, I knew I had learned what I needed to know to write any book I ever decided to write.

I have done lots of things since earning my doctoral degree. Most importantly, I worked as a publishing consultant, and, as it turned out, this work became an important "turning point" for me. Remember that ad agency I worked for when I was in Dallas? Well, while I was working as a publishing consultant, through a network of people associated with my work in publishing, I became "reconnected" with that same agency. The agency's owner then hired me to become a screenwriting consultant, to help an already-published novelist who wanted one of her unpublished books adapted into a screenplay. So, in 2004, I moved to the Los Angeles area (Orange County) where I worked for six months on the screenplay. I was fortunate to be able to hire another consultant, a man who was a real live, Emmy-winning, Hollywood screenwriter and film editor who was a professor of film at Pepperdine University. And this man? He had won acclaim working with none other than Oprah!

Although confidentiality agreements prohibit me from being able to talk about the screenplay, after six months of hard work, I completed it. Those six months involved total focus on and commitment to that project, and once I completed the screenplay, I knew well the meaning of true commitment to a project. Finishing that project, in fact, is what made me know I could commit to putting together an interesting and exciting story from beginning to end. I knew that if I could adapt someone's novel into a 120-page, well-written screenplay, I could darn well commit to starting and completing my own first novel.

In 2005, back in Texas, I became communications director for a nonprofit organization in Fort Bend County, a suburb of Houston. After more than two years there, I accepted a position at a larger nonprofit organization in Houston where I became the marketing and communications manager. After nearly three years there I decided it was time for me to do something else, maybe begin working from home. That would save at least three hours of driving every day, giving me time to start writing my first novel. So, in 2009, I resigned, moved home, and started working remotely. Since that time, I've held many remote positions, including working in sales for a book publishing company and working as a technical editor for a billion-dollar software as a service company.

In addition to doing work I enjoy to earn a living, in my spare time, I have been working on writing a "collection" of novels. I just finished book number ten, the last book in a ten-book collection I call "Living in Color." Using my many years of learning about and creating graphic design, I created the covers for all ten of my books. If I could talk to her, I think Connie Bea, my old childhood friend, would be mighty proud. In addition to completing ten novels, I have written several nonfiction books to help writers of fiction and nonfiction, and I've written and illustrated children's books (under my pen name, Bea Rivers). I've also written scores of articles and short stories that are published online (on sites owned by Maven Media Group). I even published the first two novels in my color-coded collection, but, after rethinking both, I took them off the market and I have revised them. I recently completed a course in book publishing for which I earned a certificate. I am continuing to learn as I am developing plans to release my "Living in Color" books backed by a robust marketing campaign.

MY ADVICE TO OTHERS WHO MIGHT WANT TO BEGIN THE DOCTORAL JOURNEY

Earning a doctoral degree can be a life-changing decision, and life-changing decisions are never easy. Often, what it comes down to is that you're faced with choosing between two entirely different alternatives. One of your alternatives is enticing because it will allow your life to maintain your status quo. It represents a chance to keep doing, pretty much, what you're already doing. It is a certain path that you can live with, and you know it because you've lived on a similar path for the past oh-so-many years.

The other alternative(s) would lead you to uncertain places, places representing a big, scary, gigantic change in your status quo. Uncertain places are the unknown, but there is a chance this alternative could *possibly* make you happier than you've ever been in your whole life. The problem is, you have no way of knowing for sure that happiness will be the end result of either of these alternatives or which might be the best one for you. And that's what makes what you're faced with a big, difficult decision.

Well. Here is all the help I can offer you. The only guarantee in life is that life offers no guarantees. Let's face it: Sometimes you will make decisions that will end up not being the best ones for you. That's a fact of life. But even though life does not come with guarantees, when it comes to making big decisions—such as whether to go for the doctoral degree—there are certain steps you can take to give yourself a chance to make a sound decision you can live with.

Listen to your inner voice. What is it trying to tell you? Are you acting hastily in making your decision? Do you need to devote more time to consider your alternatives? Perhaps you need to consult a friend or a loved one, or someone you know and trust, who may have been faced with making a similar decision in the past.

Consider how each alternative you consider aligns with your values, beliefs, and purpose. Any choice that is right for you will be aligned with these. Becoming more self-aware will help you, now and in the future, to know what choices are more likely to be best for your life, in the short and long term. Be sure you can and will want to live with the decision you make. Involve your heart as well as your mind. What is it telling you? If you find yourself needing to be "talked into" making a particular choice, it may not be the right decision for you. If no alternative you've considered feels "right" for you, give more thought to the situation. Perhaps a better alternative will emerge that you have not yet considered.

Think about how each alternative might affect other parts of your life. Will the decision "sit well" and "fit well" with other people who are important to you? Remember, it is important to consider the effects your final decision will have on the lives of those you love. Still, the best decision will be one that is aligned with your values, beliefs, and purpose.

Use your mind's eye to visualize what your life might look like once you've made your decision. When you imagine your life with each alternative, how does your decision "look" and "feel" as part of your life? Do you feel relieved with your first alternative as your choice? Do you feel more relieved with another alternative as your final choice?

Look closely at the consequences or possible end results of each alternative. How will the consequences affect you and any loved ones whose lives might be affected by your decision? Examine each alternative from as many angles and perspectives as possible.

If you're a person of faith, pray, and then listen for God's response. Pay close attention to your life and make sure you don't miss out on the answers God is sending to you when you pray or when you ask for wisdom and guidance. Make sure, first, you're asking out of a sincere desire to do God's will. God always sends us answers, but sometimes we're too busy living our lives or we're too consumed with the affairs and business of the secular world to look around, listen, and receive messages from God.

In the final analysis, learning to be optimistic and confident in yourself and your ability to make decisions is key to helping you calm your mind. And as long as you are willing to put in the time it takes to consider the possible steps you'll need to take; you should find some comfort in knowing you will always do your best to give decision-making your all. After deciding to give it your all, take a deep breath and a step back. Doing this will help you replace negative thoughts, feelings, and behavior with positive thoughts, feelings, and activities. And you'll be on your way to making a good decision that has a good chance of being the best decision for you.

CHAPTER 9

The Big Questions, Answered

THIS CHAPTER IS DEVOTED TO QUESTIONS AND ANSWERS. EVERY author of *Inspired to Climb Higher* was asked to come up with some of the biggest questions she encountered when deciding whether the doctoral journey was something she would pursue. And, since knowledge is power, we decided compiling our questions and answers in one place would make it easy to reference these valuable insights to aid your decision-making process. We hope both the questions and our responses will help you find the answers you need to make decisions about your academic pursuits.

There are myriad questions and oh, so many challenges that students face when pursuing a doctoral degree. However, with the right mindset and support, any and all challenges can be overcome.

The first challenge is often financial. Many students take on significant debt to attend graduate school. However, there are many ways to avoid this obstacle. You can find scholarships, grants, or employee reimbursements that cover a significant portion of tuition and other costs. Another option is to take or change to a job that supports working during graduate studies. Additional strategies include reducing living expenses through downsizing, getting a roommate, or moving back home. There are endless options.

Another challenge that students face is the workload. Many doctoral programs are extremely demanding, and students must devote a large amount of time to their studies. This can be difficult, especially when students are also working full-time. Here are some ways to make the workload easier. Find study groups or tutors that can help with focusing on studies. Use online resources to help with homework. Invest in software, equipment, and tools that save you time and effort like buying your own printer instead of using the one at the library. Learn to become more efficient with your time. Consider using your lunch hour or commute time to study.

Finally, rigorous doctoral programs require extensive research skills. Potential students often wonder if they have what it will take to see them through the rigors of advanced academic research. If you have not had extensive experience in research before starting doctoral study, hire a tutor or join a study group to help you overcome this obstacle.

The following is a compilation of all the questions the authors of *Inspired to Climb Higher* offered in chapters where we shared our stories. We want you to know that even though the challenges prospective doctoral students face are significant, they are all manageable. With the right mindset and outlook, most students can overcome any type of adversity to achieve their goals. If you choose to pursue this journey, you might even find yourself having "mid-program" questions about whether you should continue. If this happens to you, it might be a good idea to think about when you first considered earning a doctoral degree, when you first asked yourself, "Why?" Remember the moment you first considered ascending higher. Were you inspired by someone else, or was advancing your knowledge or your career your primary motivation? After you reconnect with your reasons and motivations for starting your journey, you will be closer to answering the question of whether it is right for you to continue.

To help you as much as we can before you begin your journey, we are inserting here questions we had before deciding to pursue our doctoral degrees. The questions and responses are presented in the order our chapters appear in the book. Each section is labeled with a subhead indicating which author's chapter the questions and answers come from. You may notice some questions are asked multiple times in similar or slightly different ways. We intentionally left this overlap because it demonstrates the rich diversity of experience and perspective. What's right for one may be different for another.

Q&A

DR. BEVERLY MIDDLEBROOK-THOMAS (QUESTIONS AND ANSWERS FROM CHAPTER 1)

There are many questions I considered the answers to before deciding to make the commitment to the life-changing leap of pursuing a doctorate degree. Many of the answers to the questions you may have will be unique to your own life situations. It is important to consider the pros and cons when answering the questions that you have about whether to pursue a doctorate degree, but finding the answers will help you make the best decision and be better prepared for success. The following are some of the questions I entertained before making the decision to pursue the degree.

Is a doctorate degree right for me?

A good way to decide if the doctorate degree is right for you is to ask yourself some key questions regarding why you want to pursue the degree. The answers to such questions may range from a desire for personal fulfillment to show your mastery or expertise in your field to career advancement reasons. When you have satisfactory answers to the questions, it's up to you to take the first step. As an educator, my decision to pursue the EdD degree was based on my desire to be among the most educated in my field.

Which institution should I consider?

Institutions may vary greatly in programs of focus, financial support, and time commitment for the doctoral degree; therefore, choosing a school will involve doing your research well in advance. You will need to determine which accredited traditional or online schools best fit your needs. Learn the reputation of the school and the resources and opportunities offered. If you know anyone who has attended the school, talk to them about their experience. Do your research, because weighing the pros and cons and choosing a school that will help you be successful during your journey and in your personal and future endeavors is important.

How do I decide between the PhD and EdD?

Both the PhD and the EdD are high-level terminal degrees with rigorous programs, but the program you choose will depend on your reason for pursuing the degree. The PhD degree is more suitable for those who want to conduct research or teach at the university level. On the other hand, the EdD degree prepares one to work in the field of education as a teacher or educational leader. As an EdD career candidate, you can expect to be involved in roles that are mostly practice-based, meaning you will likely manage or oversee other people. In my role as a K–12 schoolteacher and adjunct professor, the EdD degree was the best fit for me.

Is there a good time to start a doctoral journey (age, career or family status, etc.)?

Getting a doctorate can be highly rewarding. However, choosing the right time to start is unique to each person's life situation and goals. Life will not stop. Therefore, among other things, it will ultimately depend on choosing a time when you feel that you can be confident, focused, and productive as you juggle the demands of doctoral coursework and obligations with other demands of your life. At the time I chose to enter my doctoral program, I was an adjunct professor at University of Phoenix Online. I made my decision to enroll in the doctorate program based partly on the fact that, as an employee, I would receive a considerable discount on the coursework.

Dr. Jyenny Babcock (questions and answers from chapter 2)

Deciding to attend a doctoral program is a big decision. It's right up there with buying a house, choosing a career, or getting married because it requires a lot of resources, dedication, and time. There are so many questions, large and small, to answer before, during, and after the journey.

How do I choose where to attend?

The first big question was where to attend. Choosing a program was easy once I established a hierarchy of wants and needs. In weighted order, I looked for a program that was accredited, offered online, cost less than twenty-five thousand dollars, could be completed in three years, did not require travel or extensive group work, and had an easy application process. Every requirement on my list was a deal-breaker. Had I not been able to find a program that fit those criteria, I would not have enrolled in a program. I know other students who prioritized institutional prestige, mentorship opportunities, and research funding when choosing where to attend. If I were younger and looking to build a career, my criteria would have been similar to the other students I know.

What do I want to use this degree for?

After starting the doctoral program, the next big question to answer was what do I want to use this degree for? Ideally, this question is answered as part of the decision to pursue a doctorate so it can direct the choice of institution. If you don't answer this question at that stage, the next best time to answer it is at the start of your program because the answer should drive how you select your dissertation topic, to leverage or support your postgraduate plans. In my case, since my primary reason for getting the degree was to assuage my fear of missing out, I decided to not put any pressure on myself to use the degree for anything beyond professional credentials in the circles where it matters.

Has the investment in this doctoral program been worth it so far?

A final big question emerged about halfway through my program. A colossal question in fact. How would I graduate with my sanity intact? Phrased another way, was the investment worth it? Being in the program was costing me money, degrading the quality of my personal and professional relationships, and eroding my mental health. I worried every day that the return on my investment was absurdly small. What did the title of doctor mean if I was unhappy with life, unable to pull myself out of the hole it seemed I was digging in double time?

Finding the answer took a lot of soul-searching, which I've already covered. My answer was to continue, but in a healthier way than I had been doing. That was the best decision I made on my doctoral journey. But I want to take this opportunity to point out there is no shame in changing your mind about what you want out of life. If the doctorate program is not what you imagined it would be and you believe the cost does not outweigh the value, then please make a graceful exit, and get on with the rest of your life. Changing your mind is not quitting. Quitting is giving up. Changing your mind is acknowledging your needs.

DR. NOHA ABDOU (QUESTIONS AND ANSWERS FROM CHAPTER 3)

It is not every day one decides to pursue a terminal degree, such as a PhD or an EdD. Since this is a life-changing experience, one must go into it with their eyes wide open. So many questions flooded my brain when I first pondered the possibility of pursuing a doctorate that I needed answers to before taking on this endeavor.

Will earning a doctorate be worth the time, effort, and money to get this degree in my field?

The first question was, is it worth the time, effort, and money to get this degree in my field? Since stumbling on and falling in love with higher education, I knew I would never return to the information technology world in the private sector. I also knew that a terminal degree was desirable in higher education if I wanted to pursue a leadership position, regardless of my field. Attaining such a degree would open doors for me. So, yes, it would be worth it, and my return on investment should be worthwhile.

Do I want to burden myself and my family with the cost of paying for my degree?

Speaking of cost, I also pondered whether I wanted to burden my family excessively financially since we had college-going kids at the time. So, while there may have been more distinguished schools that I could have applied to and possibly attended, with costly tuition, California State University, Fullerton's rankings in their EdD leadership program convinced me that it was a rigorous, affordable program, especially since I was getting some tuition reimbursement as I worked in the California State University system. So this was a win-win for me.

Do you enjoy studying alone or with a group?

Another reason I chose California State University, Fullerton, was because their EdD was a cohort program. Being part of a cohort was very important to me. The bonds formed when you spend three years of your life taking courses alongside your peers and progressing through the program together would be the peer support system I needed lest life throw a curveball at me. Sure enough, it did.

Do you want to pursue a PhD or an EdD, and does it matter which you choose?

Another question I asked myself was whether I should pursue a PhD or an EdD. I knew I was not interested in a primarily instructional and research role in higher education. Instead, I enjoyed higher education administration more, and thus an EdD would allow me to apply the knowledge I learned to practice. An EdD would give me the skills necessary to succeed in leadership levels, and that's why I chose the EdD route.

Are you prepared and ready to take on several years of demanding study?

I also doubted myself and thought I could not take on such rigorous academics after graduating with my bachelor's degree some twenty-plus years ago. That is why I challenged myself that if I could retake college-level calculus and pass with an "A" grade, I would be graduate school material. I not only surprised myself with getting "As" but also rose to the occasion when I raised the bar for myself. Thus, I felt ready to take on the world and this doctorate.

How will you manage your marriage and family obligations?

When I started my program, we were empty nesters, so I did not have to worry about attending to my kids' needs or demands. However, you must consider this if your kids are still home. I did worry that my commitment to the rigorous program could impact my marriage. Luckily, I had my husband's buy-in from the get-go, and we both understood that we were a team going into this journey together. True, he ended up golfing a lot, and it sometimes felt unfair that I was studying while he played golf, but I constantly reminded myself that it was my choice to get my doctorate.

Besides, he needed a way to fill the void of my not being there; for him, that filler was golf.

While these are just a flavor of some of the questions you may ponder when considering a doctoral degree, the important thing is to address every one of your concerns before committing to this journey. Going in with your eyes wide open, with all your questions answered, will set you up for success and, ultimately, degree completion.

DR. HELGA MCCULLOUGH (QUESTIONS AND ANSWERS FROM CHAPTER 4)

How would I pay for this?

I was not making much money when I started my doctorate, and I was also the sole supporter of a family of four. There was no funding available for the program I had chosen. I did not have any money in savings. I knew I would have to take out many loans to complete the degree. What I *didn't* realize at the time was that most positions in higher education qualify for the Public Service Loan Forgiveness program as long as the institution is not-for-profit. Thankfully, my employer is a not-for-profit, and I am on track to having the remainder of my loans fully forgiven.

Would the benefits outweigh the negatives?

I knew that pursuing a doctorate would entail a great deal of work, leading to missing out on social and family time. I also knew that it would be very stressful, potentially negatively impacting relationships and overall well-being. That said, I really enjoyed learning, and I really wanted to achieve this goal. I also felt somewhat stale in my career, and I knew this could be a way to remedy that. For me, it really helped to keep the benefits in mind. I knew my primary goal for earning a doctorate was securing a tenure-track role in higher education. I also knew that such a position could potentially afford tuition remission for my kids, a better work-life balance, and more flexibility with my schedule.

Am I capable?

A doctorate just seemed so prestigious. I knew that I was smart, but was I *that* smart? I always tend to feel this way when embarking on new journeys. I have always shied away from doing things unless I am confident I can succeed. Clearly, I was capable, and I am grateful that I did not let those doubts stop me.

Does this particular degree have the potential to get me where I want to go?

I knew I wanted to pursue a tenure-track faculty position in a speech-language pathology program. I also knew that not just *any* doctoral degree was the best bet for this goal. Students wishing to become certified speech-language pathologists need to attend a graduate program that is accredited by the Council on Academic Accreditation in Audiology and Speech-Language Pathology. The Council on Academic Accreditation in Audiology and Speech-Language Pathology mandates that terminal degree holders must teach the majority of graduate-level courses in an accredited program. The Council on Academic Accreditation in Audiology and Speech-Language Pathology also specifies that they only recognize the PhD and EdD as appropriate academic terminal degrees in our field. Therefore, I knew that pursuing a clinical doctorate in speech-language pathology (SLPD or CScD) would not afford me the best opportunities for the goals I wished to achieve.

Would I have the support that I needed?

I had two small children. I was working full-time. I could not afford *not* to work full-time. I knew I would primarily have to use weekends to complete the bulk of my schoolwork. Thankfully, at the time, my kids' dad was very involved in their lives and did the vast majority of child-related work. If he had not been so willing to be their primary caretaker, I likely would not have been able to keep up with my coursework, so I am very grateful that he was so involved in their lives when they were so young.

DR. WANDA EBRIGHT (QUESTIONS AND ANSWERS FROM CHAPTER 5)

There are several important questions to ask yourself if you are considering pursuing a doctoral degree.

Do you enjoy conducting research?

It's important to know that the purpose of a doctoral degree is to contribute new knowledge or a new interpretation to your field of study. That requires you to select one or more research questions, develop a research project, choose a methodology, conduct the research, sort and analyze data, and then write and publish the findings and analysis. If you find all of this distasteful, a doctorate will be torture for you.

Do you enjoy writing, or do you dread it?

If you enjoy the writing, that is helpful in doctoral study. If you struggle with clarity of thought, grammar, punctuation, or spelling, you will likely need to budget for an editor. An editor will not write your papers for you, but they will let you know where your thoughts are unclear and where you need to review and revise grammar issues. I had a lot of trouble with formatting and sought a colleague's help with that, so I could focus on the writing itself.

Do you want to be an educator, or is it the only career you could think of in your field?

As a professional dancer, I have known many peers in dance who considered teaching as the only option they could think of once their performing years came to an end. This is not an ideal reason to teach and could lead to resentment and bitterness on the job when the educator is asked to do unpleasant or unsatisfying work. If you have a passion for education and for being the positive change your field needs, then doctoral study may be right for you.

If you want to be an educator, what ages and levels of education do you most enjoy teaching?

You want to be sure to pursue a degree program, institution, and research topic focused on the demographics of most interest to you. It is your passion for your topic and the students whose lives you will change that will get you through the time and effort required to complete a doctorate.

What are the qualifications for and salaries attributed to teaching those ages and levels?
I have encountered many people who were surprised by the change, or lack of change, in their salaries upon completion of their doctoral studies. Monetary gain can be a motivating factor, but it should not be your only motivating factor. Do your research before starting a doctoral program. If you know you want to teach K–12 in your hometown, know the typical salaries there in public and private schools. Know how much the pay increases upon completion of your doctorate.

What funding exists to offset the expense of your doctoral study?
Be sure to ask the schools to which you apply about departmental scholarships, graduate school scholarships, fellowships, student employment options, and the Academic Common Market. Ask financial aid if they are aware of any additional opportunities for which you should apply. If you are already teaching, your institution may offer professional development funds that can help offset the cost of tuition or textbooks.

Will you be able to work full-time while pursuing your doctorate, or is that frowned upon?
Some doctoral programs require you to be in residence on campus at all times, which would make keeping your day job difficult or impossible. Some programs are low residency, as mine was. It allowed me to continue to work full-time and keep my benefits while pursuing my doctorate. I did have to manage one week in residence each fall and spring, and multiple weeks in residence each summer.

If you are a parent, do you have help with your children, your home, and your finances so that you can focus on the overwhelming amount of reading and writing necessary to finish the degree that you start?
My husband and I established blocks of weekend time when he would take the kids out so I could read, write, and make notes for my classes. At my job, I found the holes in my schedule that allowed me to book a study room in my campus libraries, so I could do more reading and writing. You

will need to plan the necessary time and block it as an ongoing commitment to yourself.

Does the history of your marriage or relationship suggest that prioritizing your studies will bring you closer to each other or drive a wedge between you?

Not every doctoral student who is in a committed relationship struggles as a result of their studies. However, I recommend taking the time to think through past levels of support from your significant other when you have taken on huge tasks. I also recommend that you discuss the blocks of time you will need to read and process an overwhelming amount of information, so you can write and speak about it. I am certain many partners feel neglected at times and wish the entire process would move more quickly. Know that you control the pace of your research and writing, but the pace of degree completion is up to your advisor and committee. This is a long commitment for you, but it may feel like an eternity for the most supportive significant other.

If a prospective doctoral student enters into coursework without having thought through all of these things, they may be set up to fail bitterly and discourage all others from pursuing degrees.

DR. DEBORAH BROOM-COOLEY (QUESTIONS AND ANSWERS FROM CHAPTER 6)

Prior to embarking on my dissertation journey, I had a variety of questions and concerns. It was my hope to complete my educational journey in a unique way; I did not want to continue in a traditional learning environment, attending all my classes in person during a weeknight. Immediately, I understood that returning to graduate school in the era of online teaching and learning meant navigating multiple platforms of learning was what I needed for flexibility and ease in successfully completing my doctorate. The transition was initially challenging; however, my teaching job and graduate school experiences assisted me in understanding the new ways of learning. Additionally, the multiple opportunities to mentor educators in the Atlanta Public Schools and DeKalb County Schools afforded me a unique perspective in asking probing questions and making appropriate decisions regarding my doctoral journey by asking the following.

What institutions of higher learning would provide diverse teaching and learning experiences in the field of educational leadership that would implement practical and applicable strategies in the twenty-first-century learning environment?

From multiple professional encounters, I found the best-suited institution for completing my specialist and doctoral degrees in educational leadership that would prepare me for meeting my academic and career goals ahead.

Would the faculty, department chairs, and auxiliary personnel have the training, experience, and sensitivity in guiding and supporting all doctoral students in multiple disciplines?

The professionals at Argosy University, Sarasota, Florida, had vast career, knowledge, and work experiences in leadership, in and outside the field of education. Dissertation defense teams were supportive, direct, caring, and professional; they were known as no-nonsense, experienced in guiding doctoral students in multiple disciplines. A great institution of higher learning, knowledgeable content professors, and an experienced defense team assisted me in completing my doctoral journey in three years.

What would be the cost of my doctoral journey for three to five years, and how would it be financed?

After deciding on the institution, I developed a plan to pay for courses for the next three years, travel, hotel, and other expenses.

What employment opportunities and career advancement might be available after completion of my program?

I was familiar with various career options that would be available after attaining my doctorate, all I needed was to enter and successfully complete the program of study. Once beginning the EdS program in educational leadership, I had questions regarding topics I wanted to research in leadership, but I wasn't certain, so my writings were centered around a variety of current topics and issues.

What personal and professional sacrifices would occur during my tenure in doctoral studies?
It was vitally important that I develop a plan of action for time management and effectively communicate that plan to family, friends, coworkers, and organizations in which I held membership.

Dr. Jennifer Malone (questions and answers from chapter 7)

Why do I want a doctorate degree?
This is a question that must be answered on an individual basis. Every person has a different "why" for wanting to pursue a doctorate degree. I encourage you to be very clear when answering this question because your answer will be the light that guides you when times get tough and become difficult, especially in the beginning when you are trying to find your footing. I personally desired to pursue a doctorate degree in order to set a high, yet attainable bar for Black children to aim toward. I knew they needed a voice and an example of what Black excellence looks like. I had a mission to prove the self-fulfilling prophecy was a fallacy. I needed to be the one to make a difference in the classrooms across America whose curriculum was historically built on the goal of preserving the Eurocentric curriculum.

Which university best meets your needs?
You have to decide on which higher education institution best meets your needs: both professionally and personally. I chose Saint Louis University because this particular institution displayed a keen interest in diversity and inclusion. Again, I was accepted into their doctorate program, not based on my GRE scores, but rather, based on my research platform and my unwavering desire to pursue the degree. The campus location was a four-hour drive from Kansas City, Missouri; close enough to make the journey to and back during the summers of my residency. I also had a very close network of friends in Saint Louis, so I was well aware there

was no need to concern myself with lodging, food, transportation, and most importantly, childcare. Not only was the university located in Saint Louis, but they also had a satellite campus which was only a couple of miles away from my home where my cohort and I would meet for class once weekly.

What am I passionate about?

I encourage you to think about what you are most passionate about concerning your field. This will serve as a backdrop when forming your research question. It's important to keep a journal with you at all times during the process of entertaining your research question. I wrote down everything that came to my mind for at least a year before making a solid decision on my question. Then began the deconstruction process: which question or topic brought me the most satisfaction? Finally, I chose my research question based on my deliberate analysis of my journal entries. I shared my topic with my chair who was then able to support me in the process of narrowing it down to something that could be accomplished within my two-year time frame.

Forming your hypotheses should be fashioned in a manner that allows you to formulate solid research-driven answers. Your focus should be hinged in the context of solving a current problem or adding further solutions to a recently solved dilemma. I caution you to steer away from questions that you might not find an appropriate answer or solution to per your research. It would behoove you to look carefully at your literature review while seeking answers to your research question(s). It is not an admirable practice to gather literature that does not serve your research purpose. Your literature gathering should be significantly tied to your question. You do not want unnecessary articles, books, magazines, and other publications to clutter your mind and thinking. Staying focused on your question requires you to cross-examine any and all inquiries for substantive information that can support you in proving your hypothesis.

What do I want to accomplish through my research?

It's important to know with certainty what your end goal is regarding your research. Answer these questions: What am I seeking through my research results? What am I attempting to prove? This is going to serve a stupendous purpose as you outline your research question. Being confident in answering your research question will serve as your hypothesis. Your literature review should be robust enough to support your research topic and answer your question.

Joining an online research organization is very helpful. Some of the major research platforms are ResearchGate, Google Scholar, JSTOR, Library of Congress, Google Books, and of course your university library. These sites will be instrumental in allowing you to narrow your research focus simply by entering your topic into the search bar. You might have one hypothesis or several. I chose to have five hypotheses because my research question required results from several grade levels. I questioned the impact of the Afrocentric curriculum across sundry grade levels. Your research results must be tightly aligned with your question(s). If the configuration is absent your research might possibly be viewed as invalid in nature.

How will I pay for my classes?

I believed in the principle of "if they make room for me it will come." I am referring to funding your doctorate. I was accepted into my program late; therefore, there was no time for me to apply for scholarships or funding. My chair suggested I take out a second mortgage on my recently purchased home. I knew there was not enough equity there because I had bought my house just three months before I began my doctorate. I did what many of us do: I applied for student loans. I paid for my master's degree as well as my educational specialist degree out of my own pocket. I wasn't financially able to do the same for my doctoral degree. I attended a very prestigious university which called for steep tuition. Student loans would be the answer for me. If you have scholarships and internships available for you to apply for, that might serve as a more lucrative route for you. I was also blessed with a full-time teaching position in a local school district while pursuing my doctorate.

Who will serve as my support system?

Knowing who is for you during this process is key to your success. I am a very gregarious person. That being said, I had a large number of friends and acquaintances around me all the time. Once I began to dive deeper into the doctorate work, I began to realize which people, both individuals and groups, should remain in my close circle. If drama was your forte, you had to be put on hold and I would "see you on the other side." My circle of support included my family, church members, my pastor, and my very close friends. These people became my tribe and propelled me to greatness on more than one occasion. They listened to my writings, proofread my writings, and provided a shoulder to cry on if needed. They provided shelter, sanctuary, love, and so much more. You might also consider joining a group on Facebook. There are several assemblies, and this platform that can provide support for individuals on the doctoral journey. I joined at least two of these myself.

My father, who was well into his seventies at the time of my studies, would find so much joy in listening to me read my chapters to him. He called me "doctor" even before I was entrusted with the title. He was to pass away only two years following the conferring of my degree.

Am I too young or too old to pursue my doctorate degree?

People told me I was too young to pursue a doctorate degree and should put my dream on hold until my son finished high school. This didn't sit well with me, and I dismissed this theory swiftly. My son needed to witness his mother achieve greatness.

I was thirty-three years old when I began my journey to become a doctor of education and was thirty-five upon my completion. There are no age restrictions in the world of academia. I have students in my current position who are my age and some are even older; some are younger of course. It doesn't matter your age; instead, it's your desire for your life and fulfilling your dreams and desires. You can accomplish this feat at any age.

Are my writing skills up to par?

I had achieved two graduate degrees prior to my doctorate; therefore, I had an advantage regarding academic writing. One piece of advice I can offer is to invest in purchasing the latest edition of the American Psychological Association writing manual. I procured my copy of its current edition, and it served as my academic writing guide during and after my doctoral degree. Being an academic calls for academic writing. The seventh edition of the *Publication Manual of the American Psychological Association* is available online in the form of a PDF.

In the event you need support in the area of writing, there are numerous online resources available to you. I found Citation Generator, Scribbr, Research Rabbit, and Grammarly to be most helpful and the best part is that these platforms provide free services. Citation Generator will be useful when you are at the point of citing your literature review sources. Grammarly is known for checking your document for proper structure and word usage. Scribbr has a reputation for providing editing services as well as checks for plagiarism and clarity. Most university campuses have writing labs on-site. This might serve as an additional layer of support for you when formulating your research question. There is an abundance of online groups and platforms designed to underpin your writing by providing editing and proofreading services. The majority of these services are available for free; however, there are a handful that require a fee. I caution you against using the services that ask for a fee or subscription. Paying for your classes can be financially burdensome. You don't need an extra expense on top of your tuition.

DR. SALLIE MIDDLEBROOK (QUESTIONS AND ANSWERS FROM CHAPTER 8)

Some of the most important questions I had are questions you might need to ask. It is not easy to provide a list of questions and answers because the questions and the answers will vary depending on both the student and the specific higher education provider. In other words, considerations about earning your doctoral degree are personal, based on your needs and preferences. However, as a doctoral-degree graduate of a university providing distance education, exclusively, and as someone who has read survey responses from more than five hundred adult students learning through distance education, many of the major concerns I and other students had many years ago (when I conducted my research study) are still relevant today.

Is the school I'm choosing regionally accredited?

If you are considering distance education providers, you will need to be concerned about accreditation because it is important to employers, licensing agencies, and financial and lending institutions. Accreditation is an ongoing process that schools must go through periodically, and accreditation can be attained or lost. Therefore, you need to know if the distance providers you are considering have continually maintained the standards of quality that are required by regional accrediting agencies.

This, I believe, is the first and most important question you should find the answer to as you look at distance providers. It is extremely important for a college or university to earn and keep regional accreditation—the highest (and most important) form of accreditation that any college or university, traditional or nontraditional, can attain. You need to know that many employers, licensing authorities, and financial lending institutions view regional accreditation as the standard, most vital indicator of quality when it comes to colleges and universities.

Most distance education providers are aware that potential students are concerned about whether schools have attained regional accreditation. Schools that are not regionally accredited are considered to be "diploma mills," and you should avoid them at all costs. Accreditation information is usually contained in marketing and advertising materials used to reach prospective students. If you are unable to find this information in printed material, you should contact the school's administrative offices or check out their website to find out if they're regionally accredited. Depending on the region of the nation where the school's main offices are located, the school should be accredited by one of the following six regional accrediting authorities in the United States: Middle State Association of Colleges and Schools (Commission on Higher Education), New England Association of Schools and Colleges (Commission on Technical and Career Institutions and Commission on Institutions of

Higher Education), North Central Association of Colleges and Schools (The Higher Learning Commission), Northwest Association of Schools and Colleges and Southern Association of Colleges and Schools (Commission on Colleges), and Western Association of Schools and Colleges (Accrediting Commission for Community and Junior Colleges and Accrediting Commission for Senior Colleges and Universities).

Will I be able to manage my life and my time so that I can devote needed time to reading, research, and study?
The question of time management is important. Education and learning require a great degree of time management and self-discipline. Doctoral students who do not learn to manage their time effectively while pursuing a degree often find themselves getting nowhere fast. Learning and/or adhering to good time management habits was the main problem area cited by respondents to my national survey. If you decide to study via distance education, you should first determine your own needs and how you like to study, keeping in mind your lifestyle and what you plan to accomplish as a result of your education.

After looking for a school that offers a program of study suited to your needs, learning preferences, and lifestyle, you need to think about, ask, and answer questions related to things that will help or hinder you as you strive to accomplish your educational goals.

I've decided to pursue distance education, but if I later decide to transfer to a different school (traditional or nontraditional), will I be able to transfer the credits I've earned?
If you decide to study through a "nontraditional" education provider (distance education provider), you will need to ask and get answers to questions you might not need to think about if you choose a traditional university. These days, especially post-COVID-19, more and more traditional schools are offering degree options using distance learning/distance education modalities. This fact alone has enhanced the "image" of distance education/distance learning. Some people who choose a nontraditional provider sometimes decide to transfer to a traditional university to complete their degree. The problem is some providers of

online/distance education offer courses that may not be transferable to state-supported/public or other private colleges and universities. Therefore, you need to ask if you will be able to transfer your credit before choosing between nontraditional or traditional schools and before committing to any distance provider.

Most schools have policies governing transfer coursework and will only transfer certain coursework completed at US and foreign colleges and universities/institutions that meet/have obtained the proper academic accreditation standards. For this reason, if you know you might need to be able to transfer your earned credits to another institution, you need to find out about the transfer policies for the school you're attending and for the one you're planning to attend in the future.

What about financial aid to help pay for school-related expenses?

Many providers of distance or nontraditional education allow students to apply for the same types of financial aid as students attending traditional colleges and universities. Distance education institutions, when they are accredited, are eligible to receive certain types of financial aid. Since there are so many different kinds of financial aid, and since schools may have different offerings, when you request information about a particular school, you should always ask them to send you information about their arrangements for student financial aid.

END-OF-CHAPTER WORDS OF WISDOM

There are a few simple things you can do to help overcome potential academic obstacles. First and foremost, establish an academic plan and stay focused on your goals. If you have set realistic expectations for yourself, it will be much easier to stay motivated when faced with difficulties along the way. Second, get help from those who know more than you do—your professors, advisors, and other students who have been through the process can be excellent sources of support. Finally, remember to investigate financial aid and other sources of monetary support if necessary.

Earning a doctoral degree can be one of the most rewarding and challenging endeavors of your life. While there may be times when you feel overwhelmed, underprepared, or unqualified, remember to hold on to your motivation and stay focused on why you want to pursue this endeavor in the first place. With dedication and perseverance, along with insight from those who have gone before you and an established support network to help guide you through the challenges that come with pursuing a doctorate degree, success is possible.

CHAPTER 10

Seek Support (When You Need It) for Your Doctoral Journey

IT'S UNANIMOUS. WE ALL AGREE THAT PURSUING A DOCTORAL DEGREE can be a long, demanding journey filled with many and varied kinds of highs and lows. When you decide to take this arduous journey, finding the right support will be a critical component of success. To help you manage the ups and downs of your journey, we added this chapter as an easy way for you to access advice from us (from our chapters).

We know it can sometimes be difficult to manage the roller coaster of challenges that come with earning a doctoral degree, but with the right attitude, tools, and strategies, it's possible to scale any mountain. When you experience the inevitable setbacks during your journey, your ability to "bounce back" will be most crucial. Following the advice in this chapter will help you strengthen your self-confidence and improve your resilience to stay the course through graduation.

As you are considering pursuing a doctoral degree, there is one substantial piece of advice we'd like to offer at the outset, and that is to make sure you have clear motivation for choosing to pursue this degree. While many people go for the doctorate to gain the prestige and career opportunities it can offer, there are also many other valid reasons to pursue a doctoral degree. Some people simply crave new knowledge and new research skills to help them advance in their current careers. Others earn the degree to explore new areas of research that interest them, and some get their doctorate prior to setting up their own independent consulting practice.

Knowing your motivation is paramount if you choose to embark upon this journey. Be honest with yourself about your desires and needs; give serious thought to what you are looking for in a doctoral program. Ultimately, we want you to be sure that the school and the program you choose to attend is one that you believe will help you meet your goals.

After establishing your motivation, it is important to build a support network of people who will help you during your doctoral journey. This network can include family members, friends, business associates, and colleagues from your undergraduate years, as well as people who you meet during your doctoral program. Having a supportive network will help you manage the ups and downs of your studies and will provide encouragement when you need it most.

Seeking support from peers and mentors can be invaluable during your doctoral journey. Peers can provide advice and support during the early stages of research, while mentors can provide guidance and support as you progress through your doctoral program. Your support network might also include fellow students and faculty members at your institution. Not only will this network help you through tough times, but it will also provide practical support, such as someone who can point you in the right direction when you are choosing a research project or help you find affordable housing near campus.

The following is a compilation of all the advice authors of *Inspired to Climb Higher* offered in the personal story chapters. We have inserted here the personal advice that was offered in each author's chapter in the order the chapters appear in the book. Each of the following sections is labeled with a subhead indicating which author's chapter the advice comes from. Keep in mind advice topics may be presented multiple times since the advice is coming from people with differing life experiences and perspectives. That means the discussion will be different (though sometimes only slightly). We intentionally left this overlap because it demonstrates the rich diversity of experiences and perspectives we all have. What's right for one may be different for another. Ultimately, we are offering you our advice as a sort of "decision-making" support system based on the twenty/twenty hindsight we have now that we've climbed higher and earned our doctoral degrees.

Personal Advice from Dr. Beverly Middlebrook-Thomas (Chapter 1)

Conducting a primary research study and writing a dissertation based on that study is a long and arduous journey that is very mentally and physically demanding. It is a formidable task that can be, at times, utterly exhausting as each phase of the journey has its own challenges. On the other hand, I think it is one of the most important and rewarding journeys I have taken in my life. In hindsight, I would offer four Ps that must be there for anyone who is thinking of starting a doctoral journey and staying the course. The four Ps are passion, positivity, patience, and persistence.

Passion and Positivity

Before you start this journey, you must have a burning desire to do it. That's passion! When you make the decision to take the "leap," you have to stay positive, because negativity will enter your world. There will be moments, people, and things that test you. During the dissertation journey, you also have to *take ownership of the obstacles you can control along the way*. Don't sweat the things that you cannot control; instead, seek professional help to get over those humps. Be positive that the topic you have chosen to write about is something that you are passionate about, because you will spend a lot of time researching the topic. It is therefore critical that you choose a subject in which you are highly interested; one you feel confident that you can enjoy researching, learning more about, and writing about for years, and finally, one that you will share the results of years of research and study with a committee of judges who are there not just to listen, but to critique the defense of your study.

If you have made the decision to start this marathon of a journey, I hope you are excited about beginning one of the most important voyages of your life. I hope you *have in mind a vision of the "big picture" at the finish line* because you will need to be able to bring this vision to mind sometimes to get you to the next part of your journey. In your vision, I hope you have also seen "Dr." in front of your name or the initials for your PhD or EdD that will follow your name. I hope you've seen that new nameplate on your office desk. Keeping these things in mind and being able to recall them at will, I promise, will help get you through some of the toughest days you will face as a doctoral student.

If you've chosen to go on this journey, it means you are not a person who gives up when the going gets tough. It means you have a fire burning inside and you're the kind of person who'll *step over and go around any "potholes" you run into along the way*. And, even if you take a misstep and fall into a few of the "potholes," you are the type of person who will get up, dust yourself off, and continue. Because you know you will not give up because you want this and because you have what it takes to get this job done. In other words, you know you have the hunger for the knowledge you need to prevail, and you have the confidence you need to stay the course. You know you can reach the finish line and you are ready and prepared to stay positive. Even when your committee chair or perhaps a member of your committee makes you feel less than competent (oh yes, it can happen). Even when people around you sometimes make you feel like you could be in "over your head." You know you're not. You are just feeling a few "growing pains," and those are expected and should be welcomed because you are on a journey of growth. Through it all, you know you have what it takes to stay positive and to remain passionate as you continue on your journey.

Patience and Persistence

Once you begin the dissertation process, at some point, you must *become inspired and empowered to continue*, because the urge to quit may enter your mind. Keep in mind that this is a journey that can take a few years, or it can take many years. Know, however, that during your doctoral journey, you will learn a lot about yourself because, *among other things, your patience and persistence will be tested*.

Whoever described patience as a virtue was right. The doctoral journey will be fraught with "wait times." For example, you must wait for feedback from draft submissions, wait for the return of graded assignments, wait for answers to your emails, and so on. During such times, you must be patient. Getting stressed could cause you to lose focus, so don't let impatience affect your progress. *Lean on your support system.* I cannot overemphasize how much my support system (my family, my committee) meant to me, and how much they helped me focus and remain patient during the wait times.

Be reminded: writing a dissertation is quite a daunting task. Can you believe *some experts even suggest that you have a second project to work on while writing your dissertation?* Some believe that having other projects (such as a job) to think about can provide both perspective and distance while enabling you to remain productive as you persist with your dissertation. During my journey, I was a middle school teacher with lesson planning to do while also having to do research for classroom activities. I found perspective and was able to achieve the needed distance from my doctoral studies by focusing on my work as a teacher when I wasn't doing work related to my doctoral studies. This helped me to persist and not give up on my doctoral studies and research.

Since the June 2022 defense of my dissertation is still fresh in my mind, a *final piece of advice involves the critical oral defense.* The success of the oral defense will depend on how confident you are as you present your topic and how well you are prepared to respond to questions from your doctoral committee. *It pays to be well-rested, practiced, focused, and ready for the defense.* I think I was ready for my defense after spending many hours practicing, and I truly believe that practice is key.

Additionally, *be sure to have a thorough understanding of the nature of your research topic and key issues surrounding your research problem.* Finally, it is paramount that you be thoroughly familiar with the theory and the framework associated with your research study. These things are the core of your study and will help ensure success on your "big day" as you present your topic and answer questions directed at you by your committee.

PERSONAL ADVICE FROM DR. JYENNY BABCOCK (CHAPTER 2)

Hold on, dear reader, because I'm about to go all woo on you. Every doctoral journey is unique, shaped by the student's personal experiences and expectations. The expectations you place on yourself and your program are the primary drivers of your experience. If your thoughts are filled with worries or questions about your capabilities or deservingness, your doctoral journey will be stressful in a way that leads to burnout. But when your thoughts about your ability and worthiness are at least half filled with self-compassion, curiosity, and courage, your path will be more straightforward. There will be no need for stress, anxiety, or overwhelm.

My advice to those entering a doctoral program soon is to *spend some time clarifying exactly what kind of experience you want to have.* Picture how you want to move through your program. What kind of student do you want to be? How do you want to manage your time? What levels of energy will you maintain? What types of connections will you form? What will be the outcome of earning the degree? What would make the outcome worth the investment of time and money? Are there other ways to obtain what you desire besides getting a doctorate? Are those ways more attractive?

For students already on the doctoral path, I offer you this advice. *More than anything else, be kind to yourself.* You do not need to be hard on yourself to accomplish this dream. You can be, but it isn't necessary, even if that's the way you have gotten to where you are now. I promise you that self-compassion produces much better results because you enjoy the journey more. Managing your mind and energy throughout the journey is critical to success. Self-judgment creates negative conditions in the mind that consume energy better spent on being productive. Cultivate the ability to slip into a positive mindset on demand. Yes, this is possible. You have more control over your emotional states than you may understand.

Don't worry about meeting anyone's expectations besides your own. Partners, employers, faculty members, mentors, family, and friends will all have expectations about how you do the doctorate. Their opinions do not matter as much as your own. As an adult, you are 100 percent entitled to live your life in any way you choose to and you are 100 percent worthy, no matter what you do. You are also 100 percent responsible for your choices. Step into the power of that. Own your choices 100 percent of the time. Forget about complaining about circumstances. Every day, choose your path to graduation.

Start leading your process right away by making choices and moving to the next step. You don't need to overthink your choices about the dissertation.

Explore your interests, evaluate the options, choose a viable option, commit to one option, and continue until you are finished or need to pivot. The sooner you choose a path, the sooner you will arrive at your destination.

No path is a straight line to graduation, only decisions that delay or speed up your time to graduation. The path to graduation will be circuitous and obscured with lots of twists and turns. The key to not getting lost along the way is trusting that the territory you explore is necessary to get you to where you want to be. When you stay curious and committed, you will learn from each obstacle, detour, and setback. Don't be in such a hurry to graduate that you put too much pressure on yourself to perform. Have patience with the process and trust in yourself.

On a practical note, be organized. Organized with your thoughts, your ideas, your documentation, and your files. If you haven't yet, create tracking files to organize your dissertation articles and create folders to organize your files. Create schedules to organize your writing activities. Schedule reminders to do the tasks on your schedule. Set yourself up for success. I cannot emphasize enough how necessary organization is to a successful dissertation and defense. Being disorganized wastes time, leads to frustration, and undermines progress. Use all the tools available to make organization easier like citation management software, whiteboards, and learning how to properly format Word documents using style guides.

My last bit of advice should be obvious, but many students, including myself, overlook this. *Get help when you need it.* If you need academic help, look to classmates, mentors, reputable internet sources, and various university resources like the writing center or librarian (you'd be surprised at how helpful librarians can be). When emotional support is needed, check in with your normal sources such as a partner, friends, family, and trusted colleagues. Be open to seeking additional support from professionals such as therapists, coaches, and doctors. And there's one more source of support that you should not overlook—yourself!

Starting a daily self-coaching habit can turn you into your best source of support. There are so many tools and techniques for self-coaching that promote well-being and mental fitness. *A self-coaching routine can strengthen your resilience, reduce your stress level, and improve your quality of life.* If you aren't sure how to begin a self-coaching routine, I recommend you reach out to a life coach to get you started. Look for a life coach who offers causal coaching, which addresses the reasons students struggle so those struggles can be resolved instead of just treating the symptoms.

You can engage in life coaching at any point in your program. A life coach will help you clarify your goals, identify obstacles holding you back, and find the right strategies for overcoming each obstacle. Engaging in coaching at the beginning of the doctoral program provides a strong foundation from which to build school-life balance, ensuring a positive educational experience. Engaging in coaching when you need assistance to resolve some difficulty can be the support that keeps you from burning out, dropping out, or taking longer than planned to graduate.

The bottom line is that earning a doctoral degree requires managing sustained personal growth over years, which is decidedly uncomfortable. Leverage all of your resources to make the best of your educational experience.

PERSONAL ADVICE FROM DR. NOHA ABDOU (CHAPTER 3)

Reflecting upon my doctoral journey, I have some practical, pragmatic pearls of wisdom that I wished someone had told me before I began and when I concluded my program.

You should start the program with the end in mind, from the get-go. It is a good idea to start thinking about your potential dissertation topic from day one or before you even start the program. If there is an area that you are passionate about, start reading about all the prior research that has been done on it so you can identify the gaps in the literature. The holes you find are what you should focus on, so you can add to the empirical research that is available.

With regard to your dissertation topic, you will usually start with a general area you are interested in. Then you should narrow down the scope of your research until you eventually discover the small niche or angle you will take to add to the body of literature on the topic. Having a very focused topic makes it easier to run specific statistical or qualitative analyses, and, hopefully, adds significance to the empirical research.

As far as adding to the empirical research, we all embark on our dissertation journeys hoping to find a cure for cancer or solving for world peace, metaphorically speaking. The fact of the matter is, that will not be the case for most of the doctoral candidates, and that is okay. Do not feel like your research was a waste of time or less than. You are sometimes not going to find statistical significance in your findings. This is part of the journey. The most important thing is that you finished and beat the odds of all those doctoral candidates that are "All but Dissertation," meaning they are done with all their coursework but have not finished their dissertation and have dropped out.

Once you have successfully defended your dissertation, while you are still on autopilot, why not publish your research findings in a journal article? It will require tweaking and reformatting your dissertation to fit the publication. However, if you wait a little, it is much harder to get back into the groove. Additionally, if a lot of time has elapsed, you may find that your research findings are no longer the latest and greatest or relevant. This is something I regretted not doing right away.

Additionally, during your coursework, you will have a deluge of writing assignments for each course you enroll in. If possible, focus your writing so you can make it fit some chapter in your dissertation. When it's time to start writing your dissertation, you can just take paragraphs from your prior work and paste them into the relevant areas of your dissertation. I wish someone had given me this advice when I first started my program. For my writing assignments, I wrote about a wide variety of topics. Then, when it was time for my dissertation, I felt like I was, unnecessarily, starting from scratch again, and it was very overwhelming.

Typically, at the end of the first year in the program, all students must take a candidacy exam. During this exam, program administrators will weed out the students they do not think are proficient enough to advance to candidacy. The exam will consist of several prompts, and students are tasked to solve the issues at hand or write position papers about them during a limited amount of time. In my program, we were given the prompts on Friday night, and we had to submit our papers by Sunday at 4 p.m. During the candidacy exam weekend, it is a good idea that you be in complete isolation, away from the distractions of your friends and family. Choose an area where you can be completely focused and removed from the hustle and bustle of your everyday life. Personally, I chose to take the exam in my office. I stayed in my office that Friday evening after work and prepared the outline of how I was going to answer the prompts. Then I returned to my office early in the morning to start the writing process and stayed there until late that night. I returned Sunday morning to finalize my responses and submitted my exam.

Do not underestimate the power of a good peer support system. Luckily, my EdD was a cohort program. In a cohort, all the students are admitted at the same time, take the same courses, and progress along the curriculum together. While our cohort was not large to begin with, a group of us naturally gravitated together and began a friendship that resulted in an amazing peer support system. We helped each other out whenever anyone needed help with any subject, analyses, position paper, or problem at hand. It was this peer support system that managed to get me through to the finish line, especially when the going got tough. I am indebted to them for getting me out of my "funk" when my father passed away. The bond we formed has transcended academics and we are now lifelong friends, checking in on each other and our families on a continual basis. Since life happens to all of us, make sure you surround yourself with a good peer support system, lest life throws a curveball your way.

Lastly, don't forget to celebrate the little wins along the journey. It does the body and mind a lot of good. I used to reward myself with milk tea with boba every time I finished writing a paper. As trivial as this seemed, I looked forward to getting my boba drinks from my local juice bar. Most importantly, sit down, buckle up, and enjoy the ride!

PERSONAL ADVICE FROM DR. HELGA M. MCCULLOUGH (CHAPTER 4)

What is your motivation for earning a doctorate? That is going to be different for everyone, right? Regardless of your motivation, make a note of it and refer to it *frequently*. I would also suggest finding an accountability partner. I had absolutely *no one* holding me accountable for my dissertation. My dissertation chair was supportive of me, but she definitely was not going to hold my hand, nor did I expect her to do so. That said, I should have asked someone close to me, a colleague, or a fellow doctoral student to be an accountability buddy. I also can't stress this enough: *just write*. I was so intimidated by starting that I just didn't start. If I had even just committed myself to one paragraph per day or one page per week, I would have been so much better off. I think I was so stressed out by looking at the big picture of a more than one hundred page dissertation that I let fear paralyze me. Treat it like any ol' research paper that you will expand on later. *Just start writing.*

Also, don't be afraid to ask for help. I am sure that if I had asked my dissertation chair to hold me more accountable or put some extra pressure on me to get things done, she would have done so. I just never asked. I am not the type to ask for help, nor do I talk about my struggles, and sometimes both of those things bite me in the butt.

Personal Advice from Dr. Wanda K. W. Ebright (Chapter 5)

If you or someone you care for is contemplating whether to begin the doctoral journey, please *take the time to help think through the answers to every question you can imagine about how to make the completion of the degree both possible and useful.* Know how you best study, alone in quiet or with a group, with a set writing time each day or week or if you prefer to be sporadic about when you can go into writing overdrive.

Design your methodology so that you can easily get to any sites or resources you need for your research. Remember that your dissertation is not necessarily the last thing you will ever write or publish. Don't hold on to control of it so tightly that your committee will not let you defend or pass. You have the rest of your life to write the way you want to write on subjects of your choosing. You will get it done by simply accepting the feedback you receive and applying it. Get done, get out, then write as you like, but *only start a doctorate if what you want to do and be requires one, then think about how your life will change to make completion possible.*

On the social media doctoral and dissertation support groups, I so often see people asking if the degree is worth the time and expense. Unhappy people rush in like predators to say a doctorate is a waste of time, energy, and money, and that they have not advanced enough in their careers to justify their choices to obtain them. This frustrates me not only because they are discouraging people as a result of their own lack of research and planning, but because they made a decision to obtain a degree specifically for money, not because it helped to advance knowledge in their chosen field of study. Anyone who enters into education at any level without thinking through their own intrinsic motivation, prospects for employment in the field, average starting salaries, and rate of upward mobility in the field has set themselves up for disappointment and debt.

You are capable, and my PhD has been worth everything I went through to acquire it.

PERSONAL ADVICE FROM DR. DEBORAH J. BROOM-COOLEY (CHAPTER 6)

Before starting your dissertation journey, I would advise you to question your motives for seeking a doctorate. Think about how you plan to use it in the future, for personal and professional reasons. First, evaluate the cost and time needed to complete your coursework from dissertation writing to defense, and how the financial cost will impact you over time. Reflect on this important investment to make sure it is worth your time and effort. Second, select the right institution, one that reflects your values and would provide professional support from professors, academic deans, and personnel from your program of study throughout the doctoral journey. Third, please talk with your immediate family and seek their support in developing a plan of action for family time, completing household chores, schooling, and emergencies. Fourth, carve out daily study and research time with no interruptions, so that you can complete a myriad of assignments and research tasks. If you are employed, keep in mind your duties and responsibilities to your employer. Any problems, concerns, or issues that may impact your daily routines and obligations should be discussed immediately with supervisors. Always maintain an open line of communication to avoid any misunderstandings. Finally, find a mentor and doctoral group that would provide needed support during your journey. Please allow for alone time to reflect and rest from conducting your dissertation research study and writing. Find the best way for you to remain focused because everybody's journey is different and unique.

Personal Advice from Dr. Jennifer Malone (Chapter 7)

Dismantling any lies you've been told should be your first priority, not just by the ones in pursuit of the doctorate degree, but everyone who has a keen interest in making our world a better place of acceptance and love for all, especially in academia.

Accountability means taking a look in the mirror and asking yourself, "Am I dismantling the lies or am I magnifying them?" This is a question only you can answer for yourself. Determine what you are passionate about and what brings you joy. Ask yourself the question, "What needs to either change or be brought to light?" Envision yourself answering this question through your research and sharing your results with others, for the good of course: with an overwhelming goal to make things better as a result of your research. For me, I had a mission to change and eliminate the errors of the curriculum on our Black students. My desire was to give educators a new way of teaching and learning as it pertains to Black children. With this in mind, it's important to choose the right higher education institution for you. Find out which institutions support your area of research, talk to faculty members about your research interest, meet with current doctoral students, share your research ideas with family and friends for feedback, and lastly, pray for wisdom and guidance. Once you have settled on a research topic, allow space for your research to become a part of your soul, with the intention of becoming an expert. Talk about your research every chance you get; this will only make your voice stronger upon your defense.

Don't be afraid to look to others in your field of research for advice and direction. You will be amazed at what you might uncover just by reaching out to those who have walked in the path of your research topic. Remember, it's all right to be selective about who you welcome into your life while you are on your mission. From the moment you determine your topic, it's imperative that all future conversations are aligned with your topic.

As I stated earlier in my chapter, everyone who you think is for you may not be your ally. Most importantly, do not allow a test to define your destiny. If the GRE is giving you anxiety, try a different approach to your destination. Allow your research to become your best friend, your traveling buddy. I brought my research with me to church, basketball games, soccer games, and any other event that might be long-winded. I had no time to waste, and every second counted toward my big day,"which was my defense.

Understanding and having the foresight to speak about your research is paramount to your success. Build your knowledge base regularly including both past and present theories that surround and support your topic. *Become very familiar with authors, who have successful publications in your area of research.* Attend conferences and workshops both virtually and in person that will propel you to a deeper understanding of your work. It is also beneficial to join organizations that are aligned with your goals. For instance, Learning for Justice is a platform that I am associated with as this organization provided me with current information including webinars, literature, and a variety of resources that proved to be invaluable to my study. There are a host of resources available simply by searching for your topic in groups or organizations.

Writing a dissertation can and will be a very overwhelming task, especially when you have doubts. *Once you begin the writing process, it's important to erase any and all negative thoughts.* Surrounding yourself with positive people who you know will provide candid and meaningful feedback is paramount. Keep in mind that all feedback is not actionable feedback; in other words, you are not required to respond to every piece of advice you are given. If you act upon all advice, you will be thrown into a vicious cycle of trying to please everyone. Make a T-chart; one side highlighting the feedback you will utilize and the opposite side highlighting the points that you might not use. This process will decrease the probability of you becoming overwhelmed and engulfed with making copious and unnecessary changes to your writing.

Personal Advice from Dr. Sallie B. Middlebrook (Chapter 8)

Earning a doctoral degree can be a life-changing decision, and life-changing decisions are never easy. Often, what it comes down to is that you're faced with choosing between two entirely different alternatives. One of your alternatives is enticing because it will allow your life to maintain your status quo. It represents a chance to keep doing, pretty much, what you're already doing. It is a certain path that you can live with, and you know it because you've lived on a similar path for the past oh-so-many years.

The other alternative(s) would lead you to uncertain places, places representing a big, scary, gigantic change in your status quo. Uncertain places are the unknown, but there is a chance this alternative could *possibly* make you happier than you've ever been in your whole life. The problem is, you have no way of knowing for sure that happiness will be the end result of either of these alternatives or which might be the best one for you. And that's what makes what you're faced with a big, difficult decision.

Here is all the help I can offer you. The only guarantee in life is that life offers no guarantees. Let's face it: Sometimes you will make decisions that will end up not being the best ones for you. That's a fact of life. But even though life does not come with guarantees, when it comes to making big decisions—such as whether to go for the doctoral degree—there are certain steps you can take to give yourself a chance to make a sound decision you can live with.

Listen to your inner voice. What is it trying to tell you? Are you acting hastily in making your decision? Do you need to devote more time to consider your alternatives? Perhaps you need to consult a friend or a loved one, or someone you know and trust, who may have been faced with making a similar decision in the past.

Consider how each alternative you consider aligns with your values, beliefs, and purpose. Any choice that is right for you will be aligned with these. Becoming more self-aware will help you, now and in the future, to know what choices are more likely to be best for your life, in the short and long term. Be sure you can and will want to live with the decision you make. Involve your heart as well as your mind. What is it telling you? If you find yourself needing to be "talked into" making a particular choice, it may not be the right decision for you. If no alternative you've considered feels "right" for you, give more thought to the situation. Perhaps a better alternative will emerge that you have not yet considered.

Think about how each alternative might affect other parts of your life. Will the decision "sit well" and "fit well" with other people who are important to you? Remember, it is important to consider the effects your final decision will have on the lives of those you love. Still, the best decision will be one that is aligned with your values, beliefs, and purpose.

Use your mind's eye to visualize what your life might look like once you've made your decision. When you imagine your life with each alternative, how does your decision "look" and "feel" as part of your life? Do you feel relieved with your first alternative as your choice? Do you feel more relieved with another alternative as your final choice?

Look closely at the consequences or possible end results of each alternative. How will the consequences affect you and any loved ones whose lives might be affected by your decision? Examine each alternative from as many angles and perspectives as possible.

If you're a person of faith, pray, and then listen for God's response. Pay close attention to your life and make sure you don't miss out on the answers God is sending to you when you pray or when you ask for wisdom and guidance. Make sure, first, you're asking out of a sincere desire to do God's will. God always sends us answers, but sometimes we're too busy living our lives, or we're too consumed with the affairs and business of the secular world to look around, listen, and receive messages from God.

In the final analysis, learning to be optimistic and confident in yourself and your ability to make decisions is key to helping you calm your mind. And as long as you are willing to put in the time it takes to consider the possible steps you'll need to take, you should find some comfort in knowing you will always do your best to give decision-making your all. After deciding to give it your all, take a deep breath and a step back. Doing this will help you replace negative thoughts, feelings, and behavior with positive thoughts, feelings, and activities. And you'll be on your way to making a good decision that has a good chance of being the best decision for you.

END-OF-CHAPTER WORDS OF WISDOM

In these last pages of *Inspired to Climb Higher*, we—the authors—want to remind you about the risk of stress and burnout that can crop up during your doctorate studies. Being stressed out has negative consequences for both physical health and mental well-being. Accordingly, let us encourage you to make sure to establish healthy work-life balance habits early on in your doctoral journey so that you're better equipped to deal with inevitable stressors along the way. As we conclude this chapter, we leave you with several pointers with regard to setting realistic goals and understanding the time commitment of a doctoral program.

When you are ready to pursue a doctoral degree, it is important to understand the time commitment and to be realistic about what you can accomplish. Doctoral degrees require a lot of hard work and dedication, but they also come with many rewards. Be prepared for the difficulties that go along with pursuing this challenging academic path. Here are five tips to help you manage stress and stay motivated during your doctoral studies:

Set realistic goals and expectations. Don't expect to complete your doctorate in less time than the advertised program length. For example, many EdD programs are structured as three-year programs. Expect that completing your program may take more time than is advertised. While it might be possible to complete your program faster, at the outset, you should expect that it will take at least the amount of time the school has set for it to take.

Break up your study program into manageable chunks. When everything feels overwhelming, take breaks between sections or course modules to help refresh your mind and motivation levels.

Mindfully allocate time for sleep and recreation. It's crucial to recharge your batteries every day so you can maintain focus throughout your studies.

Connect with friends and family members who support academic achievement. Connecting with and hearing words of support from those who care about you can be essential in maintaining high morale during tough times. Spend quality time around people who care about you, even if they don't have an academic background.

Take advantage of online resources and services to supplement classroom learning. Use technology to extend the reach of education beyond traditional classrooms. Look for and take advantage of opportunities for interactive learning both inside and outside the classroom environment.

In addition to the need to set realistic expectations, managing the lengthy time commitment of a doctoral program is also necessary. It is important to remember that it's not all work and no play. You will need to balance your studies with a healthy lifestyle and social life. Don't let the pressure of a long program or an extended journey drive you crazy—getting a doctorate is going to take all the time it takes. Being impatient will only make the program seem longer than it is. With this in mind, the following are some final tips to help you manage the required time commitment:

Stay organized. Keep all of your materials organized and easy to access so that you can focus on your studies without distractions.

Get help from your professors and classmates. Ask your professors for help with specific tasks or problems you're having with your program and reach out to classmates for advice and support.

Take "mental and physical health" breaks. Whenever you start feeling overwhelmed or stressed, take a break to relax and rejuvenate yourself. This will help you stay focused and motivated throughout your program.

And last, but not least, keep in mind that one common challenge during doctoral studies is self-doubt about one's ability to complete the program successfully. To combat self-doubt, set realistic goals for yourself based on what *you* believe is achievable rather than what others expect from you (e.g., completing all coursework within two years instead of four). And remember—no one is perfect. Even Nobel Prize winners have failed at some point during their careers. So, rather than beating yourself up over mistakes made along the way, learn from them and move forward accordingly. After all, failures are often essential learning experiences that, ultimately, contribute to success down the road.

CHAPTER 11

General Advice (and Help) for Writing the Dissertation

We are including this chapter to inspire you, to give you a general overview of all you will need to know, and to put your mind at ease when it comes to going for your doctorate. Most students regard writing a dissertation as a "scary" proposition. But, looking at the whole process, through the twenty/twenty vision of women who have gone through it, can reduce the intimidation factor.

This chapter is meant to help put you at ease when it is time for you to begin writing your dissertation. Although this chapter is not an exact "how to" or a detailed blueprint of all the "technical details" you will need when preparing your dissertation, it does provide what we see as the basic building blocks you will need to write your dissertation. It gives you a "bird's eye view" of most of the basics you will need by going through the steps of a typical dissertation preparation. The chapter also touches on and even elaborates on some of what the authors of this book went through to craft their dissertations—before starting and while they were completing the doctoral journey.

Think about this. If you were getting ready to go on a long walk of maybe a mile or more, you'd want to be wearing your best gym shoes. Getting ready to take a mile-long walk is not the time to be trying out a brand new pair of shoes. You need to know the feel of the shoes you will wear. You need to know they already feel good on your feet and that you won't get halfway through your walk only to discover that the shoes you're wearing are pinching your toes.

You can think of this chapter as a way to put on your comfortable shoes before going on that mile-long walk. It is no secret that many doctoral students have a tough time when it comes to writing their dissertations. In fact, some students are so worried about this aspect of earning their degree that they never even start writing. For some, this is the point where they simply give up on the goal of earning their doctorate.

With this book and this chapter, we are doing our best to help, encourage, and inspire so that this does not happen to you. We don't want you to become one of those students who will throw in the towel. Knowing ahead of time what will be required of you to write a dissertation reduces the likelihood you will be underprepared when you get to the dissertation phase of your doctoral program. Utilize the tips and tricks in this chapter to improve your writing and make the process of writing your dissertation a little less daunting.

A doctoral dissertation is a long and strenuous writing project that requires advanced writing skills. This chapter is here to help you improve your understanding of the writing and other skills required to complete a doctoral dissertation. We hope what we've included herein will help you understand the steps involved in preparing the dissertation while teaching you how important it is that you write clearly, efficiently, effectively, and persuasively.

ESTABLISHING YOUR RESEARCH QUESTION

When writing a doctoral dissertation, it is essential to develop an effective research question. Take the time to thoroughly research your topic before defining your research question. A good place to start is by identifying any gaps in the literature. This can be done by scanning future recommendations in articles or by reviewing current professional practices. By doing this, you can establish an agenda for your study and begin to explore potential research questions.

Another way to find a research question is to look at problems of practice that are currently being faced by professionals in your particular field. Finding this information can help you develop hypotheses about why those problems of practice exist, and that will prepare you to offer insights into possible solutions.

Defining your topic, exploring existing literature to identify gaps in knowledge, scanning the professional environment for potential problems of practice that can be addressed through your work, and applying unused theories or techniques as needed to fill those gaps will support you in creating a strong research question upon which you can base your dissertation project. With careful consideration and effort up front, you will be well on your way toward completing an engaging doctoral dissertation that furthers the understanding of a particular area, in a particular field.

Assess Your Writing Skills; Strengthen if Needed

There are a number of different academic writing skills that you will need to have in order to write your dissertation successfully. First and foremost, you'll need to be able to compile a comprehensive, well-organized body of work. Secondly, you'll need strong argumentation and reasoning abilities which will allow you to make persuasive arguments for your thesis claims. Additionally, you need proficiency in grammar, syntax, and vocabulary, so that your writing is clear and concise.

Reviewing the literature related to your research study can be helpful in improving your writing skills because it will help you develop a better understanding of the topic you are writing about. When it comes to writing your dissertation, having a good understanding of your topic is essential. You will also need to develop good analytical thinking and purposeful writing skills if you are not already proficient in these skills.

It could be that you already possess all the writing skills needed to write your dissertation and that there is no need for improvement before you begin. But if you feel like your current academic writing skills may not be adequate for the task of writing your dissertation, you will need to do all you can to start improving your skills before you begin writing. Therefore, after assessing your writing skills, if you believe you need to improve, keep in mind that a writing coach or tutor can be an invaluable tool when writing a doctoral dissertation. By working with a coach or tutor, you can ensure that your dissertation is well-written and cohesive.

Additionally, a coach or tutor can provide feedback on your writing and help you to refine it, and they can provide guidance on how to structure your dissertation and help you learn how to stay organized. Working with a coach or tutor can ensure that your dissertation is written in a clear, concise, and easy to understand manner.

There are many resources available that can help you improve your academic writing skills. Start by assessing which areas of your writing may need improvement before embarking on a full-blown workshop or course in these areas. Additionally, using online tools such as Grammarly can also help catch common mistakes before they become errors in your final work product.

What Types of Academic Writing Skills Are Needed for a Successful Dissertation?

There are a variety of academic writing skills that are needed for a successful dissertation. These skills can be broken down into three categories: argumentation, reasoning, and grammar/syntax. Each of these areas can be improved with practice and study.

Argumentation: In order to effectively argue your points, you need to be able to clearly state your position and provide evidence to support it. You also need to be able to refute opposing arguments with appropriate evidence.

Reasoning: In order to come to a reasoned conclusion, you need to be able to identify relevant sources of information, synthesize the information, and discern meaningful arguments. Reasoning also requires explaining how your evidence supports your claims.

Grammar/Syntax: In order to write effectively, you need to know the basics of grammar and syntax. This includes knowing how to use proper punctuation and capitalization, as well as understanding the rules of grammar.

BASIC STEPS INCLUDED IN WRITING A DOCTORAL DISSERTATION

Most doctoral dissertations are written using a rigorous and academic style. However, many graduate students find that they need to improve their writing skills in order to produce a high-quality dissertation. One of the goals of this chapter is to give you the basics of effective expository writing.

1. Your dissertation should start with a strong thesis statement. Your thesis statement should be the main focus of your paper and it must be well-supported by evidence from the text. A strong thesis statement will help you organize your thoughts on the topic and make it clear to readers what your paper is about. It is the stance you will support and defend throughout your dissertation. Without something to defend, your argument will come crashing down and your discussion will wander around like a lost soul, without a definite purpose or destination.

2. You will need to use specific and concrete language when discussing your research findings. Do not use general or abstract terms unless you are specifically discussing those terms in relation to your research findings. For example, when describing an experiment, do not say "the study examined" but rather "the experiment found." When stating a fact, use unambiguous wording such as "John eats pie for breakfast every day." Clarity is crucial in all types of writing, but it is especially important when writing about topics that most people are not familiar with. Using concrete words and language will help to improve, for your readers, the readability and comprehension of your dissertation.

3. You need to pay close attention to grammar, punctuation, and word choice. These factors can affect how people perceive and react to what you have said. For example, make sure each sentence has a subject and verb, avoid beginning sentences with prepositions (e.g., in spite of), place commas where they belong, choose carefully which words to use, etc. Citations should be formatted properly according to your university's style guidelines.

One of the purposes of this chapter is to help you improve your writing skills for a doctoral dissertation. In order to be successful in writing a dissertation, you will need to have strong grammar and punctuation skills.

In addition to the steps presented here, you will want to pay attention to university-specified style guidelines, such as those by the American Psychological Association, Modern Language Association, or Chicago Manual of Style, when formatting your document. Why? Because you will need to be sure to use properly structured citations when referencing the sources you used in preparing your work. Finally, practice makes perfect. Over time, as you share different parts of your dissertation with your doctoral committee members, you will become better at crafting clear and engaging prose.

THE IMPORTANCE OF EDITING AND PROOFREADING

Editing and proofreading are important steps in the writing process for any document, but they are critical for doctoral dissertations. The dissertation is a significant piece of research that must be error-free. Furthermore, it is important to have someone else, such as a dissertation editor, review your work for potential errors before you submit it to your academic institution. This can help ensure that your dissertation is accurate and meets the standards of your discipline. Since hiring an editor is usually a personal decision, it is a good idea to check with your dissertation chair or advisor to see if your school offers resources to support dissertation research, writing, and editing. Your program may require or endorse specific editors, so be aware of such requirements.

Many students either edit their own dissertations simply because they cannot afford to hire a dissertation editor or they might ask another student or a friend (who is a good writer and editor) to help them out. However, if you are considering hiring a dissertation editor, you may be wondering how to choose the right editor for the job. Since a good dissertation editor can make or break your project, it is important to make an informed decision.

When choosing a dissertation editor, it is necessary to evaluate their qualifications and experience. Not all editors are created equal, so it is important to find the right fit for your needs. When evaluating the qualifications of potential editors, it is helpful to consider their experience in the field, as well as their education and experience in dissertation editing. Some editors may have more experience than others when it comes to having edited distinct types of research papers or dissertations. Choose an editor who is qualified and has the right experience for your topic. When looking for the right editor, you should verify the qualifications of potential candidates by looking at their online portfolio or by contacting them directly. If you talk to them, be sure to ask about their editing experience and how they approach dissertation writing and editing.

Different types of editing services offer different advantages and disadvantages. For example, comprehensive editing offers more thorough coverage of all aspects of the dissertation, while line editing is more focused on correcting grammar and spelling errors. As a result, a comprehensive editor may be more expensive than a line editor, but they might be more likely to provide a higher level of dissertation editing services that will help ensure strong overall developmental benefits.

An editor's fee can vary depending on the specific services they offer and the complexity of the project. Generally speaking, an editor with more experience will charge more than one with less experience. The cost of a dissertation editor can range from a few hundred dollars up to several thousand dollars or more, depending on the amount of work required and the number of modifications or revisions requested.

Once you have found a dissertation editor who meets your qualifications and who can help you complete your project efficiently, it is important to establish good working relationships with them. One way to do this is to be sure that you take the time to review their qualifications and experience before hiring them. It may also be helpful to ask for references from other researchers who have worked with the editor in the past.

The Role of Research in Writing a Doctoral Dissertation

As you think about the process of writing a doctoral dissertation, keep in mind the role of research. The purpose of your research is to develop solid evidence that supports your thesis and assertions. Don't rely solely on anecdotal evidence or personal opinion when compiling your findings; use data and statistics to support your claims.

Understanding What a Doctoral Dissertation Is

A doctoral dissertation is an especially important document that is critical to completing your work toward obtaining your degree. In writing it, you will need to showcase your academic knowledge, your research knowledge and skills, and your writing skills. It is important to plan and organize your work carefully in order to produce a high-quality document.

Understanding what a doctoral dissertation is can help you to plan your work more effectively. A doctoral dissertation is a research-based document that typically contains between sixty thousand and eighty thousand words. It should be organized around a specific thesis or argument and should be written in an academic style.

It is important to have a clear idea of what you want to achieve when writing your dissertation. You should also be aware of the different types of research that are possible for a doctoral dissertation. Finally, you should plan how you will structure your document so that it is easy to read and understand.

Knowing the Audience for Whom You Are Writing

There are many different types of doctoral dissertations, so it is important to plan your writing accordingly. Knowing who you are writing for will help make sure that your dissertation is tailored specifically to their needs and expectations. Additionally, an understanding of the audience's research context can help you create more effective arguments and develop richer explanations.

First of all, you'll want to make sure you have the topic that is right for you. You need to be sure that you are interested in the topic you choose so that you will apply the commitment and dedication necessary to sustain you as you work to complete your project. The point is that the more dedicated you are to your research, the more you're going to enjoy and be passionate about doing everything that's needed to produce output that creates knowledge in your field. This is why you will need to develop a plan for your dissertation before actually writing or conducting research for it. Finally, keep in mind the readership you are targeting. For example, a thesis aimed at a general audience may be more concise and less technical than one written for your dissertation advising committee.

When writing for an audience, it is important to focus on clear and concise communication. Use simple language that everyone can understand without having to read between the lines. In addition, use concise images and graphs when necessary in order to visualize complex concepts. Your goal should be to make your argument as easy as possible for the reader to follow, no matter their level of expertise.

Finally, always remember that dissertations are meant to challenge common assumptions and provoke discussion around controversial topics. By doing this, you can help move scholarship forward by inspiring others to think critically about the world around them.

Determining the Purpose of Your Dissertation

It is important to plan and organize your work when writing a doctoral dissertation. This will help you to achieve specific goals, as well as provide a structure for your research. Additionally, knowing the purpose of your dissertation will help you to stay focused and motivated while writing.

One of the most important factors when planning a doctoral dissertation is determining its purpose. You need to understand what it is you want to achieve with your research, and how it ties into your overall thesis. Once you know this, you can begin setting goals for yourself and organizing your research accordingly.

If the purpose of your dissertation changes over time, be sure to revise your objectives accordingly. It can be easy to lose focus if you don't have an established goal in mind.

The next step in planning your dissertation is determining the scope of your research. This can be a difficult task, as it involves balancing the needs of your thesis with the restrictions imposed by university rules and guidelines. It is important to be realistic when making this decision, as you don't want to spend excessive time or money on research that won't fit into your thesis.

Once you have determined the scope of your work, you can begin narrowing down your focus. This process will require careful analysis of your data and literature sources, as well as an assessment of how each category relates to the overall goal of your research.

If you find yourself struggling to stay focused while writing, it may be helpful to take a step back and reassess your goals. This process can be difficult, but it is essential for achieving success in your doctoral dissertation.

More on Improving Your Skills for Writing Your Dissertation

One of the most important things you can do in preparation for writing your doctoral dissertation is to develop good organizational skills. This will help ensure that all your research is properly documented and that any relevant insights are communicated clearly and coherently.

Another key factor in effective writing for a doctoral dissertation is good research methodology. By following a structured approach, you will increase the likelihood of capturing accurate data and making sound conclusions. As such, it is essential to familiarize yourself with both classic and contemporary research methodologies before you begin writing your dissertation.

Finally, be sure to take time to proofread your work multiple times before submitting it to an advisor or publisher. Any errors or omissions may lead to unnecessary criticism or even rejection from your peers. By taking these steps, you can ensure that your doctoral dissertation is well-written and that once you defend your work, you will know you are deserving of receiving the prestigious title of "Doctor."

The Importance of Time Management for Doctoral Students

Time management is one of the most important skills a doctoral student can develop. By planning and organizing their time, students can make the most of their opportunities and achieve their goals.

There are a number of time management techniques that can be used to improve the efficiency of a doctoral student's work. Some of these include the following:

1. *Set realistic goals.* Don't try to accomplish too much at once; instead, break your tasks down into manageable chunks. This will help you stay focused and avoid feeling overwhelmed.

2. *Make a schedule.* Create a timetable that reflects your priorities and allows you to account for unexpected events. This will help you stay on track and avoid wasting time on tasks that are not important.

3. *Use technology to your advantage.* There are many online tools that can help you manage your time more effectively, such as calendars, to-do lists, and timer applications.

4. *Set up effective deadlines.* Establish specific dates by which you need to have completed a task or submitted a paper. This will help you stay motivated and avoid putting off important work until later in the semester or year.

5. *Prioritize your tasks.* When organizing your time, make sure that the most important tasks take precedence over less important ones. This will help you stay focused and minimize distractions from other activities.

By following these tips, doctoral students can maximize their productivity and manage their time more effectively.

Dealing with Writer's Block

If you find yourself struggling to write your doctoral dissertation, there are a few things you can do to help you get your writing juices flowing. First, make sure you have a clear goal in mind. If you don't know what you're trying to achieve, it will be difficult to write anything at all. Second, break your dissertation down into small, manageable tasks. This will help you stay focused and avoid getting bogged down by the larger project.

Some students find it helpful to start out by preparing an outline of what will be included in the dissertation. After that, write the first draft just as you would speak it to a friend (to take the pressure off from trying to write in an academic writing style at the outset). Once you have finished writing the dissertation, convert or translate the finished first draft into academic language.

Finally, you might consider finding a writing buddy or tutor. Having someone critique your work and offer constructive feedback can be incredibly helpful in getting your dissertation finished on time.

The Final Stages of Writing Your Dissertation

When you have completed all the writing tasks for your doctoral dissertation, it's time to finalize the document. Here are some tips to help you polish your work:

1. Proofread your dissertation for grammar and spelling mistakes.

2. Check for continuity and organization problems.

3. Check for factual accuracy.

4. Make sure that all sources are cited correctly.

5. Check for language that is too technical or obscure.

6. Rewrite any sections that need improvement.

7. Review the document to make sure that it flows smoothly and makes sense.

8. Inspect to ensure formatting conforms to university writing style guidelines.

The process of writing a doctoral dissertation can be daunting, but there are many ways to improve your writing skills. The most important thing is to get started and keep going. Don't worry about perfection, just focus on getting your ideas down on paper. Editing and proofreading are important, but don't let them hold you back from finishing your dissertation. A writing coach or tutor can be a great help, but ultimately it is up to you to do the work. Research is important, but don't get bogged down in it. Plan and organize your work, and manage your time wisely. If you hit a wall, don't give up. Find those comfortable gym shoes, get them on, tie them up, get out there, start walking, and keep going until you reach the finish line.

Tips to Help Manage Your Study, Your Writing, and Your Time
The following are some helpful strategies for overcoming obstacles and building up study and time management skills:

1. *Choose a degree that is right for you.* When it comes to choosing a doctoral degree, there are many options available. You need to get an idea of which degree might be the best fit for your goals and interests. However, before making any decisions, it is important to learn as much as you can about the different programs and what they offer. Do some research online, speak with a friend who has achieved the level of education you are seeking, or find an academic advisor at a college or a university who might be willing to help you.

2. *Build up study and time management skills.* Completing such a lengthy and rigorous program intimidates many people. However, with the right strategies and support, anyone can overcome any academic obstacle. This means learning how to manage your time effectively and setting realistic goals for yourself. It is also important to have a support system, whether that be family or friends, who can help you stay on track. If you are feeling overwhelmed by the task of studying, it is important to seek out mentorship from experienced educators. They can provide guidance and support as you work toward your degree. In addition, they can offer tips on how to overcome any *academic obstacle* you may face.

3. *Set reasonable expectations.* One of the biggest obstacles students face when trying to achieve success in their academic pursuits is setting unrealistic expectations of themselves. Instead of thinking about completing a doctoral degree within three years or becoming a published author overnight, make sure to have realistic expectations about what it will take for you to achieve your goals. Think about the amount of time, energy, and resources that you will need to be prepared to commit. To earn your degree and gain the knowledge you desire, none of the goals you set will happen all by themselves, and relegating them to someone else will not provide you with what

you need. That means you will need to be the engine that drives everything, and nothing is going to happen without your input.

4. *Take advantage of resources.* There are many resources available to help students achieve success in their academic pursuits. In addition to online resources, there are libraries that offer free consultations and workshops on a variety of topics. Additionally, there are many scholarships and fellowships available that can help cover the costs of tuition and fees. Do your due diligence. Do your research and find out as much as you can so that you can discover the resources you need.

5. *Stay organized.* One of the most important skills that a doctoral student can develop is organizational skills. This includes being able to keep track of what is due when, as well as being able to manage time effectively. One way to improve your organizational skills is to use a system like Evernote (a free, downloadable note-taking application at evernote.com that makes it easy to write and keep track of notes). Additionally, try to set up a routine for studying that you can stick to. This will help you to avoid feeling overwhelmed and will help you to better focus on your studies.

6. *Know your budget.* Before starting any degree program, it is essential to familiarize yourself with your budget and make sure you have realistic expectations about what you can afford. To figure out how much money you will need to cover tuition, room, board, and other expenses, start by creating a budget using a free resource like Mint. com or Personal Capital. Once you have an idea of how much money you will need each month, you can begin to look for ways to fund your doctoral pursuit.

7. *Another important resource for doctoral students is their professional networks.* Networks can provide access to funding opportunities, contacts within the academic community, mentorship, and other valuable resources. It is important for doctoral students to take advantage of these networks, as they can help them achieve their goals faster and more easily. One of the best ways to get ahead in

your doctoral studies is to utilize the professional networks you have built up over the course of your career. By reaching out to colleagues and friends, you can gain insight into potential research opportunities and connect with professors who could provide valuable guidance during your dissertation process.

8. *Additional writing tips that will help you save time.* Use a citation manager from the start to save time and improve accuracy (such as EndNote, Mendeley, or Zotero). Adjust the spellcheck and grammar features in your word processor to support academic writing and consider services such as Grammarly. Also, familiarize yourself with formatting and style guide functions in word processing software such as Microsoft Word to save time and get consistent formatting results. For example, set a paragraph style using an indent instead of a tab or spaces.

In conclusion, the most important thing a person who is pursuing a doctoral degree can do is to remain focused and consistently strive for the finish line. It is our hope that what we have presented to you in *Inspired to Climb Higher* demonstrates, most of all, that no one is perfect, and that even the best doctors make mistakes occasionally. However, learning from mistakes is essential if a person ever hopes to become a top scholar in their field.

Successful people are usually those who are dedicated to their goals, who are determined to succeed, and who keep going, no matter what obstacles they face on their way there. When it comes to doctoral studies, you must prepare yourself both physically and mentally for an intense academic program that lasts several years. It's also important not to give up during times of difficulty—persisting through tough times can lead to great accomplishments.

All these factors, including dedication, focus, and perseverance, are essential for anyone pursuing a doctoral degree. By recognizing and learning from the efforts of those who have succeeded before us, we can all help pave the way to success for those who are yet to pursue a doctorate or are currently studying and struggling with obstacles as they pursue their degrees.

REFERENCES

Babers, Jasmine. 2016. "For Women of Color, the Glass Ceiling is Actually Made of Concrete." *Aspen Institute* (blog), April 19. https://www.aspeninstitute.org/blog-posts/for-women-of-color-the-glass-ceiling-is-actually-made-of-concrete/.

Broom-Cooley, Deborah. 2007. "An Investigation of the Impact of High-Stakes Testing on the Graduation Rates at a Suburban High School in the State of Georgia." EdD dissertation, Argosy University.

Butrymowicz, Sarah, Jeff Amy, and Larry Fenn. 2020. "How Career and Technical Education Shuts out Black and Latino Students from High-paying Professions." *The Hechinger Report* (blog), October 22. https://hechingerreport.org/how-career-and-technical-education-shuts-out-black-and-latino-students-from-high-paying-professions/.

Clance, P. R. 1985. Clance Impostor Phenomenon Scale (CIPS). APA PsycTests.

Delpit, Lisa. 2006. *Other People's Children: Cultural Conflict in the Classroom*. New York, NY: The New Press.

Firestone, Robert W., Lisa Firestone, and Joyce Catlett. 2002. *Conquer Your Critical Inner Voice: A Revolutionary Program to Counter Negative Thoughts and Live Free From Imagined Limitations*. Oakland, CA: New Harbinger Publications, Inc.

Guffey, Gary C., and Wanda K. W. Ebright. 2019. *Dance on the Historically Black College Campus: The Familiar and the Foreign*. London: Palgrave Macmillan.

Honeman, B. 1990. "Rationale and Suggestions for Emphasizing Afrocentricity in the Public Schools." Paper presented at the conference on Rhetoric and the Teaching of Writing, Indiana.

Jackson, Derrick Z. 2022. "Black College Students: An Endangered Species, Unless They Play Ball." *The American Prospect*, December 23. https://prospect.org/education/black-college-student-athletes-supreme-court-affirmative-action/.

Nieto, Sonia. 2010. *The Light in Their Eyes: Creating Multicultural Learning Communities*. Tenth edition. New York, NY: Teachers College Press.

Quote Investigator. 2016. "Do All the Good You Can; In All the Ways You Can." Accessed February 23, 2023. https://quoteinvestigator.com/2016/09/24/all-good/#:~:text=In%20conclusion%2C%20John%20Wesley%20may,the%201799%20%2Ucollection%20of%20sermons.

Woodson, Carter G. 1933. *The Mis-Education of the Negro*. Washington, DC: The Associated Publishers.

Index

ABD. *See* All but dissertation, 197
academic writing skills, 184,
    209–10

balancing life, strategies, 13, 34,
    49, 51, 57, 89, 114, 115, 128,
    153, 196, 205, 206

choosing an institution and
    program, 169, 170–71, 179,
    180, 185, 219
coping strategies 191–
    95, 198;faith-based, 89,
    116–17, 204; self-coaching,
    38–9, 95–6

dissertation defense: act of
    defending 17, 40, 61, 100–1,
    117–19, 132, 158–59; post-
    defense 61, 101, 118,
    132, 159; preparation 16–17,
    39–40, 60–1, 100, 117, 132,
    157–58; strategies 193, 195,
    200, 201, 202
dissertation topic, strategies for
    choosing, 10, 41–3, 55–7, 78,

97–9, 112–13, 131–32, 152–53,
    176, 191, 196
distance education, deciding to
    pursue, 151, 153, 169, 178,
    184–87

EdD degree. *See* PhD vs EdD,
    deciding between

financial considerations, 32, 115,
    126, 167, 169, 172, 174, 177,
    182, 184, 185, 187, 200, 220

general advice, pursuit of
    doctorate, 207–21
general questions, pursuit of doc-
    torate, 167–188
GRE, 202

imposter syndrome, 30, 32, 35,
    73, 128
Institutional Review Board (IRB),
    15–16, 118, 131
IRB. *See* Institutional Review
    Board

online doctoral programs. *See* distance education

PhD vs EdD, deciding between, 74–5, 170, 173, 175
Public Service Loan Forgiveness program, 82, 174

regionally accredited program, choosing, 170, 175, 185
research in writing, role of, 213
research methodology, selecting, 12, 97–99, 199, 216
research platforms, 182
research questions, 181–82, 208–09

self-judgment, effects of, 194

sorority, pledging, 28, 71

time management, strategies 177, 180, 186, 193, 198, 199, 200, 202, 216–217, 219

value of doctoral degree, 172, 174, 175, 177, 179, 191, 199

writer's block, 91, 217
writing: editing and proofreading 176, 184, 212–13, 216; final stages of, 218; skills, 209, 210, 216; strategies 176, 177, 183, 193, 197, 199, 200, 202, 214–16, 221; style guides 184, 212; support and resources 184, 195, 209–10, 221

About the Authors

Beverley Middlebrook-Thomas, EdD, senior business and computer science teacher, Dekalb County, GA

Dr. Beverly Middlebrook-Thomas is a senior business and computer science teacher in Dekalb County (metro Atlanta, Georgia). She is also a mentor/coach to new teachers. Dr. Middlebrook-Thomas received her bachelor of science in business education from Alcorn State University (Lorman, Mississippi) and a master's in liberal arts from Houston Baptist University (Houston, Texas). She earned her EdD in educational leadership with an emphasis on technology from the University of Phoenix.

Dr. Middlebrook-Thomas began her working career as a Medicaid field auditor for the state of Mississippi, where she was responsible for reviewing and performing risk assessments and quality analyses of nursing homes and hospitals and creating, compiling, and reporting the results. She held this position for eight years before relocating to Houston, Texas, with her husband and family. In Houston, she began her career in education as a teacher for the Alief Independent School District, where she taught business and computer science to high school students and served as chair for her department during her eleven years in the district. Additionally, Dr. Middlebrook-Thomas has worked for more than seven years as an online adjunct professor of liberal arts at the University of Phoenix. The desire to be closer to family members led to her decision to relocate to Atlanta, Georgia, after residing in Houston for over twenty-five years.

Dr. Middlebrook-Thomas's personal business endeavors have included being the owner of an accessories and apparel business, Pashminas by Beverly, and an "unfranchise" owner of Market America marketing company. She is a widow with three grown children, Michael, Candis, and Christopher. In her spare time, she enjoys traveling and spending quality time with family.

Dr. Middlebrook-Thomas is the architect of the idea for the *Inspired to Climb Higher* book project. After completing her doctorate and excited to have finished her dissertation, she felt compelled to continue writing. This led to her coming up with the idea to write a book to inform and advise others who might be considering beginning the doctoral journey. She then sought and recruited others who had completed the doctoral journey and who shared in her excitement to engage in an autobiographical reflection of their experiences.

Jyenny Babcock, EdD, higher education data consultant, certified professional life coach, and artist

Dr. Jyenny Babcock is a retired higher education professional turned doctoral student life coach who resides in the greater Sacramento, California, area. She splits her time between coaching doctoral students, consulting within higher education, and pursuing artistic endeavors. She coaches doctoral students on how to thrive throughout the degree-earning process so they can reach the finish line emotionally intact, ready to achieve their postgraduation goals.

Dr. Babcock earned an associate of arts in liberal arts/business administration from Foothill College, Los

Altos Hills, California; a bachelor of arts in psychology and an master of arts in sociology: research skills option from California State University, Dominguez Hills, Carson, California; and an EdD in leadership with a health and wellness focus of study from American College of Education, Indianapolis, Indiana.

After spending fifteen years working in higher education, eight years as a research analyst at California State University, Dominguez Hills, and seven years as an assessment professional at California State University, Fullerton, Dr. Babcock retired as associate director, assessment and institutional effectiveness. Prior to her higher education career, she was a marketing professional within the architecture, engineering, and construction sector for nearly a decade. Her last position in corporate America was as director of marketing for a landscape architecture firm in downtown Los Angeles, California.

Over the years, Dr. Babcock has engaged in many entrepreneurial enterprises, the two most notable and enjoyable were Babcock Business Consulting, where she helped small business owners improve their business practices, and Crafted by Jyenny, where she sold handmade sterling silver jewelry. She began silversmithing in 1999 and was active until 2011. Her current artistic endeavors are focused on painting and woodturning.

Noha Abdou, EdD, director of institutional research, adjunct faculty in computer science

Dr. Noha Abdou is the director of institutional research in the Office of Institutional Effectiveness and Planning at California State University, Fullerton. She earned her bachelor of arts in economics with a minor in computer science from the American University in Cairo and her master's in public administration from California State Polytechnic University, Pomona. She earned her doctorate in educational leadership from California State University, Fullerton.

Dr. Abdou has taught in the computer science department as an adjunct faculty member, and also University 100, an introductory course for undeclared freshmen students, at California State University, Fullerton. She has worked at California State University, Fullerton, for the last five years, and prior to that, she was a senior systems analyst in the Division of Information Technology at California State University, Pomona, for ten years. Before her higher education career, Dr. Abdou worked in the private sector for a decade as a software developer in the construction and banking sectors.

Dr. Abdou is a proud mother of three young men, Shereef, Shaddy, and Rami; a dedicated wife to her husband of thirty-six years, Tarek; and is still seeking the love of their cat, Jojo. In her free time, she enjoys traveling, playing pickleball—her latest infatuation—cooking, and spending quality time with family and friends.

Dr. McCullough is a first-generation college student who earned her bachelor of science in speech-language pathology and audiology and her master of science in speech-language pathology from the East Stroudsburg University of Pennsylvania. She earned her EdD with a concentration in speech-language pathology from Nova Southeastern University.

Dr. McCullough has been a practicing speech-language pathologist for over twenty years and specializes in adult and geriatric swallowing disorders. She has worked in many settings, including acute care, acute inpatient rehabilitation, outpatient rehabilitation, skilled nursing, home health, schools, and higher education.

Helga M. McCullough, EdD, CCC-SLP, assistant professor of communication science and disorders/speech-language pathology

Dr. McCullough is tenure-track faculty in the Department of Communication Sciences and Disorders/Speech-Language Pathology at Lebanon Valley College. She teaches both undergraduate- and graduate-level courses primarily geared toward medical speech-language pathology. Her research interests include the work ethic of speech-language pathologists, best practices in dysphagia rehabilitation, and caregiver quality-of-life issues in the dysphagia population.

Dr. McCullough lives in Easton, Pennsylvania, with her two teenagers Samarah and Xander; fiancé Phil; cats Lehigh, Poppy, and Sesame; and bird Rosco. She enjoys reading and exploring new places with Phil in her free time.

Wanda K. W. Ebright, PhD, professor of dance, author, and arts administrator

Dr. Ebright is a tenured, full professor of dance, serving in her second year as dean of the College of the Arts at Columbus State University in Georgia. Prior to this, she served as associate dean for the College of Visual and Performing Arts at Winthrop University in Rock Hill, South Carolina; chair of the Department of Visual, Performing, and Communication Arts at Johnson C. Smith University in Charlotte, North Carolina; dance program coordinator at Coker College in Hartsville, South Carolina; assistant professor of dance at Kansas State University in Manhattan, Kansas; and dance program coordinator for the DeKalb Center for the Performing Arts in the metropolitan Atlanta, Georgia, area.

Dr. Ebright holds a bachelor of arts in French and a history minor from Memphis State University (now University of Memphis), a master of fine arts in dance performance and choreography from Florida State University, and a PhD in dance from Texas Woman's University in Denton, Texas. Her master's thesis explored the history of Black people in classical ballet, and her doctoral dissertation focused on the myriad ways in which dance exists on historically Black college and university campuses. Her book, *Dance on the Historically Black College Campus: The Familiar and the Foreign*, was published in 2019.

Dr. Broom-Cooley is a native and part-time resident of New Orleans, Louisiana, with a residence in Decatur, Georgia. Henry Cooley Jr., is her spouse of forty-seven years, and they are the parents of two adult sons, Henry Cooley III, and William Simon. As a recently retired educator with forty-five years of teaching and leadership experience in the K–12 and postsecondary arenas, it has been Dr. Broom-Cooley's sincere and distinct pleasure to have become an educator. She has worked in Louisiana and Georgia as a teacher support and coaching specialist; professional learning coordinator; content coordinator and liaison; mentor to teachers, leaders, and students; and adjunct instructor.

Deborah J. Broom-Cooley, EdD, educational consultant, minister, and mentor

Her teaching experiences have encompassed the following disciplines: Spanish, English as a second language, reading, curriculum and instruction, and early child education. Currently, Dr. Broom-Cooley serves as a director on the Foundation Board for Southern University at New Orleans and chair of the following committees: Policy and Procedure Development, Content Creator, Foundation Scholarship, and Foundation Newsletter. She is a lifetime and active member of the SUNO Alumni Association and Sigma Gamma Rho Sorority, Inc.

Dr. Broom-Cooley's career legacy and accomplishments have been cited in the *HBCU Times Magazine*, August 2021, with regard to her work in literacy and the positive impact of historically Black colleges and universities. Prior to this honor, the Celebrity Series Unsung Heroes Project, which was started by the late travel writer Michael Andre Adams in July 2012, focused on her work with students in alternative schools in the DeKalb County School District in Georgia.

A proud graduate of Southern University at New Orleans, Louisiana, there, Dr. Broom-Cooley earned a bachelor of arts in Spanish education. She later earned a master of education in curriculum and instruction, and a master's plus thirty hours in educational leadership at the University of New Orleans, Louisiana (formerly known as LSUNO). At Argosy University (University of Sarasota), in Sarasota, Florida, she earned an educational specialist and a doctorate in educational leadership. She currently holds teaching and leadership certificates in Louisiana and Georgia, and her motto is: *"Literacy is everyone's business, not just the children's!"*

Jennifer Malone received her bachelor of science degree in special education from Truman State University in 1985. In 1992 she earned a master of arts in special education and in 1996 an educational specialist degree in educational administration both from the University of Missouri. She earned her EdD in 1999 from Saint Louis University in the area of educational leadership.

Dr. Malone is a first-generation college graduate who had the desire to change the trajectory of the number of Black women graduating from college. She performed the necessary tasks to break through the barriers including the glass ceiling and the concrete ceiling to create a space for other Black women to do the same.

Jennifer Malone, EdD, assistant professor, Missouri Western State University

An educator for thirty-eight years, she spent eighteen years as a K–12 classroom special education teacher and an additional eighteen years as a K–12 principal. She spent two years in the central office as an executive director and as an assistant of student services. Her tenure includes the Kansas City, Missouri, public school district, Kansas City,

Kansas, district, Topeka public schools, and Center schools. Dr. Malone served as an adjunct professor for sixteen years at two different universities before becoming a full-time professor at Missouri Western State University in the Department of Education.

Her scholarship encompasses the shortage of Black teachers serving special education students, dismantling the self-fulfilling prophecy encroached upon students of color, uncovering the disparities of the graduate records exam concerning Black women, best instructional practices in higher education, tackling the achievement gap, and supporting Black students who attend predominantly white universities and colleges.

A member of the Council for Exceptional Children, Black Women in Higher Education, Teaching for Learning, and Black Doctors in Higher Education, Dr. Malone is also a proud, lifetime member of Alpha Kappa Alpha Sorority, Inc., and is active in the Xi Tau Omega chapter in Grandview, Missouri. In addition, she serves on the board of Bridge Leadership Academy.

She lives in Kansas City, Missouri, with her husband Kevin, and they have four beautiful children, Joseph (thirty-seven), Judon (thirty-three), Jaylen (twenty-two), and Tempest (twenty-one).

Dr. Middlebrook is a writer, an editor, and a writing coach who lives in a small town near Houston, Texas. She has worked independently for the past thirteen years as a writer/editor and as a fiction and nonfiction writing and editing coach helping her clients do their best work as they write/create their first fiction or nonfiction books. She also writes for an online platform (Hub Pages) where her articles and short stories have amassed close to one million views.

Sallie B. Middlebrook, PhD, writer, editor, and book writing coach

A graduate of traditional and nontraditional institutions,

Dr. Middlebrook holds a bachelor of science degree in mass communications/journalism from Jackson State University, Jackson, Mississippi, where she also completed two-thirds of a master's degree in English. She also earned a master of science in advertising from the University of Illinois, Urbana-Champaign, Illinois; and a PhD in business administration and management (with a specialization in marketing) from Walden University, Minneapolis, Minnesota.

In the corporate world, she has worked as a communications director, a graphic designer, a marketing and communications manager, an assistant director of marketing and planning, and a magazine and newspaper journalist and editor, among other roles. Her career history also includes serving twelve years in the academic arena as a full-time faculty member at Jackson State University, the University of Nebraska (Lincoln, Nebraska), and the University of Florida (Gainesville, Florida), and part-time at the University of Phoenix (Katy, Texas), the University of Houston (Sugar Land, Texas), and the University of St. Thomas (Houston, Texas).

Single with no children, these days Dr. Middlebrook spends most of her time writing and editing books (fiction and nonfiction, print, and e-books), while also coaching writers and writing and editing articles about writing (and other topics) for a variety of websites.

www.ingramcontent.com/pod-product-compliance
Lightning Source LLC
Chambersburg PA
CBHW020402100426
42812CB00001B/164